Oceans Governance in the Twenty-first Century

Oceans Governance in the Twenty-first Century

Managing the Blue Planet

Marcus Haward

Associate Professor, University of Tasmania, Australia

Joanna Vince

Lecturer, University of Tasmania, Australia

Edward Elgar
Cheltenham, UK • Northampton, MA, USA

Published by
Edward Elgar Publishing Limited
The Lypiatts
15 Lansdown Road
Cheltenham
Glos GL50 2JA
UK

Edward Elgar Publishing, Inc.
William Pratt House
9 Dewey Court
Northampton
Massachusetts 01060
USA

A catalogue record for this book
is available from the British Library

Library of Congress Control Number: 2008932865

ISBN 978 1 84720 111 9

Printed and bound in Great Britain by MPG Books Ltd, Bodmin, Cornwall

Contents

Figures and tables

Preface

This book developed from our interest in national, regional and international arrangements directed towards governance of the world's oceans that have been implemented from the 1980s to the present. We note, too, that major challenges remain even where states have made concerted efforts to develop new approaches to oceans management. We are interested in the factors shaping oceans governance, the supports and constraints affecting policy development and implementation, and the links between and within international, regional and national initiatives.

We have benefited greatly from the opportunities to discuss oceans governance with colleagues at the University of Tasmania and around the globe. At the University of Tasmania we have been fortunate to work with Bruce Davis, Fred Gale, Rob Hall, Richard Herr, Julia Jabour, Aynsley Kellow and Lorne Kriwoken, and with inspiring undergraduate and postgraduate students.

To our publishers, we thank Edward Elgar for his enthusiasm for the initial proposal, and to the staff at Edward Elgar Publishing Limited for their efforts in turning our manuscript into a book. Our editor Alexandra O'Connell, and editorial assistant Elizabeth Clack, provided excellent advice, support and encouragement. We would like to acknowledge the efforts of Mel Evans for her work in producing the figures and developing a quick appreciation of the key points of maritime jurisdiction. We would like to thank *Australasian Canadian Studies* and its editor Sonia Mycak for permission to reproduce material originally published in that journal that appears in Chapter 5.

To Anne and Charles, and Brendon, our thanks for their support during the writing of 'the book'.

Introduction

The seas and oceans of the Earth have been sustaining and supporting life for millennia, while at the same time they have been seen as a hostile and alien environment to be conquered and a barrier to movement. This image of the oceans was immortalised in the poetry of Samuel Taylor Coleridge's *Rime of the Ancient Mariner:* 'Water, water, everywhere, Nor any drop to drink' (Coleridge 1797–99). More than two centuries after Coleridge's epic poem the oceans are better understood, and their significance in comprising 70 per cent of the earth's surface has been recognised. This appreciation of the scale of the world's oceans was enhanced in the late twentieth century by images of the Earth from satellites and in particular by the evocative photograph 'Earthrise' taken by Apollo astronaut William Anders during the Apollo 8 mission to the Moon on 24 December 1968. This image was produced at the time when the vulnerability of the oceans had been dramatically illustrated through a major oil spill. On 18 March 1967 the *Torrey Canyon*, one of an emerging fleet of large crude oil tankers (later to be termed 'supertankers') ran aground off southern England. The resultant oil spill devastated the marine and coastal environment and bird life in the English Channel and led to calls for action to protect the marine environment. A month after the Apollo image had been broadcast, on 29 January 1969 a blowout on an oil rig six miles offshore from Santa Barbara, California, accidentally released hundreds of thousands of gallons of crude oil, creating a major oil slick that affected large areas of the California coast.

These incidents helped to mobilise public opinion, and contributed to the rise of environmental consciousness in the late 1960s. The effects of human impacts on the environment were increasingly apparent and the calls to protect the environment had developed in response to several stimuli, including the call to arms contained in Rachel Carson's *Silent Spring*, published in 1962. Carson had earlier written *The Sea Around Us* (Carson 1951), a book described by one reviewer as 'creat[ing] a mood of awe and wonder at the marvels of the sea' (Stommel 1952, pp. 321–2). The marvels of the sea were brought to public attention through the work of pioneering underwater photography and films made by French marine explorer Jacques Cousteau in the 1950s. Cousteau developed the aqualung, the forerunner of what became known as SCUBA – 'self-contained underwater breathing apparatus' – in the 1940s, and continued to campaign for protection of the marine environment until his death in 1997. Rachel Carson's recognition of the significance of the world's seas was as pertinent as her concerns a decade later over the impacts of human activities on the terrestrial environment, but action over the marine environment has generally lagged behind terrestrial developments in environmental protection. The sea, 'out of sight, out of mind' has more often been regarded as a dumping ground.

This first wave of modern environmentalism led to Earth Day in 1970 and the first global conference on the human environment in Stockholm in 1972. While focusing generally on the problems of population growth and on the terrestrial environment, this conference recognised the threat to the world's seas and oceans and specifically, in response to recent disasters, the need to prevent marine pollution. These disasters also focused attention on the need to develop effective instruments to govern the oceans. As a result, the United Nations General Assembly in 1970 passed a resolution agreeing to establish an international conference to revivify discussions on the law of the sea. This conference, known formally as the Third United Nations Conference on the Law of the Sea (UNCLOS III), was held between 1974 and 1982 and resulted in the negotiation of the Law of the Sea Convention (LOSC), a comprehensive 'constitution for the oceans'.

The oceans also figured prominently in the 1980s. The publication of the report of the World Commission on Environment and Development (WCED) *Our Common Future* (also known as the Brundtland Report) in 1987, revived and gave clout to discussions on the environment. The WCED introduced the concept of 'sustainable development' into the lexicon of international and domestic politics. The Brundtland Report defined sustainable development as that 'which meet the needs of the present without compromising the ability of future generations to meet their own needs'. The United Nations Conference on Environment and Development (UNCED), in Rio de Janerio in 1992, 20 years after the Stockholm conference, provided a major forum to advance the agenda introduced by the Brundtland Report.

The UNCED was a major global event, providing a number of outcomes that included key international conventions and the reiteration of a number of soft law principles. Major outcomes from the UNCED were the Framework Convention on Climate Change and the Convention on Biological Diversity. A global action plan, Agenda 21, and the Rio Declaration provided further development of the soft law principles underpinning sustainable development, including integration, precaution, intergenerational equity, 'polluter pays', public participation, community-based development, indigenous rights and women in development (see VanderZwaag et al. 1996). Agenda 21 Chapter 17, dealing with oceans and coasts (including exclusive economic zones), provides a specific action plan which emphasises the requirement for 'new approaches to marine and coastal area management at the national, subregional, regional, and global levels, approaches which are integrated in content and are precautionary and anticipatory in ambit' (Agenda 21 Chapter 17.1).

By the late twentieth century the natural limits of the world's oceans had been conquered. Technological developments overcame constraints of depth and distance. Fisheries could be exploited and oil and gas extracted from depths and distances thought unattainable only three decades previously. At the same time the fragility of the marine environment and its ecosystems, and their vulnerability to overexploitation, was graphically depicted in the collapse of the northern cod fishery off Newfoundland in the early 1990s. This collapse, tearing at the economic and social fabric that had sustained Newfoundland communities for over 200 years, also destroyed – finally – the notion advanced in the nineteenth century that the world's fisheries were inexhaustible. Improvements in governance of the oceans were demanded.

The decade and a half following the conclusion of the United Nations Conference on Environment and Development (UNCED) in 1992 has led to considerable efforts given to developing and extending institutions and processes related to the management of the world's oceans and marine areas. At the same time increased emphasis has been given to moving from management of single-sector activities towards frameworks that provide integration and coordination between different uses and users of the oceans. The latter, termed integrated oceans management, has been the focus of national policy development regional initiatives and international discussions. Related to this has been an emphasis on the means by which such initiatives can be developed, implemented and evaluated, directly linked to the concept of governance. At the same time the entry into force of instruments including the Law of the Sea Convention have refocused attention on rights and responsibilities of states in the marine domain. These developments from the mid 1990s have led to increased attention towards appropriate governance of ocean and coastal areas and, effectively, a new oceans agenda.

Internationally this agenda has been addressed in reports to the Commission on Sustainable Development (CSD), the annual UN Secretary-General's report on *Oceans and the Law of the Sea* (see, for example, United Nations General Assembly 2007) and the establishment of the United Nations Informal Open-ended Consultative Process on Oceans and the Law of the Sea (UNICPOLOS). Other UN specialised agencies and programmes such as the Food and Agriculture Organization (FAO), the United Nations Environment Programme (UNEP) and United Nations Educational, Scientific and Cultural Organization (UNESCO), have all contributed significantly to raising the profile of ocean governance. Regionally the Asia-Pacific Economic Cooperation (APEC) forum has recognised the importance of integrated oceans management in the Pacific rim and the APEC Marine Resources Conservation Working Group established a major multi-year programme to facilitate exchange of information and capacity building amongst member economies. A regional oceans policy for the Pacific was developed by member states of the Pacific Islands Forum in the late 1990s. The European Union established a Maritime Policy Directive in 2005, and published *An Integrated Maritime Policy for the European Union* in 2007.

National governments, too, have been active. Canada enacted its Oceans Act in 1996, providing a legislative framework for oceans policy initiatives. Australia's national Oceans Policy was released in late 1998, eschewing a legislative approach in favour of a more collaborative effort within existing legislation. The United States of America, after developing pioneering legislation and administrative arrangements in the late 1960s and early 1970s, established a Commission on Ocean Policy following the passage of its Oceans Act of 2000. At the same time the Pew Trust established the Pew Oceans Commission to advance debate on US oceans governance. New Zealand, having established an innovative terrestrial-based resource management framework in the 1990s, and having introduced radical reforms to fisheries management at the same time, also began moves towards a national oceans policy.

Despite these considerable efforts, and the range of initiatives or actions developed, progress towards the aspirations of the UNCED's Agenda 21 for 'new approaches to marine and coastal area management at the national, subregional, regional and global levels' has been slow, tortuous and patchy. Integrated oceans management, like sustainable development, has become a 'buzzword' (Chircop and Hildebrand 2006). Implementation of integrated approaches, either as policy or legislative frameworks, has however been difficult even when states have made concerted efforts to develop new approaches to oceans management. At the same time exciting opportunities and actions are apparent, often at local or sub-national scales.

This situation invites analysis. We are interested in the factors shaping oceans governance, the supports and constraints affecting policy development and implementation, and the links between and within international, regional and national initiatives. The role of science, too, is critical, yet often poorly integrated into oceans management. Good science is a necessary element of good management although it is important to recognise that good science alone may not necessarily lead to good management (Fløistad 1990). Scientific input is an important element in the management of marine living resources and managers require adequate and timely advice from scientists to be able to formulate effective policy.

We apply a governance lens to our analysis, recognising that while this concept has attracted an ever-increasing literature, and the concept is to some extent contested (note Kjær 2004; Jose 2007), it has focused attention on tools and processes that coordinate activity. Governance has been described as 'governing without government' by a major contributor to the literature (Rhodes 1996) but we see government as a major actor in the development of oceans policy. We are thus interested in the processes that underpin development in oceans policy, and see these processes as providing the bases for the development of tools and instruments of governance. In this analysis a number of cross-cutting factors – institutional design, policy capacity, and policy frameworks – become important supports to facilitate integrated oceans management. These factors have considerable influence on the management of oceans and marine resources, and have become important parameters for oceans governance.

INSTITUTIONAL DESIGN AND POLICY CAPACITY

We believe that these two factors are central to the analysis of oceans governance. Institutional design relates to the structures and processes established to facilitate integration of ocean uses and users. Policy capacity relates to the ability to make decisions and the quality of that decision forming the substance of policy. A key question is: How is government organised to manage the oceans?

POLICY FRAMEWORKS TO FACILITATE INTEGRATED OCEANS MANAGEMENT

A focus on governance helps shift away from a concentration on traditional regulatory models towards alternative policy instruments and/or increasing partnerships with private and non-governmental organisations. The key question, and one that underpins any assessment of oceans governance, is: How effective and efficient are alternative policy frameworks in delivering desired goals of integrated oceans management?

OUTLINE OF THE BOOK

We develop our discussion of oceans governance in Chapter 1, focusing on concepts, processes and practices. This chapter outlines key analytical issues and provides a framework for examining oceans governance at different scales – international, regional and national. We are conscious of the interaction between domestic policy development and initiatives pursued in regional and international arenas. This chapter helps us develop a framework that allows us to assess the development and implementation of oceans policy initiatives. We also explore how traditional governance approaches based on bureaucratic and regulatory state-directed models relate to the emerging use of alternative tools and instruments associated with market-based approaches and community involvement.

Chapter 2 focuses on oceans governance in international arenas. This chapter outlines key instruments, initiatives and institutions that have shaped, and continue to play influential roles in, contemporary oceans governance. We discuss the international framework for oceans governance, separating instruments into either binding 'hard law' or voluntary, hortatory 'soft law' categories for ease of classification rather than from any value judgement on effectiveness. We note that non-binding agreements may contribute directly to improved national capacity through integration in national legislation, while compliance with formal binding instruments may be superficial.

Oceans governance has also been addressed at the regional or supra-national level. A number of representative regional initiatives and actions are discussed in Chapter 3. This chapter provides a broad survey of current practices in the Asia-Pacific, the Caribbean, the Arctic and the Antarctic. Oceans governance initiatives within the European Union are also discussed, highlighting the particular challenges in developing and implementing policy in multi-jurisdictional political systems. Analysis of regional institutions and arrangements directs attention to opportunities for capacity building, information exchange, policy learning and/or policy transfer amongst member states.

The development of national oceans policy initiatives is the focus of the following four chapters, providing case studies of Australia (Chapter 4), Canada (Chapter 5), New Zealand (Chapter 6), and the United States of America (Chapter 7). In examining oceans policy development in each country we are influenced by the strength of the structured, focused, comparative case study methodology (George 1979; Sartori 1991). This approach adopts what has been termed the 'most-similar' systems approach (Roberts 1973). As Roberts notes: 'where the problem is one of identifying and accounting for specific differences, selection of units of analysis which possess many similarities in terms of relevant variables makes easier the identification of variables which *do* differ' (Roberts 1973, p. 246).

This analysis also aims to increase the relevance of the individual country studies by comparing experiences in oceans governance between the states. These states have faced similar challenges in oceans management yet have different institutional frameworks and have used different policy tools to address these challenges. They have also responded to regional and international developments in oceans governance in different ways.

1. Oceans governance: concepts, processes and practices

The world's maritime estate has been justly regarded as a last frontier – with scientists knowing more about parts of the Moon's surface than of the deepest areas of the earth's seas and oceans. These seas and oceans are under significant stress from 'pressures being exerted on the ocean ecosystems through over fishing, pollution, and environmental and climate change' (Costanza et al. 1998, p. 198). The oceans, traditionally seen as a vast virtually inexhaustible commons, have been utilised to the point where a majority of fisheries resources are fully exploited. The most recent United Nations Food and Agriculture Organization (FAO) analysis provides a serious assessment of the state of the world's fisheries, and 'reinforces calls for more cautious and effective fisheries management to rebuild depleted stocks' (FAO 2007, p. 7). The FAO recognises that challenges in international fisheries governance still remain, centring on improving effectiveness of arrangements to manage and conserve fish stocks (ibid).

Management of the world's maritime estate can also therefore be seen as a last frontier. Concern over overfishing and widespread recognition of the need for more 'responsible' fishing practices has led to the development of both 'hard law' agreements and conventions (such as the United Nations Fish Stocks Agreement and the FAO Compliance Agreement) as well as 'soft law' instruments such as the FAO-sponsored Code of Conduct for Responsible Fisheries. At the same time concerns over the marine environment have resulted in a range of actions. The International Maritime Organization (IMO) has continued to address the problems of ship-sourced marine pollution, while national governments and international organisations have given increased attention to land-based sources of marine pollution. The Convention on Biological Diversity has been extended to the marine environment. The development of arrangements addressing marine archaeological heritage have also covered an emerging gap in marine environmental protection.

Management of the oceans and their resources have been major items on the agenda of regional forums such as the Asia-Pacific Economic Cooperation (APEC) forum and in the Organisation for Economic

Co-operation and Development (OECD). The OECD, for example, has taken a leadership role in, and provided strong support for, action against illegal, unreported and unregulated (IUU) fishing. International and regional action includes commitments by the European Union to implement an integrated maritime policy, and oceans policy initiatives in a number of nation states. The Oceans Summit in Lisbon in October 2005 (IISD 2005) is indicative of the attention now given to 'oceans governance' at national, regional and international levels.

These recent developments have built on institutional arrangements affecting the management of the world's seas and oceans established in the preceding two decades (Vallega 2001). These arrangements provide a foundation for, and an impetus to encourage, addressing challenges faced in the management of the world's seas and oceans. The convening of the United Nations Conference on Environment and Development (UNCED) in 1992 and the entry into force of the United Nations Law of the Sea Convention (LOSC) in 1994, discussed (albeit in different ways) questions surrounding sovereign rights and ecological responsibilities in relation to the world's seas and oceans.

The development of 'customary' law of the sea was based on the acceptance of a number of key principles that had evolved from debates in the seventeenth century. These debates centred on work of the Dutch scholar and jurist Hugo Grotius, who argued for freedom of the seas, and his critics, most notably the English jurist John Selden, who claimed that states could assert rights over the sea (Cullen 1990, p. 11). The evolution and acceptance of the principle and practice of a coastal state's rights to claim waters within the range of its coastal defences – 'the cannonshot rule' – (Cullen 1990, p. 11) provided the basis for oceans governance for over 200 years. This principle and concept of the 'territorial sea' was eventually formalised within the 'law of the sea' from the late 1950s (see Chapter 2).

Attempts to codify the law of the sea in the twentieth century met first with failure with the collapse of the Hague Conference in the late 1930s. Following the action of the United States in proclaiming sovereignty over its adjacent continental shelf in 1947, a number of states took similar actions. The mid- to late 1960s saw increasing concern over significant oil spills associated with crude oil tanker groundings or collisions. These concerns were given voice by the advocacy of Arvid Pardo, Ambassador of Malta to the United Nations, who argued that the world's oceans should be the 'common heritage of mankind'. Pardo's speech was a reaction against the 'creeping jurisdiction' of coastal states asserting rights over the seabed and water column from the late 1940s onwards. Pardo's speech was also instrumental in seeing the passage of a United Nations resolution establishing a conference to address the development of a comprehensive approach to the law of the sea. The concept of the common heritage of mankind was to be a core principle discussed at the Third United Nations Conference on the Law of the Sea (UNCLOS III) and was embedded directly into the United Nations Law of the Sea Convention (LOSC). We discuss the evolving international framework for oceans governance in the following chapter.

GOVERNANCE: EXPLORING THE CONCEPT

Governance emerged in the 1980s as a conceptual tool to help explain developments in international relations and national politics that had moved beyond the traditional state-centred or bureaucratic model of administration. Traditional institutional analysis 'cover[ed] the rules, procedures and formal organisation of government' (Rhodes 1995, p. 48), yet increasingly 'government' was not the only actor involved in 'governing', either in relation to operations of international instruments or regimes or within nation states. Non-state actors – civil society organisations, national and transnational corporations, and international organisations – were important and obvious actors involved in 'governing'. International relations scholars developed the concept of 'regimes' to help explain the operation of international arrangements that moved beyond the formal establishment of international legal instruments, to focus on decision-making processes and outcomes.

At the same time, public sector reform in the 1970s and 1980s within the nation state – most notably first in Ango-American liberal democracies, but then more broadly – shifted focus towards the problem of government overload and government or regulatory failure. Increased use of market models, including privatisation, to address these failures invited new approaches to the analysis of political institutions, particularly those dealing with common pool resources (see Ostrom 1987, 1990). At the same time, these developments encouraged the emergence of the term 'governance' (see for example Pierre 2000; Kjær 2004) to help explain these new trends. Reform of government administration has been based on what Canadian political scientist Herman Bakvis identified as two overarching features: first the reorganisation of government agencies to focus on their core responsibilities; and second, separating policy responsibilities from operational responsibilities (Bakvis 1997). While the literature on 'institutionalism' and 'governance' is vast (see Kjær 2004), it has focused on the mechanisms that coordinate government activity (Rhodes 2000) resulting from this 'policy – operations split'.

The World Bank links governance to institutional capacity and to the effectiveness of public organisations (World Bank 2000) drawing attention to tools and approaches underpinning effective and efficient institutional arrangements (Kjær 2004, p. 189). Governance is more than government and involves a number of instruments and actors, 'encompassing norms, institutional arrangements and substantive policies' (Miles 1999, p. 1). Rhodes commented in a seminal article in 1996 that the 'search for new tools' is a key element of the new governance (Rhodes 1996, p. 666), as indicated by the use of market-based instruments in addressing public policy problems. In oceans governance, as in other policy areas, these market-based tools are diverse and include transferable quotas in fisheries, user fees and charges for resource users, and the external certification of products and processes. Co-management arrangements – or more broadly based community forms of governance – are also important and have been promoted as alternative means to address regulatory failure.

It is important to note that neither market nor community governance, while promoted as means to overcome such failure efficiently, are a complete replacement for regulation, the most common form of government action. Regulation, market and community are not mutually exclusive approaches. Indeed effective market or community approaches are based on appropriate legislative and regulatory instruments. At the same time market-oriented actions are being felt in interesting ways. For example the 'Give Swordfish a Break' campaign in 1998–2000 resulted in East Coast United States restaurants, hotels and cruise ships removing swordfish from menus in response to concerns over the state of Atlantic swordfish stocks (SeaWeb 2007). In Europe eco-labelling initiatives such as the Marine Stewardship Council (MSC) have attracted wide support (Potts and Haward 2007) from consumers concerned with sustainability of fisheries resources.

In analysing oceans governance we are interested in the development of new tools and approaches to management of marine areas, for example the development of ecosystem-based approaches to management, and particularly the attempt to shift from 'sectoral' to 'integrated management' (see below). We accept the important insights that the governance literature provides about means of governing but we recognise that government still has an important function in policy development, and implementation, as well as in establishing compliance and enforcement regimes to ensure policy directions are achieved. From this our assessment focuses on the concepts of policy capacity and coordination.

In examining the concept of governance we concur with Pierre and Peters's (2005) assessment that it contains four elements:

- articulating a common set of priorities (involving goal definition and mediation or conflict resolution of competing goals);
- coherence (ensuring consistency and coordination);
- steering (application of policy instruments and an implementation strategy); and
- accountability (and evaluation) (Pierre and Peters 2005, pp. 3–5).

This helps develop an analytical framework that can be applied to various national and regional initiatives in oceans governance. We are also influenced by the importance of recognising systems of governance that involve 'transnational, national and subnational institutions and actors' (Pierre and Peters 2005, p. 82). This analysis centres on:

- policy initiation (priorities);
- policy development (consistency and coordination);
- implementation (steering); and
- evaluation (accountability).

We are also interested in the mechanisms by which states develop and implement oceans policy initiatives; how traditional governance approaches based on bureaucratic and regulatory state-directed models relate to the emerging use of alternative tools and instruments associated with market based approaches and community involvement.

GOVERNANCE: GOVERNMENT, MARKET AND COMMUNITY

Wide-ranging reforms and changes in their public sectors occurred in a number of countries including Australia in the 1980s and 1990s. These reforms and changes have incorporated a number of elements that together form what has been called the new public management (NPM). The introduction of NPM attempted to change the role and functions of the public service, most notably in developing a new relationship between politics and administration. One of the major results of these wide-ranging reforms was a focus on the core roles of the public service, providing policy advice and information to ministers and politicians and managing (implementing) the eventual decision or policy.

The reasons given for public sector reform were similar in each country:

- improve standards of professional management;
- establish standards and measures of performance;

- place greater emphasis on outputs and results;
- disaggregate and downsize the public sector;
- improve competition within the public sector;
- incorporate private sector styles of management; and
- encourage discipline and parsimony is use of resources (Hood 1991, in Hughes 1998, pp. 61–2).

Thus management was emphasised over administration – the latter was seen to be concerned with process rather than with results. Just as earlier generations of scholars and practitioners grappled with the politics – administration dichotomy (Hughes 2003) and the proper role of the public servant, today the discussion centres on the appropriate role for the public servant.

The traditional model of public administration was tested and found wanting in a climate which emphasised economy, efficiency and effectiveness – the 'three "E"s' of public sector management (see Hughes 2003). The traditional model's focus on process was criticised as being unbusinesslike, constraining and costly, with government considered to be ineffective at allocating goods and services. The development of a more innovative, entrepreneurial, corporate focus to the public sector introduced a new vocabulary to describe the work of the public sector, much of it borrowed from the private sector. These phrases include '"empowerment", "total quality management", "pay for performance", and "improved services to clients"' (Savoie 1995, p. 94).

The introduction of public management principles and practices has had the effect of changing both structures and processes within the public sector, although it must be recognised that these changes may be less visible to the public. Importantly the notion of 'public service' has been redefined to include greater commitment to stakeholders and to client service, making government more responsive and accountable. The managerial reforms have as many supporters as they have critics; one important element for the future will be to evaluate the impacts of the reform agenda implemented from the 1980s, as this period has seen radical changes in approaches to public policy problems.

The introduction of market-type forms of governance is a visible feature of contemporary governments' changed approach to these problems. We are increasingly faced with shifts to 'user pays' and other economic instruments in the place of former government-based approaches to governance. The resurgence of neo-classical economics has contributed significantly to the reappraisal of the relationship between the market and the provision of services. The 1980s through to the 2000s have seen the concept of 'government failure' assert itself as a major paradigmatic feature in the debate, supplanting the earlier concept of 'market failure' that drove much of the growth of government action from the 1940s to the 1960s.

Market instruments are those that introduce pricing, as well as dynamics of supply and demand, as a means of allocating access to resources. The use of tradeable rights and the creation of quasi-market approaches by such 'trades' in fisheries management, for example, have provided an alternative paradigm for both fishers and fisheries managers. In the 1990s Australian governments have increased the use of economic instruments, chiefly through the introduction of individual transferable quotas, fishing rights and resource rent recovery. Other market instruments include user fees and charges, increasingly used in areas such as marine parks (Haward and Wilson 2000) and also includes use of certification and labelling of fisheries through non-state market-based instruments such as eco-labels (Gale and Haward 2004; Potts and Haward 2007).

Market approaches are based on the assumption that individuals are interested in maximising benefits to themselves, that is they display self-interest in determining exchange relationships. In simple terms a price of a good is determined by the relationships between supply and demand. A good which is in short supply but in high demand will have a high price, simply because sellers can charge a high price as people want the good. Conversely, the greater the supply of the good the lower the price, as sellers are forced to compete and buyers can 'shop around'. Adam Smith argued that in engaging in the marketplace the individual often sought personal advantage, but also helped the market to function, simply clearing or balancing the relationship between supply and demand. The 'invisible hand' explains how numerous individual transactions can help the market operate, and is also a means by which we can model the way in which markets clear, or adjust to increased demand or oversupply (see, for example, Larmour 1997).

Supporters of market approaches to governance argue that if left alone markets will indeed get to an equilibrium point, while critics argue that conditions can arise in which markets fail and lead to suboptimal outcomes. While the models of governance provide useful insights into aspects of public policy development and implementation, we should also be aware of the limitations of single models. Although the concept of model failure provides us with a way in which we can appreciate the dynamics of governance it is also important to recognise that real-world policy-making may well involve mixing of the models. Legislation is enacted to establish 'user pays' arrangements which have the effect of increasing the interest of those users of the goods or services or resources and increases their sense of community and encourages cooperative or self-management.

This invites a reassessment of the 'tragedy of the commons' thesis that has had significant influence on oceans management. The tragedy of the commons identified the negative consequences of individual action, and focused on regulatory and/or market regimes as solutions to the tragedy caused by individual self-interest (see Hardin 1968). Concerns over exploitation of stocks increasingly led to fisheries management 'solutions' which cast regulatory arrangements and government control as the only means of protecting fish stocks and controlling fishers. Underpinning this view of fishery management was 'a polarised view of the world, in line with Hardin's "Tragedy of the Commons": fishers were seen as selfish profit maximisers, versus regulators as protectors of the resources. This perspective, although flawed, actually became self-fulfilling' (Charles 1997, p. 108). As a result fishers, excluded from decision-making processes, had few incentives to moderate catches. Simply speaking they were seen as rapacious maulers of the commons unable or unwilling to reduce their desire for short-term profit over the need for long-term sustainability of stocks in the fishery. As a consequence government regulation was needed to control fishing. This approach dominated fisheries management arrangements but in what is a classic case of regulatory failure was less successful in restricting effort and catch levels in fisheries.

The possibility of an alternative solution to those proposed by Hardin has already been suggested. Increased support for co-management derives, first, from a reappraisal of view of the inevitability of a tragedy of the commons, and second, from the recognition of the limits of government action. A number of writers have re-appraised Hardin's pessimistic prognosis for the commons. Berkes et al. used a number of brief examples to show 'that success [in managing the commons] can be achieved in ways other than privatisation or government control' (Berkes et al. 1989, p. 91), and point out that: 'Communities dependent on common-property resources have adopted various institutional arrangements to manage those resources, with varying degrees of success in achieving sustainable use' (ibid.). These arrangements can in fact be quite complex, as shown in studies of community rights-based fishing arrangements in different parts of the world.

Co-management can be defined as: 'an arrangement where responsibility for resource management is shared between government and user groups' (Sen and Neilsen 1996, p. 46). Co-management arrangements developed at a time when traditional regulatory approaches to oceans management had been seen to have 'failed', most notably in a number of fisheries around the world. Concern with such failures has reintroduced concepts such as 'self-governance' as the basis for an alternative approaches (see Wilson et al. 1994; but see rejoinders from Parsons and Maguire 1996; Hilborn and Gunderson 1996). Cooperative management is advocated to counter regulatory failure (Wilson et al. 1994), including non-compliance with laws and regulations (see, for example, Sutinen et al. 1991), and is based on a focus on shared values or community interests.

Community is an 'open-textured concept' (Taylor 1982) subject to many definitions and uses; including what has been seen as a symbolic 'spray-on solution' to organisational failure (see Bryson and Mowbray 1981). Theoretical bases for co-management derive from Tonnies's concept of *gemeinschaft* (socially constructed order) first developed in the late 1800s (Tonnies 1957). A century later Taylor (1982) developed 'an idealized community' from 'empirical studies of stateless societies to identify the conditions under which people sustained order without centralized, hierarchical forms of government' (Larmour 1997, p. 386). For Taylor order was achieved by the community's shared norms and values, the existence of multiple relationships between members of the community and the use of shaming or retaliation against defectors from these norms and values (Taylor 1982; see also Larmour 1997, pp. 386–7). In effect co-management arrangements create a socially constructed order (including forms of 'rights') from the recognition of the shared interests and values (reciprocity) among the community defined by these interests.

Reciprocity provides the base for community self-enforcement, as mutual obligations together with shaming or ostracism can be powerful instruments encouraging compliance. Often this centres on 'speaking to' those who repeatedly flout regulations (Sturgess 1997). While this may reinforce community values, the difficulties of community self-enforcement are also significant. As Larmour points out: 'notions of governance derived from stateless societies or common pool resources do not sit easily with other notions of governance that emphasise human, economic and cultural rights' (Larmour 1997, p. 390). Commitments to justice and fairness are seen as fundamental, but such commitments can lead to increasingly complex management arrangements to implement such values. It is these institutional frameworks that, paradoxically, can contribute to management failures in common pool resources (Healey and Hennessy 1998, p. 109).

Co-management is predicated on individuals and groups (forming a community of interest around a fishery) recognising that such problems arise from their day-to-day activities. In relation to the more practical use of co-management, the attraction of 'community-based' management is obvious. Too often the community has not recognised that problems are theirs to own, or have not been able to deal with the problems. Recognition and ownership of the problems by resource users are likely to have much greater effectiveness than solutions imposed on that community. There are some obvious caveats. It is equally clear that community action cannot resolve all issues. Difficulties arise in dealing with spillover effects – for example the actions of fishers who lack kinship or community ties (thus escaping community sanction) or who fish either predator or prey species – affecting the food chain and thus the biomass.

One important aspect of community involvement relates to the role of the fishing industry itself. Seeing the industry as a community provides important theoretical and practical insights into fisheries management. In terms of theory, the developing literature dealing with common pool resources emphasises community solidarity as a means of providing effective 'self-management'. In practice, while fisheries may be fragmented and a unified view difficult to ascertain, the role of industry self-management is an integral component in ensuring compliance with both externally imposed management arrangements and community-based codes of practice. Compliance with management measures is clearly more likely when these measures can be shown to benefit directly the fisher's economic performance.

If it was concern over major tanker disasters in the mid-1960s that provided impetus for the international community to heed Ambassador Pardo's call for action, crises in the world's fisheries provided similar motivations in the 1990s. World fisheries production steadily increased after the Second World War, although capture fisheries production stabilised and then declined from the early 1990s. Distant-water catches provided much of the increase in production until the early 1970s. These fisheries declined from then as a proportion of world catch as distant water catches peaked in the late 1980s (FAO 2007). Fisheries production increased from all principal fishing areas since 1950, although the most rapid rate of increase from 1980 has been from Asian aquaculture operations (FAO 2007). While production has increased in the world's oceans, relative rates of increase from capture fisheries have declined in each ocean from the mid 1950s.

THE OCEANS: FROM SOVEREIGN RIGHTS TO ECOSYSTEM MANAGEMENT?

Effective oceans governance will build on what has been termed 'operational interplay' between instruments. This occurs where 'deliberate coordination of activities ... avoid[s] normative conflict or wasteful duplication' (Stokke 2000, p. 205), and contributes to problem-solving activities. One key element of such operational interplay is the application of relevant conservation and management measures whether a state is a party to relevant instruments or not. Despite the broadening of oceans governance through the development and entry into force of hard law instruments and soft law agreements, the effectiveness of governance remains unclear while key distant-water fishing states object to key provisions of the United

Nations Fish Stocks Agreement (see Chapter 2). The high seas regime's effectiveness is further weakened by a lack of agreement over the reach of provisions that extend compliance and enforcement regimes away from the traditional 'flag state' regime embedded in the LOSC, identified as having status as a 'sacred text' (Johnston and VanderZwaag 2000, p. 143).

Marine environmental protection has become an important focus for governments at all scales – local, national and regional or international – from the mid-1970s. As previously noted this has been a driver for both international and national attention to oceans governance. This attention was enhanced through well-publicised maritime disasters such as oil spills from tanker grounding or collisions, and increasing scientific evidence of degradation of the marine environment through dumping of pollutants, overfishing and industrial and other developments in the coastal zone. At the same time the focus on sustainable development has increased interest in the development and application of ecosystems management to marine environments and resources.

The 1970s saw increased international control over pollution from ships at sea, the development of conventions regulating and later prohibiting dumping of material at sea, and national declarations of marine protected areas (marine parks or reserves) – with Australia's declaration of the Great Barrier Reef Marine Park in 1975 a world-leading initiative. Attention shifted to management approaches as well as tools, with increasing concern at impacts on ecosystems from resource extraction. Development of ecosystems approaches began with the negotiation of the Antarctic Treaty System's Convention for the Conservation of Antarctic Marine Living Resources (CCAMLR). The CCAMLR, entering into force in 1982, attempted to ensure that ecosystem relationships – such as that between predator and prey species ('dependent and associated species') – were taken into account in marine resource activities such as fishing, traditionally managed as single stocks. The CCAMLR has been active, too, in focusing on managing incidental or by-catch of non-fish species such as seabirds, particularly albatross and petrel species, and has been a leader in developing conservation measures to address this problem (Haward et al. 1998; Hall and Haward 2001).

There are a number of international instruments that have direct or indirect relevance to the protection of the marine environment. In addition to the Convention on Biological Diversity, the World Heritage Convention does extend to marine areas (for example the Great Barrier Reef). The Convention on Biological Diversity, developed under the auspices of the United Nations Environment Programme (UNEP) came into force in December 1993. The convention was developed in recognition of the present and future value of biological diversity, including marine biodiversity and its significant reduction around the world. The intention is for the convention to be a powerful catalyst drawing together existing efforts to protect biological diversity and to provide strategic direction to the whole global effort in this area.

Biological diversity is defined in the convention as the variability among living organisms from all sources including terrestrial, marine and other aquatic ecosystems and the ecological complexes of which they are a part; this includes diversity within species, between species and of ecosystems. Each party to the Convention on Biological Diversity has responsibility for the conservation and sustainable use of its own biological diversity. Parties also have a responsibility to manage their own activities that may threaten biological diversity, regardless of where their effects may occur. Parties are to cooperate in implementing the convention in areas beyond national jurisdiction such as the high seas. There is a requirement for implementation through national plans and the integration of sustainable use into policies for sectors such as fisheries and forestry. Parties are required to give emphasis to *in situ* practices and policies (that is, conservation of ecosystems, habitats and species in their natural environment), encouraging development of protected areas. While there is a requirement for periodic reports to a conference of the parties for their review and comment, enforcement of obligations is weak.

Development of marine protected areas (MPAs) has been a highly controversial and politically charged process around the world. Often such designations have the effect of limiting or constraining existing uses or resource users from exploiting the areas within the MPA. The term 'MPA' incorporates a range of arrangements and management responses, from multiple-use areas, to 'no-take' closed areas. The term 'MPA' encompasses a diverse range of areas, from fishery nurseries to fully protected marine parks, and can be defined as an area that attempts to conserve or protect marine flora and/or fauna. The experience in designating and implementing MPAs within waters under national jurisdiction around the world is salutary. The benefits of MPAs are accepted but often their introduction is contentious and the source of friction and concern. Often marine resource users believe that their interests are sacrificed for broader political motivations in the development of these protected areas. Proposals to establish MPAs in high seas areas are even more problematic. While such initiatives are possible within existing legal regimes (and are being developed for the CCAMLR Area) they are unlikely to gain widespread support in the short term.

FROM SECTORAL TO INTEGRATED MANAGEMENT

Traditionally oceans and coastal policy has been developed in a fragmented, generally uncoordinated manner by sectoral agencies with responsibility for managing that sector, be it fisheries or shipping or marine environmental protection, based on legislation developed by government. As marine-related activities increased in scope and extent government followed with regulatory models to manage such activities. National government interests increased in the twentieth century, and influence increased significantly in the post Second World War period in response, first, to growing international attention to 'law of the sea' issues and, second, to perceived problems in managing marine activities.

We have noted elsewhere that 'the traditional institutional framework governing ocean management has considerable strength' but also that the 'challenge is to build on this framework and establish new institutions and processes' to deal with new demands (Haward 2003, p. 49). The development of a sectoral base to ocean management is understandable and is driven by traditional administrative and legislative models of government. While this approach is effective in addressing problems, challenges arise when management decisions have impacts or spillovers into other areas. This can lead to what has been termed 'the tyranny of small decisions' (HORSCERA 1991, p. 46) where significant and perhaps cumulative impacts can be felt from a decision. Land use decisions, for example, can have impacts on coastal and marine environments through fertilizers or chemical load into watercourses. Development of the coastal zone can have impacts on coastal and marine environments, yet traditional sectoral management arrangements would not necessarily address such impacts.

Attempts to develop more integrated approaches to oceans management have been promoted form the mid 1970s, supported by initiatives at the international, regional, national, sub-national and local government or community scales. These initiatives have first focused on coastal zones, and then have been adopted more broadly into oceans policy and governance They have also been centred on a shift from sectoral to integrated approaches to management of the coast, and increased recognition of the problem of cumulative impacts. Internationally the focus on integrated coastal zone management (ICZM) gained traction though the work of the World Commission on Environment and Development (WCED), also known as the Brundtland Commission, and its report Our Common Future (WCED 1990). This report noted that:

> the use of coastal areas for settlement, industry, energy facilities and recreation will accelerate .... Shore-lines and their resources will suffer ever increasing

damage if the current, business as usual approaches to policy, management, and institutions continue. (WCED 1990, p. 307)

Coastal and marine areas were also a focus of the United Nations Conference on Environment and Development (UNCED) held in Rio De Janerio, Brazil in 1992. Agenda 21, the soft law 'global action plan' developed at UNCED, for example, emphasised the need for more integrated approaches to coastal management. The World Coast Conference in 1993 held in Noordwijk in the Netherlands as an immediate follow-up to UNCED recognised that:

> ICZM has been identified as the most appropriate process to address current and long-term integrated coastal management issues including habitat loss, degradation of water quality, changes in hydrological cycles, depletion of coastal resources, and adaptation to sea-level rise and other impacts of global climate change. (Haward and Hildebrand 1996, p. 143)

The World Coast Conference helped 'to develop frameworks and methodologies (encapsulated in the Noordwijk Guidelines for Integrated Coastal Zone Management) for implementing ICZM' (Haward and Hildebrand 1996, p. 141). While the Noordwijk Guidelines provide a useful framework for development of coastal management programmes and plans (and have continuing relevance in the Indian Ocean region – see Francis and Torell 2004) key problems of government capacity and coordination still remain:

> The translation of broad global objectives into feasible programs at regional, national and provincial levels is not a simple matter. Apart from questions about jurisdiction, institutions, procedures and financial resources, there is the sheer diversity and complexity of environmental factors involved. It is not surprising that many of these issues become the province of a variety of stakeholders. Even if effective programs are devised, implementation becomes a significant problem in itself. (Davis and Haward 1994, p. 156)

In this case the relative strength of sectoral legislative and management approaches have considerable importance. Governments often have much stronger vertical links – being described as 'rods of iron' and contrasted to the 'threads of gossamer' as a metaphor for the much weaker horizontal links between agencies of the same government. These horizontal linkages and policy deliberations are at the core of integrated management. The terms 'rods of iron' and 'threads of gossamer' are derived from Warhurst's survey of 'inter-' and 'intra-governmental' linkages in Australia (Warhurst 1983). Warhurst's insights are useful in considering the opportunities and limitations in developing integrated policy and management for coasts and oceans that involves multiple stakeholders. Gaining agreement within government involving agencies with necessarily different perspectives on the marine and ocean domain may well be more difficult than gaining agreement between governments in, for example, fisheries management or principles for marine protected areas.

OCEANS GOVERNANCE, COORDINATION AND POLICY CAPACITY

Coordination in a minimal sense implies that component parts of a system work together so that they do not to impede, frustrate or negate each other's activities (Metcalfe 1994, p. 278). Policy capacity is linked to this, and has two key elements: first, the ability to make decisions (addressing processes or procedures), while the second relates to quality of decisions (addressing the substance of policy). Both elements of policy capacity are important in developing effective oceans governance. Policy capacity is affected by a number of factors including the relative size of agencies and resources, both human and financial, available to them (Peters 1996). Key agencies need to be able to maintain and extend their own capacity, and be able to display leadership in this area. These agencies also need to be able to coordinate their efforts with other agencies and actors.

Questions of coordination and policy capacity lead to consideration of the need to manage 'internal components' and 'external constituencies' (Allison 1992, p. 285). Managing internal components within agencies concerned with coastal or marine management will necessarily be complex, given the nature of such responsibilities. Managing the relationships with external constituencies is also likely to be complex given that government objectives are not always shared by other stakeholders. Non-governmental stakeholders including industry and business interests as well as environmental or conservation-oriented interest groups may have strong commitments to the policy area but may have significant differences (both with government and with other interests) in terms of priorities and policy options.

All governments have responsibilities for the development and implementation of policy. The structures and processes developed to undertake these activities form core institutional arrangements. In relation to issue areas such as oceans management these arrangements can influence the efficacy of policy responses. There is a vast range of organisational options available to address problems associated with oceans management. These options include establishing a specific agency, responsibility for management within a specified agency or coordinating a number of relevant agencies. This will lead to 'inter-institutional interaction' focusing on coordination across programmes (Pierre and Peters 2005, p. 138), and introduces the importance of horizontal governance, the 'threads of gossamer' of intra-governmental relations.

An important additional factor is the way in which policy is implemented. This introduces the concept of 'vertical' governance or the processes and relationships between central government and local agencies or governments (see Pierre and Peters 2005, p. 139). These relationships are central to establishing institutional arrangements to address problems associated with oceans management. The development of national 'plans of action' and response strategies implemented or impacting at local levels are examples of vertical governance. Such actions have utility in providing a national focus to the problem but these plans and/or strategies must be able to address problems at a local level.

One key element in any discussion of institutional arrangements focuses on the 'vertical' dimensions of governance – how such arrangements affect implementation of public policy. A centralised administrative system that delegates activities will have a different focus to a system that devolves responsibility to local levels and agencies, yet both systems necessarily involve institutions and processes to facilitate governance between central and sub-national and/or local 'government'. In federal states these institutions and processes can be complex, with intergovernmental relations forming a major area of focus in their own right. In each of the cases we examine in subsequent chapters, vertical governance is an important factor in shaping the development and implementation of ocean policy. Considerable work has been undertaken on the means to improve intergovernmental dimensions of public policy processes, particularly in policy fields such as oceans management where jurisdictional responsibilities enhance the rights and interests of sub-national governments. One consequence of focusing on 'vertical' dimensions of government may be to ignore the need for increased 'horizontal' coordination between different government agencies.

Guy Peters has noted a number of key factors that contribute to improved coordination across government agencies. These factors are:

- Structural manipulations cannot produce changes in behaviours, especially if existing behaviours are reinforced by other factors in government.
- There is often greater willingness to coordinate programmes at the bottom of organisations than at the top.
- Timing is important.

- Formal methods of coordination may not be as beneficial as the more informal techniques involving bargaining and negotiation (Peters 1998, pp. 304–9).

A focus on vertical and horizontal governance, and of institutional arrangements to address problems such as those associated with coastal zone management also addresses the question of policy capacity. Policy capacity – the ability to provide an effective solution to a problem – is linked to broader questions of institutional design. Policy capacity is affected by a number of factors including the relative size of agencies and resources, both human and financial available to them. In many economies the last 20 years have seen a reappraisal of government activities and greater use of alternative delivery mechanisms and/or increasing partnerships with private and third-sector organisations. These reforms may have increased the separation of responsibility for 'policy' from 'operations' (Bakvis 1997) and in some cases has contributed to a loss of policy capacity or effectiveness within agencies.

The identification of the 'internal management of external relationships' highlights a major factor contributing to capacity and coordination. This involves ensuring that adequate institutional arrangements and processes are in place so that national negotiating objectives can be established and appropriate strategies and tactics designed (Metcalfe 1994, p. 277). A considerable part of the work that goes into international negotiations involves negotiators negotiating with their own side to reconcile internal differences, to clarify objectives and priorities and to agree upon strategies and tactics (Metcalfe 1994, p. 277). This leads to the conclusion, also underscored by Weiss and Jacobson (1998, p. 553), that effective preparations require continual coordination among ministries at the national level.

DOMESTIC POLITICS AND INTERNATIONAL RELATIONS – OCEANS GOVERNANCE AS A 'TWO-LEVEL GAME'

The interdependence of international and domestic or national politics has been long recognized, often seen through the concept of 'linkage politics' and is most evocatively described by Putnam's image of the 'logic of two-level games':

> The politics of international negotiations can be usefully be conceived as a two-level game. At the national level, domestic groups pursue their interests by pressuring the government to adopt favourable policies, and politicians seek

power by constructing coalitions among those groups. At the international level, national governments seek to maximise their own ability to satisfy domestic pressures, while minimizing the adverse consequences of foreign developments. Neither of these two games can be ignored by central decision-makers, so long as their countries remain interdependent, yet sovereign. (Putnam 1988, p. 434)

The link between domestic interests and international aspirations can lead to complex interactions, including what has been termed the 'internationalization of domestic policy issues' (Hanf and Underdal 1998, p. 149). This affects 'the way in which the international dimensions of environmental management penetrate domestic society and politics, and how these processes within the nation state feed back upon the operation and further development of international agreements and institutions' (Hanf and Underdal 1998, p. 150). This interaction links to national policy-making, implementing commitments made in the negotiation of an international agreement or a regime. Effective decision-making is shaped by the ability to coordinate national objectives and interests as much as it involves the coordination of actions with other governments:

The impact of domestic factors on international policy-making is widely recognized, the mediating influence of co-ordination processes within national government requires careful consideration in its own right. The internal management of external relationships has a dual role in ensuring the coherent representation of national interests and in supporting the effective functioning of the international policy process. Poor internal coordination not only compromises national interests; it also adversely affects the performance of the system as a whole. (Metcalfe 1994, p. 276)

The development of national oceans policies and management arrangements as detailed in subsequent chapters owes much to the increased attention to oceans management at various international forums or initiatives. The launch of Australia's Oceans Policy in late December 1998, along with actions in Canada and the United States, for example, were driven by commitments to action within the United Nations-sponsored International Year of the Ocean.

LEARNING AND SHARING – POLICY TRANSFER

The concept of policy learning is contested – there are a number of different uses of the term and no necessarily agreed single definition. The concept of learning within policy-making is relatively old. It has links to the decision-making theory debates in the 1950s, and arguments for incremental changes to using small gradual adjustments to the existing decision. More recently the concept of learning has been linked closely to the concept of 'policy transfer', the process by which initiatives are adopted in other places, yet the two approaches are distinct (see below). There are a number of approaches to policy learning. Bennett and Howlett (1992), for example, distinguish between the instrumental and experiential – the former linked closely to concerns to ensure goal attainment and improve practical outcomes. The latter is a more normative approach – focusing on policy-makers' approaches to policy development.

This approach is also found in the work of Sabatier and the concept of policy-oriented learning (Sabatier 1986). This concept is integral to Sabatier's model of implementation, with learning occurring through interaction between advocacy coalitions. More recently learning has been linked to policy evaluation through the ideas such as 'evidenced-based policy making' (Sanderson 2002) that have currency among both policy practitioners and academic analysts. Scientific organisations and individuals form what Haas termed the 'epistemic community' (Haas 1989), ongoing links developed by shared interests in scientific discovery and, particularly, in large-scale marine science, the need for this science to progress through international collaborative scientific research programmes.

The concept of policy transfer provides insights into understanding policy change on the global, macro, meso and micro levels (Evans 2004, p. 212; Jacobs and Barnett 2000, p. 187; Evans and Davies 1999, p. 367). Policy transfer occurs when 'knowledge about policies, administrative arrangements, institutions and ideas in one political system (past or present) is used in the development of policies, administrative arrangements, institutions and ideas in another political system' (Dolowitz and Marsh 2000, p. 5). Levi-Faur and Vigoda-Gadot emphasise that policy transfer contributes to a 'better understanding of the process of policy change and governance in a global polity by improving [knowledge] of cross-cultural collaboration' (2006, p. 260). The policy transfer approach can be used to explain a variety of situations including in conjunction with other approaches and/or theories, and it has been applied in a range of policy areas including oceans policy development (see Vince 2004, 2008).

According to Dolowitz and Marsh there are a number of 'degrees of transfer' that range from 'copying' a policy to 'emulation' where only certain elements of the policy are transferred (Dolowitz and Marsh 2000, p. 13). Others have argued that it is a deeper process of learning 'about different concepts and approaches rather than specific policy designs' (Wolman 1992, p. 41; also see Stone 2000, p. 59). Dolowitz and Marsh identify nine categories of actors that are involved in the policy transfer process and these include 'elected officials, political parties, bureaucrats/civil servants, pressure groups, policy entrepreneurs and experts, transnational corporations, think tanks, supra-national governmental and nongovernmental institutions and consultants' (Dolowitz and Marsh 2000, p. 10). The utility of the insights from the policy transfer literature for the analysis of oceans governance arises from its interest in identifying the linkages between policies, and the means by which transfer occurrs. This analysis returns attention to the way in which domestic policy is developed and implemented.

DOMESTIC POLICY-MAKING – ACTORS, INSTITUTIONS, PROCESSES

Policy-making is a central activity of government, but as noted previously the focus on governance reinforces the point that government is not the only actor interested or influential in deliberations over policy. While a focus on government as policy-maker has always caricatured the reality of involvement in an engagement of multiple interests and in policy deliberations, it was not until the 1970s that the literature on policy-making addressed limitations in traditional approaches to policy development, or at least the traditional influences on policy-making, that focused solely on governmental processes. The emergence of policy subsystems approaches, the policy community and network models (Richardson and Jordan 1979; Rhodes 1985) and the advocacy coalition framework (Sabatier 1986; Sabatier and Jenkins-Smith 1993) are examples of attempts to broaden this analysis.

The sub-systems approach to the analysis of public policy-making recognised non-governmental groups as important actors, active in policy development and implementation not just as agitators for action or 'agenda setters'. Indeed some policies required the active help of these groups to implement and evaluate policy. This is particularly obvious in areas such as fisheries management where catch returns and related data are essential for modelling of stock abundance, and reinforces the partnership role of non-governmental actors in these management systems. In an early articulation of the subsystem approach Richardson and Jordan identified policy as

being made (and administered) between a myriad of interconnecting, interpenetrating organisations. It is the relationships involved in committees, the policy community of departments and groups, the practices of co-option and the consensual style, that perhaps better account for policy outcomes than do examinations of party stances, of manifestoes or of parliamentary influence. (Richardson and Jordan 1979, p. 74)

Following Richardson and Jordan's work many others developed the concept and utilised it in a range of areas, with some confusion over the use of terms such as 'community' and 'network'. Despite this confusion, work on clarifying the policy community had utility and the identification of actors based on their influence – the sub-government and the attentive public (Pross 1992) – provided further opportunities for analysis. The sub-government includes government agencies and institutionalised interest groups, while the attentive public includes other government agencies, private institutions pressure groups, specific interests, and individuals – including academics (Pross 1992). Further work has provided three important additional categories within the policy community: first, the executive core of key central agencies of ministers; second, the coordinating sub-government – key agencies within the sub-government; and third, the influence of international actors – for example foreign governments, scientific organisations and individuals (Homeshaw 1995). In terms of the latter, Homeshaw (1995) argued that the category of the international attentive public needed to be included in certain policy areas. Vince (2004) noted that international actors were often more than attentive observers and used the term 'international collaborators', emphasising their close interaction with other members of the sub-government. This included active involvement in policy development and as possible agents of policy transfer (Vince 2004, p. 61).

Analysis of oceans governance reiterates the salience of Homeshaw's categories; the executive core – ministers, the ministerial offices and lead agencies – provide important drivers of policy and of the policy process, while international scientific linkages and the roles of 'international collaborators' are central to achieving many of the goals related to improving knowledge of the oceans.

OCEANS GOVERNANCE – MANAGING THE BLUE PLANET

As noted above we concur with Pierre and Peters's (2005) evaluation of governance that centres on how priorities are set, the coherence of policy proposals, how policy is developed and implemented, and how it is evaluated. These criteria provide a framework for the analysis of ocean and coastal policy.

In analysing oceans governance we are interested in the development of new approaches to managing the world marine estate, such as ecosystem-based integrated oceans management, but we are also interested in the means by which these approaches are developed, implemented and evaluated. We are influenced, too, by Johnston's insights that a focus on governance 'embracing economic and societal as well as political values, coincides with a new determination to achieve a higher degree of effectiveness in the highly complex field of ocean management' (Johnston 2002, p. 3).

The preceding discussion has attempted to elaborate the concept of governance and develop a framework through which we can explore developments of international, regional and national initiatives directed at managing the world's oceanic domain. Governance, while increasingly a contested concept with no agreed definition, allows us to explore the development of responses to the challenges of oceans management that highlight the importance of policy development and implementation, and accountability for and evaluation of policy. While we recognise the importance of institutional frameworks, a 'governance lens' enables us to recognise that while governing can occur without government, 'government' still remains an important actor in both international and national arenas.

2. International instruments, initiatives and institutions

The contemporary framework for oceans governance has been influenced by a number of international instruments (primarily, but not exclusively, associated with the law of the sea) as well as initiatives and institutions that complement and extend these instruments. The 'law of the sea' has its antecedents in the Ancient Roman Empire with 'Pax Romana' governing the Mediterranean Sea and protecting vessels bringing people and cargo to and from Rome (Johnston 1994). The Law of the Sea Convention, entering into force in 1994, has been influential both as an instrument in its own right and as a framework to manage maritime activities.

The 'law of the sea' developed as European states established colonies and trading routes in the Americas, and in South and South-East Asia. Protecting these interests saw maritime power expand, and at the same time so did the ability to exert this power well beyond the coastal margin of the state. This enabled freedom of passage of ships on trade routes to be guaranteed, most notably by the power and presence of the British Royal Navy (Herman 2004). The power of the Royal Navy 'regularly intervened to protect the Briton and non-Briton alike for tyranny and violence' (Herman 2004, p. xix) – an early expression of intervention foreshadowed under the Proliferation Security Initiative developed by the United States of America in the early twenty-first century. As a state's maritime power expanded it was widely accepted, as noted in the preceding chapter, that it could also control that area of sea that it could defend from the shore, a right later to be incorporated into the concept of a territorial sea. This is an example of what is termed 'customary law', one of the two drivers of international law. The other driver is the establishment of legal instruments that formalise principles or practice and become binding on states that accept these provisions.

This chapter discusses the international framework for oceans governance, outlining key instruments initiatives and institutions. We also provide a short coverage on non-state actors, increasingly influential in this arena. We separate instruments into either binding 'hard law' or voluntary, hortatory 'soft law' categories but recognise that this dichotomy may be limited. International non-binding agreements may contribute directly to improved national capacity through integration in national legislation, while compliance with formal binding instruments may be superficial. Johnston's metaphor of the box of chocolates is appropriate here. The performance, effectiveness or influence of instruments is difficult to ascertain prior to operation, just as it may be impossible to distinguish those chocolates with soft or hard centres before consuming them (Johnson 1994). An instrument may appear robust but have a soft centre that limits its effectiveness.

INSTRUMENTS

The Law of the Sea Convention

The 1982 Law of the Sea Convention (LOSC) is at the centre of regimes governing the world's seas and oceans, providing the basis for what was described as a comprehensive 'constitution for the oceans' (Koh 1983). The LOSC is built upon a key principle – the elaboration of the rights of states brings related obligations and responsibilities. The LOSC is a classic hard law instrument that includes mandatory provisions – language that includes the words 'states shall ...'. Despite these provisions the LOSC, centred on traditional concepts such as flag state responsibility, has weaker provisions affecting actions outside the exclusive economic zone – exhorting states to seek cooperative arrangements to manage activities.

The twentieth century saw considerable progress in the codification of the law of the sea, although initial attempts in the 1930s to draft a binding convention under the auspices of the League of Nations failed. This failure occurred for a number of reasons, most notably the collapse of the League and the increasing belligerence of key states in the march towards what became the Second World War. The establishment of the International Law Commission (ILC) by the United Nations in 1949 provided an opportunity to revisit questions surrounding the law of the sea. The ILC's work was encouraged by President Truman's announcement in 1945 that the United States claimed sovereignty over the continental shelf off the coast of the United States. The 'Truman Proclamation' encouraged similar actions from other states, and these actions were a major impetus for resuming international discussions on the law of the sea. The agenda of the ILC's meeting in 1952 covered the 'regime of high seas' and the 'regime of territorial waters' (United Nations International Law Commission 2007).

In 1958 the first United Nations-sponsored Conference on the Law of the Sea (UNCLOS I) resulted in the drafting of a number of instruments that became known as the Geneva Conventions on the Law of the Sea. These were conventions on:

- the High Seas;
- the Continental Shelf;
- the Territorial Sea and Contiguous Zone; and
- Fishing and Conservation of the Living Resources of the High Seas.

These conventions, with the exception of the Convention on the Continental Shelf, did not achieve widespread acceptance or sufficient ratifications. In 1960 a second, but inconclusive, United Nations Conference on the Law of the Sea (UNCLOS II) was held in an attempt to progress these matters. It was not until after a number of high profile marine environmental disasters occurred in the mid-1960s that a further attempt within the United Nations General Assembly was made to discuss the law of the sea. The Third United Nations Conference on the Law of the Sea (UNCLOS III) was established by a General Assembly resolution in 1970. This outcome was influenced, as noted in Chapter 1, by the impassioned advocacy of Arvid Pardo, Ambassador of Malta to the United Nations. The focus of the UNCLOS III was set by the words of the resolution to address:

> all matters relating to the law of the sea ... bearing in mind the problems of ocean space are closely interrelated and need to be considered as a whole. (United Nations General Assembly 1970)

This focus was to remain as the convention was negotiated as a comprehensive 'package deal' rather than, as followed by the 1958 Conference, separate instruments.

The UNCLOS III was a complex multilateral exercise in diplomacy. The conference was held between 1974 and 1982, over 15 formal sessions of 585 days in total as well as numerous inter-sessional meetings. The conference had an open-ended time frame and involved between 2000 and 3000 delegates representing 150 countries. Following the eight years of negotiations, key issues remained sticking points – particularly surrounding deep-seabed mining – and it took another 12 years for the required 60 states to ratify the convention. The Law of the Sea Convention (LOSC) entered into force in November 1994.

The LOSC contains 320 articles in 17 parts and nine annexes (see Table 2.1). It provides the basis for managing ocean space and provides definitions of key maritime zones for costal states, based on establishing baselines from which these zones are delimited. These zones include the territorial sea and contiguous zone, the exclusive economic zone (EEZ), the continental shelf and the high seas (see Figure 2.1). While providing a comprehensive framework 'constitution' for the oceans it embodies 1960s and 1970s worldviews and can be read as emphasising a developmental rather than a conservation approach to exploitation of marine resources. The LOSC predates ideas such as the precautionary approach and ecosystem-based management that developed in the 1980s and 1990s. The inclusion of these latter principles in later hard and soft law instruments that are linked – even implicitly – to the LOSC shows, however, that the regime established and supported by this convention can adapt to new and emergent customary practice, even if this is not yet accepted as customary law.

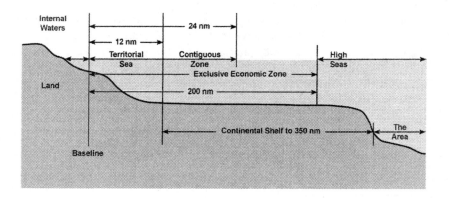

Figure 2.1 Maritime zones under the Law of the Sea Convention

The LOSC provides clear rights for coastal states, yet these rights have concomitant obligations. Article 61, for example, notes that 'the coastal state shall determine the allowable catch of the living resources of its exclusive economic zone' but also introduces the need to 'take into consideration the effects on species associated or dependent upon harvested species with a view to maintaining or restoring populations of such associated and dependent species'. This introduces a broader focus than just target species and foreshadows what has become known as the ecosystem approach to fisheries harvesting. Articles 63 and 64 indicate that coastal states and other states shall cooperate over the utilisation of straddling and highly migratory stocks. The limitations apparent in these articles, particularly over cooperation between coastal and distant-water fishing states, led to negotiation of further instruments.

Part XI dealt with the area outside the exclusive economic zone or the extended continental shelf of coastal states' national jurisdiction and elaborated the common heritage of mankind principles and established institutions and regimes governing deep seabed mining. This was the most controversial component of the convention, and concern amongst Western industrial states contributed to their reluctance to ratify the convention.

Between 1990 and 1994, 15 meetings were convened following the UN Secretary-General's initiative for informal consultation to resolve 'problems with some aspects of the deep seabed mining provisions of the Convention that had prevented some states from ratifying or acceding to the Convention' (UNDOALOS 2007). In August 1993 an informal paper prepared by representatives of a number of states was circulated as a contribution to the ongoing consultations.

The 'Boat Paper' provided further impetus to resolve outstanding issues, with additional encouragement occurring on 16 November 1993 when the sixtieth instrument of ratification or accession for the LOSC was lodged. This meant that the convention would enter into force one year later.

In April 1994 further consultations took place based on a 'further updated version of the Boat Paper entitled "Draft Resolution and Draft Agreement Relating to Implementation of Part XI of the 1982 United Nations Convention on the Law of the Sea dated 14 February 1994"' (UNDOALOS 2007). On 3 June 1994 a revised implementation agreement and resolution was concluded, with the resolution put to a session of the General Assembly. The Agreement Relating to Implementation of Part XI of the 1982 United Nations Convention on the Law of the Sea was then open for signature, and facilitated ratification of the convention by a number of states.

While the question of deep-seabed mining exercised considerable diplomatic efforts in the early 1990s, other aspects of the LOSC also influenced debates shaping international oceans governance. Article 87 elaborates the 'freedom of the high seas' that includes 'freedom of fishing, subject to the conditions laid down in section 2'. This, in accordance with the 'rights – obligations' principle, was never seen as an unfettered freedom. Article 87 (2) notes that: 'these freedoms shall be exercised by all states with due regard for the interests of other states in their exercise of the freedom of the high seas.' Article 91 (on the nationality of ships), and Article 94 (on the duties of the flag state) are important bases for the high seas regime, despite the development and application of 'port state controls' to fisheries in more recent instruments (see following section).

Table 2.1 Provisions of the United Nations Law of the Sea Convention

Part	Article Number	Content
I	1	Terms and Scope
II	2–33	Territorial Sea and Contiguous Zone
III	34–45	Straits Used for International Navigation
IV	46–54	Archipelagic States
V	55–75	Exclusive Economic Zone
VI	76–85	Continental Shelf
VII	86–120	High Seas
VIII	121	Regime of Islands
IX	122–123	Enclosed or Semi-Enclosed Seas
X	124–132	Rights of Access of Land-Locked States to and From the Sea and Freedom of Transit
XI	133–191	The Area
XII	192–237	Protection and Preservation of the Marine Environment
XIII	238–265	Marine Scientific Research
XIV	266–278	Development and Transfer of Marine Technology
XV	279–299	Settlement of Disputes
XVI	300–304	General Provisions
XVII	305–320	Final Provisions
Annex I		Highly Migratory Species
Annex II		Commission on the Limits of the Continental Shelf
Annex III	1–22	Basic Conditions of Prospecting, Exploration and Exploitation
Annex IV	1–13	Statute of the Enterprise
Annex V	1–14	Conciliation
Annex VI	1–41	Statute of the International Tribunal for the Law of the Sea
Annex VII	1–13	Arbitration
Annex VIII	1–5	Special Arbitration
Annex IX	1–8	Participation by International Organizations

Source: United Nations (1983, pp. i–xviii).

Articles 116, 117, 118 and 119 of the LOSC provide key provisions related to the conservation and management of living resources of the high seas. Article 117, the duty of states to adopt measures related to their nationals as necessary for conservation of living resources of the high seas, provides a powerful tool. The LOSC also outlines the need for the protection and preservation of various marine environments (Articles 192–237). Special regimes for the fishing of anadromous and highly migratory fish species are established in Articles 64–67. The management and protection of marine mammals is addressed in Articles 65 and 120 of the LOSC.

Fisheries

United Nations Fish Stocks Agreement

Problems in managing straddling stocks – those that were found both inside and outside a coastal state's EEZ – emerged forcefully in the early 1990s, particularly off the Canadian Atlantic Grand Banks. Perceptions of overfishing by distant-water fleets on the high seas encouraged Canada and a number of other like-minded states to convene a number of meetings prior to the scheduled United Nations Conference on Environment and Development (UNCED) meeting in June 1992. As a result, a provision calling for an international conference on highly migratory and straddling fish stocks was included in the UNCED's Agenda 21, Chapter 17.

The United Nations Agreement for the Implementation of the Provisions of the United Nations Convention on the Law of the Sea of 10 December 1982 Relating to the Conservation and Management of Straddling Fish Stocks and Highly Migratory Fish Stocks (United Nations Fish Stocks Agreement or UNFSA) is based on key principles incorporated in the LOSC related to cooperation between states. The agreement was negotiated over six sessions from April 1993 to August 1995. Following the final session and its adoption the UNFSA opened for signature on 4 December 1995 and entered into force on 11 December 2001, one month after the lodgement of the thirtieth instrument of ratification.

The compliance and enforcement provisions within the UNFSA – Articles 19, 20, 21 and 23 – provide that states will ensure that vessels under their flag comply with regional and subregional measures and that states shall enforce such measures irrespective of where violations occur. A state shall immediately and fully investigate any alleged violation of such measures. It shall require its vessels to give information to the investigating authority regarding vessel position, catches, fishing gear, fishing operations and related activities in the area of an alleged violation.

The UNFSA includes significant non-flag-state enforcement powers (Rayfuse 2004). States parties that are members of regional or subregional fisheries management organisations may detain vessels that have engaged in activities that undermine the effectiveness of the organisations' conservation and management measures on the high seas until such time as appropriate action is taken by the flag-state (see Article 21 (8), also Article 23 (1)). A port state has the right and duty to take certain measures such as inspect documents, fishing gear and catch on board vessels when such vessels are voluntarily in its ports. A port state may adopt regulations prohibiting landings and trans-shipments where it has been established that the catch has been taken in a manner which undermines the effectiveness of subregional, regional or global conservation and management measures on the high seas. The provisions of these port state controls have been described as 'controversial element of compliance regimes' (Stokke 2000, p. 220).

Regional Fisheries Management Organizations (RFMOs) have a number of key functions under the UNFSA. They are charged with the development of 'participatory rights' that include 'allocation of allowable catches or levels of fishing effort'. This is a difficult and contentious issue as RFMOs vary considerably in their methods of allocation. These vary from national allocations (for example the Commission for the Conservation of Southern Bluefin Tuna – CCSBT) or broad-based catch limits (for example the Commission for the Conservation of Antarctic Marine Living Resources – CCAMLR). Allocation methods may include a range of tools including closures as soon as the total allowable catch (TAC) is reached – what has been termed a 'Olympic-style' fishery, as used, for example, by the CCAMLR. Other tools, such as constraints on fishing effort, can be used. This includes, for example, limits on the number of vessels or on gear, and these can be issued in conjunction with other measures. The International Commission for the Conservation of Atlantic Tunas (ICCAT) has developed complex criteria for allocations, yet arguably the more complex the criteria the less effective it will be. Catch history is the traditional basis for arguing for allocation. This can sometimes be seen to reward unsustainable practices. One possible development is a stronger international commitment opposing claims of past (unregulated) catch as the basis for allocations under RFMOs. Catch history is not the only criterion in determining 'participatory rights' in RFMOs. The importance of other criteria was identified in the early years of the CCAMLR – 'no data, no fish' became shorthand for determining interests and allocation.

The UNFSA provides that where a competent RFMO exists states should either become members or they should agree to apply the conservation and management measures established by such organisations. Only states which are members of RFMOs, or which agree to apply the relevant RFMO conservation and management measures, shall have access to the fishery resources to which these measures apply. Membership of relevant RFMOs is open to states having a 'real interest' in the fisheries concerned (see Molenaar 2000). While not defined, this is a test to be determined by the existing membership of the RFMO. Certain criteria for determining 'real interest' by RFMOs are found within the UNFSA. These include: fishing patterns and practices; contributions to conservation and management of stocks; collection and provision of data; and the conduct of scientific research on the stocks. These criteria are supplemented by consideration of the needs of coastal communities, coastal states that are 'overwhelmingly dependent' on exploitation of living marine resources, and the interests of developing states.

The problem of catches from non-parties has been traditionally addressed by RFMOs through resolutions and diplomatic *démarches* aimed at persuading particular non-party states to withdraw an authorisation of vessels or to comply with relevant fisheries management regulations through effort limitation and national regulation. It should be noted that in the UNFSA non-members or non-participants are not discharged from their obligations to cooperate, such as not issuing licenses for straddling or highly migratory fish stocks subject to conservation and management measures by regional organisations. There is also a duty on members of RFMOs to exchange information on non-member fishing operations. Parties are also obligated to encourage non-parties to become parties and adopt appropriate laws. The potential of these bodies is illustrated by measures such as limiting or refusing port access and/or introducing trade-related controls to deter catches from non-party vessels that have been initiated in several RFMOs.

States party to the UNFSA take part in regular, annual informal consultations, with the first of these meetings held in 2002. The review mechanism included in the agreement saw a Review Conference on the Agreement for the Implementation of the Provisions of the United Nations Convention on the Law of the Sea of 10 December 1982 Relating to the Conservation and Management of Straddling Fish Stocks and Highly Migratory Fish Stocks held in New York from 22 to 26 May 2006. This review conference 'was mandated to assess the effectiveness of the agreement in securing the conservation and management of straddling and highly migratory fish stocks by reviewing and assessing the adequacy of its provisions and, if necessary, proposing means to strengthening the substance and methods of implementation of those provisions' (United Nations General Assembly 2005, p. 6).

The Compliance Agreement

The Agreement to Promote Compliance with International Conservation and Management Measures by Fishing Vessels on the High Seas (Compliance Agreement) seeks to ensure that there is effective flag-state control over fishing vessels operating on the high seas. It was created to deter the practice of reflagging of vessels to avoid compliance with conservation and management rules for fishing activities on the high seas. The Compliance Agreement entered into force on 24 April 2003, with 35 acceptances at the end of March 2007. The Compliance Agreement is an integral part of the Code of Conduct for Responsible Fisheries (see below) and is a legally binding (hard law) instrument. It is designed to apply to all fishing vessels that are used or intended for fishing on the high seas, although parties may exempt vessels of less than 24 metres in length. The exemption of vessels under 24 metres in length has been seen as a major weakness, but this provision must be read in conjunction with Article III (b) of the Compliance Agreement. If a party exempts vessels less than 24 metres in length, the party 'shall … take effective measures in respect of any such fishing vessel that undermines the effectiveness of international conservation and management measures'.

The Compliance Agreement also allows a port state 'to promptly notify the flag state' if it has 'reasonable grounds for believing that a fishing vessel has been used for an activity that undermines the effectiveness of international conservation and management measures' (Article V (2)). This provision also states that 'parties may make arrangements' to enable the port state 'to undertake such investigatory measures as may be considered necessary'.

The Food and Agriculture Organization (FAO) is also requesting, on an ad hoc basis, that countries which have not accepted the Compliance Agreement make information available for the organisation concerning their vessels authorised to fish on the high seas. A database to support the implementation of the agreement has already been established.

The Code of Conduct for Responsible Fisheries

The Code of Conduct for Responsible Fisheries encourages states and fishers to use selective and environmentally safe fishing gear and practices. It is a voluntary, soft law instrument that is directly linked to 'relevant rules of international law', including the LOSC. The code contains six thematic areas or chapters for which guidelines should be developed:

1. fishery management practices;
2. fishing operations;
3. aquaculture development;

4. integrating of fisheries into coastal area management;
5. post-harvest practices and trade; and
6. fishery research.

The Compliance Agreement is an integral part of the Code of Conduct. States should ensure compliance with and enforcement of conservation and management measures. States authorising fishing and fishing support vessels flying their flag should exercise effective control over those vessels. The code 'provides guidance which may be used where appropriate in the formulation and implementation of international agreements and other legal instruments, both binding and voluntary'. It is this provision that has been used to support the development of a series of International Plans of Action (IPOAs).

The first three IPOAs addressed fishing capacity, sharks and seabirds:

- the International Plan of Action for the Management of Fishing Capacity;
- the International Plan of Action for the Conservation and Management of Sharks; and
- the International Plan of Action for Reducing Incidental Catch of Seabirds in Longline Fisheries.

These IPOAs were developed following concerns expressed by member state at the FAO's Committee on Fisheries (COFI) meeting in 1997. Two intergovernmental meetings were held in 1998 and the three IPOAs were adopted at the 23rd meeting of the COFI in February 1999, and endorsed by the FAO Council in June 1999.

Australia raised the problem of illegal, unreported, and unregulated Fishing (IUU) fishing at the COFI meeting in February 1999. At the FAO Ministerial Conference in Rome on 10–11 March 1999, following the COFI meeting, the FAO declared that it would develop an international plan of action to deal effectively with all forms of IUU fishing (FAO 1999) to be tabled at the next COFI meeting in February 2001. This decision was supported by a number of member states, including Australia, Canada and the European Community. As with other IPOAs the IPOA-IUU is voluntary, and 'elaborated within the framework of the Code of Conduct' (FAO 2000). The Code of Conduct provides the basis for 'the interpretation and application of the IPOA and its relationship with other international instruments' (FAO 2000). Application of the IPOA-IUU to vessels flying 'flag of convenience', would occur through coordinated efforts by states, RFMOs and other relevant agencies including the FAO.

The International Plan of Action to Prevent, Deter and Eliminate Illegal, Unreported and Unregulated Fishing (IPOA-IUU)

The IPOA-IUU was developed from an initial expert consultation in May 2000 and two sessions of a technical consultation (October 2000 and February 2001). The first session of the technical consultation produced a preliminary draft IPOA, working initially from, but extensively reviewing and revising, the document produced at the Expert Consultation. Emphasis was placed on linking the IPOA-IUU to the provisions of the LOSC, particularly the centrality of flag-state controls. There was not unanimous agreement over the text: 11 delegations requested reservations on specific paragraphs, and Mexico placed a general reservation on two sections related to 'Port State Measures' and 'Internationally Agreed Market-Related Measures'. The group of Latin American and Caribbean states placed a general reservation on the Spanish text.

The second session of the Technical Consultation on Illegal, Unreported and Unregulated Fishing was held in Rome on 22–23 February 2001 concluded the IPOA-IUU. The COFI approved the IPOA on 2 March 2001 by consensus (with Canada noting a reservation on the text), and urged all members 'to take necessary steps to effectively implement' the plan of action. The focus of the plan of action on 'fisheries specific issues' was reinforced. The status of the IPOA as a 'soft law', hortatory instrument was reinforced by the sentence: 'nothing in this IPOA affects, or should be interpreted as affecting, the rights and obligations of States under international law' (IPOA-IUU paragraph 13, see FAO 2002, p. 87).

The IPOA-IUU addressed a number of emerging issues and extended the range of tools that could be used to combat IUU fishing. A paragraph on 'Economic Incentives' noted the problem of economic support to the fishing industry being used by 'companies, vessels or person that are involved in IUU fishing'. The sections on 'Port State Measures' and 'Internationally-Agreed Market-Related Measures' attracted considerable attention. The IPOA also includes the provision that 'where a port State has clear evidence that a vessel having been granted access to its ports has engaged in IUU fishing activity, the port State should not allow that vessel to land or tranship fish in its ports, and should report the matter to the flag State of the vessel' (paragraph 56, see FAO 2002, p. 97).

The provisions related to internationally agreed market-related measures (paragraphs 66–76) were anchored to World Trade Organization (WTO) 'principles, rights and obligations' in a new paragraph added in the February session (paragraph 65). Paragraph 66 reinforced the nexus with WTO rules and disciplines, and notes that: 'trade-related measures should only be used in exceptional circumstances, where other measures have proven unsuccessful to prevent, deter and eliminate IUU fishing, and only after consultation with interested states' (FAO 2002, p. 98). Paragraph 68 of the IPOA emphasises, too, that trade-related measures are seen as supporting 'cooperative efforts' by states to ensure that trade in fish and fish products 'does not in any way encourage IUU fishing'. This paragraph notes that RFMOs may use such multilateral trade-related measures in ways that do not in any way 'undermine the effectiveness of conservation and management measures which are consistent with the 1982 UN [Law of the Sea] Convention' (FAO 2002, p. 99).

The IPOA-IUU, linking traditional flag-state responsibilities with port state and market or trade-related measures, reflects a significant development in fisheries governance, yet at the same time builds on provisions of the LOSC, UNFSA and the Compliance Agreement.

Whaling

Whaling began as artisanal subsistence operations developed around cultural and social traditions centred on operations in semi-enclosed bays or from shore-based whaling stations. Development in technology, both in relation to ship construction and design and in terms of harpoons, together with the decline in northern hemisphere (North Atlantic) whale stocks led to the development of what has been termed 'modern whaling' in around 1865 with the invention of the cannon-fired harpoon by the Norwegian Svend Foyn. By the early twentieth century whaling was centred in the southern hemisphere and by the outbreak of First World War two-thirds of world whaling was concentrated on the Falkland Islands.

Concern over the state of whale stocks led to a 1928 agreement between UK and Norway over licensing and 'management' – the same rules for shore-based and pelagic whaling. The International Council for the Exploration of the Seas (ICES) in 1929 told the League of Nations that 'expansion of industry in recent years constitutes a real menace to maintenance of whale stocks'. Attempts at international regulation of whaling followed in 1931 with the negotiation of the Geneva Convention for Whaling that entered into force in 1934. This convention had limited efficacy but was a template for later developments through the introduction of the 'blue whale unit' (1 blue = 2 fin = 2.5 humpback = 6 sei whales) as the basis of managing catch. Lack of consensus over whaling led to a 1937 conference called to restrict catches being described by leading commentators as a 'a total fiasco' (Tønnessen and Johnsen 1982, p. 453).

After the Second World War, when stocks rebuilt and alternatives to whale oil developed, a more concerted effort to ensure regulation of whaling saw the International Convention for the Regulation of Whaling (ICRW) negotiated in 1946, creating the International Whaling Commission (IWC).

The ICRW Preamble emphasises the importance of management of whaling in 'the interest of nations in safeguarding natural resources for future generations' and 'proper conservation ... orderly development of the whaling industry'. This 'wise use' model emphasises that the ICRW and IWC were designed to manage the harvest of whales, not to stop whaling. The ICRW entered into force on 10 November 1948, with the first meeting of the IWC held in May 1949.

The IWC has had a challenging task in ensuring the management of whale stocks. Initial debate focused on establishing catch regimes and quota negotiations began in 1958. Debate over the state of stocks occurred in the late 1960s with the new management procedure introduced in 1975 together with catch limits. Objections to commercial whaling increased in the 1970s and 1980s, with moves to establish sanctuaries and a moratorium being supported. The membership of the IWC increased with many of the states committed to a moratorium. The Indian Ocean sanctuary was established in 1979 and a moratorium was supported in 1982 to take effect in 1986.

Following the introduction of the moratorium the IWC Scientific Committee

> embarked on a major review of the status of whale stocks (including an examination of current stock size, recent population trends and productivity) which it called the Comprehensive Assessment . (IWC 2007)

This led to the development of the Revised Management Procedure (RMP), after eight years of discussion. The RMP was developed as 'a scientifically robust method of setting safe catch limits for certain stocks (groups of whales of the same species living in a particular area) where the numbers are plentiful' (IWC 2007). In addition members of the IWC agreed that 'an inspection and observation scheme must be in place to ensure that agreed catch limits are not exceeded' (IWC 2007), prior to any action taken to lift the moratorium and return to commercial whaling. Improving reporting was designed to overcome problems with under-reporting of whale catches that had been widespread in the past (see Holt 2001). This system of inspection, together with the RMP, formed the Revised Management Scheme.

Japan, Norway and Iceland have opposed the moratorium on whaling and Japan in particular has continued to undertake 'scientific whaling' as permitted under the IWC, despite criticisms of need for lethal research on whales (Jabour et al. 2007). Japan (and like-minded pro-whaling countries) have been marshalling supporters within the IWC to overturn the moratorium, while Australia, the USA, New Zealand and the United Kingdom (with other like-minded anti-whaling countries) have been pushing to extend the status quo, and limit current Japanese scientific whaling programmes and lethal whale research. Progress in implementing the Revised Management Scheme has also stalled. Following the 2007 meeting of the IWC an inter-sessional meeting was held in March 2008 to address the future of the IWC.

Marine Pollution

As noted in Chapter 1, marine pollution has been a focusing issue related to calls to strengthen and improve governance of the world's seas and oceans. This attention has intensified in the aftermath of large scale of disasters arising from accidental discharge of crude oil from oil tankers such as the Torrey Canyon in 1967, the Amoco Cadiz in 1978 and the Exxon Valdez in 1989. The impact of discharges of oil, even in amounts regarded as relatively small in comparison with these disasters, can be significant and foul the sea and shorelines, affecting birds and marine animals. The disasters emphasise the significance of arrangements to combat and mitigate the effects of ship-sourced marine pollution, and the integrated nature of such clean-up operations that often involve different agencies, local governments, port authorities, shipping and salvage companies and the community.

Increasing use of very large bulk carriers ('supertankers') to transport raw materials such as crude oil in the second half of the twentieth century increased concern over the management of such shipping, the mitigation of potential disasters and the development of agreed measures in case of discharges. While most public attention is directed at the effects of oil spills through groundings, collisions or structural failure of ships, pollution of the marine environment from land-based sources is by far the most problematic.

Ship-sourced pollution has attracted considerable international attention: first, in response to the accidental discharge of pollutants; and second, from the dumping of wastes (including ballast water and plastics and other material) from vessels. Ship-sourced pollution is regulated under two international conventions, MARPOL 1973/78 (the International Convention for the Prevention of Pollution from Ships) and the London Convention (International Convention on Offshore Dumping 1975) and its 1996 Protocol. Annexes to MARPOL deal with different ship-sourced pollutants, with Annex V (governing garbage) totally prohibiting the disposal of plastics, including fishing gear, into the sea.

The International Convention for Control and Management of Ships' Ballast Water and Sediments was adopted by consensus at a diplomatic conference at the International Maritime Organization (IMO) in London on Friday 13 February 2004. Seventy-four states, one associate member of the IMO, two international governmental organisations and eight international non-governmental organisations attended this conference. This convention will enter force 12 months after ratification by 30 states representing 35 per cent of the world's merchant fleet. At 31 March 2008 the convention had 13 contracting states representing 3.6 per cent of the world's fleet.

Marine Environmental Protection

A number of other relevant international instruments address aspects of coastal and marine environmental protection. The Convention on Biological Diversity (CBD) entered into force in December 1993. This convention was developed in recognition of the present and future value of biological diversity, including marine biodiversity (Norse 1993), and its significant reduction around the world. Each party to the convention has responsibility for the conservation and sustainable use of its own biological diversity, and they are to cooperate in implementing the convention in areas beyond national jurisdiction such as the high seas. The CBD gave more explicit focus to marine and coastal issues through the 'Jakarta Mandate' negotiated at the second meeting of state parties to the CBD in 1995. The Jakarta Mandate provided a programme of action that would focus on implementing the provisions of the convention as they related to marine and coastal environments.

Other environmental instruments include the Convention on Conservation of Migratory Species of Wild Animals (CMS or the Bonn Convention) and the Convention on Trade in Endangered Species of Wild Fauna and Flora (CITES). While the CMS has addressed issues related to the impacts of incidental catch of seabirds associated with fishing, CITES appears to provide opportunities to monitor and regulate trade in some fish species.

Convention on Trade in Endangered Species of Wild Fauna and Flora

CITES regulates trade in species that are threatened with extinction or may become so as a result of international trade driven by commercial demand (Kimball 2001, p. 33). Article II of CITES provides for the inclusion in Appendix I of species threatened with extinction that are or may be affected by trade. Listing on Appendix I prohibits international trade in wild specimens but does not prohibit the harvest of or domestic sale of fish caught by recreational or commercial fishers within a state's EEZ. Such species, though, could not be exported and such restrictions would apply to foreign fishing within a state's EEZ where the fish are actually landed in another state. Article II further provides for the inclusion in Appendix II of species that are not necessarily threatened but may become so unless trade is strictly controlled.

Appendix II allows regulated trade to continue under a permit system that allows for trade monitoring. CITES, too:

expressly reaffirmed the benefits of commercial trade for conserving species and ecosystems and/or for the development of local people when carried out at a level that is not detrimental to the survival of the species in question. (Kimball 2001, p. 33)

Few marine species are currently listed under CITES appendices and these are primarily higher vertebrates, such as great whales, sea turtles and salt-water crocodiles. Only a limited number of fish species are listed under CITES: anadromous sturgeons, coelacanth and totoaba. It should be noted that CITES can apply to species that are subject to regulation under other treaties, although '[e]fforts to date to designate certain depleted fish species (e.g., Atlantic Bluefin tuna) for protection pursuant to CITES have not been successful' (Kimball 2001, p. 33; see also Haward 2004).

In 1992, Sweden attempted to include the western Atlantic bluefin tuna in Appendix I of CITES and the eastern Atlantic population on Appendix II. This was the first time a highly migratory species subject to a commercial fishery had been proposed for listing under CITES. The proposal was opposed by the bulk of ICCAT members and was unsuccessful. In June 1994, Kenya proposed listing of both northern and southern bluefin tuna on Appendix II but the proposal was withdrawn shortly afterwards, supposedly after pressure from Japan. Opposition from ICCAT members to the proposal to list bluefin tuna on CITES centred on concerns that such a listing would reduce the ICCAT's efficacy as the appropriate management body and that the proposal failed to recognise the steps the ICCAT had taken to reduce bluefin catches (Bergin and Haward 1996, pp. 89–93).

Australia proposed listing of Patagonian toothfish on CITES Appendix II at the 12th Conference of the Parties (COP 12) held in Santiago, Chile in November 2002. This listing was seen by Australia as strengthening the CCAMLR's management and trade monitoring arrangements. The Antarctic and Southern Oceans Coalition (ASOC) argued that as CITES can designate the CCAMLR as the management and/or scientific authority, the CCAMLR would remain 'the appropriate body for management of toothfish' (ASOC 2002). Australia attracted broad opposition to this proposal at the CCAMLR XXI meeting, with only New Zealand supporting the proposal (CCAMLR 2002). Australia's proposal for Appendix II listing was withdrawn at the CITES meeting and instead a non-binding resolution that 'encourages all CITES parties to voluntarily participate in the pre-existing trade tracking system managed by the Commission for the Conservation of Antarctic Marine Living Resources' (ASOC 2002) was agreed.

Convention on the Conservation of Migratory Species of Wild Animals
The Convention on the Conservation of Migratory Species of Wild Animals (CMS or the Bonn Convention) has not had a major direct influence on marine species. It has, however, provided a hard law instrument to address the issue of seabird by-catch associated with fishing. This convention 'provides a framework for further action by its parties both to protect migratory species as such during their trans-boundary migrations and to preserve their habitats' (Birnie and Boyle 1995, p. 433). Appendix I of the Bonn Convention provides a list of those migratory species which are endangered. Range states are required to prohibit the taking of these animals, with few exceptions, so as to give them full protection. Appendix II lists 'migratory species which have an unfavourable conservation status and which require international agreements for their conservation and management, as well as those that would significantly benefit from the international cooperation that could be achieved by an international agreement' (CMS Article IV (1).

The convention provides for two types of agreements for species listed in Appendix II. First, there are 'AGREEMENTs' (the capitalisation is intentional) intended to benefit migratory species – especially those with an unfavourable conservation status – over their entire range, as provided for in Articles IV and V of the convention. Parties are also encouraged to conclude a second type of agreement (spelt in lower case, to differentiate them from 'AGREEMENTs') for populations of species that periodically cross national jurisdictional boundaries. As at May 2008 there are seven CMS AGREEMENTS, including the Agreement on the Conservation of Albatrosses and Petrels ACAP (CMS 2008).

Agreement on the Conservation of Albatrosses and Petrels (ACAP)
At the 1999 meeting of state parties to the CMS a Resolution on Southern Hemisphere Albatross Conservation was passed. This resolution, inter alia, accepted Australia's offer to initiate further discussions in early 2000 with all parties that are range states, with a view to the development of a CMS AGREEMENT directed at the conservation of these species. This aspect of the resolution built on previous discussions conducted during the late 1990s and increased scientific concern over the state of these stocks. The first international conference on the conservation and management of albatrosses was held in Hobart, Australia in late 1995 (Robertson and Gales 1998). A second conference was held in Honolulu in 2000. These conferences provided opportunities for discussions on the status of albatross and petrel species and discussions on the development of mitigation measures and approaches to conservation. The Valdivia Group (the Group of Temperate Southern Hemisphere Countries on the Environment) also addressed the

issues of albatross and petrel conservation. Under the leadership of Australia the members of the Valdivia Group (Argentina, Australia, Brazil, Chile, New Zealand, South Africa and Uruguay) agreed to advance the proposed CMS AGREEMENT on the conservation of albatrosses and petrels.

The ACAP was negotiated in two sessions in 2000 and early 2001. Australia convened a meeting in Hobart on 10–14 July 2000 to which all southern hemisphere albatross and petrel range states were invited. Twelve range states and five international organisations attended the meeting that supported fundamental principles to develop the Agreement. Following a meeting in Cape Town on 29 January–2 February 2001, the ACAP was adopted by consensus. ACAP was opened for signature at a formal ceremony in Canberra, Australia on 19 June 2001. Seven states – Australia, Brazil, Chile, France, New Zealand, Peru and the United Kingdom – signed the ACAP at this ceremony.

The ACAP recognises that other international instruments contain measures that are or can be directed to the conservation of albatross and petrel species. The Preamble to the ACAP recites the Law of the Sea Convention; the Antarctic Treaty; the CCAMLR; the CCSBT; the FAO International Plan of Action for Reducing Incidental Catch of Seabirds in Longline Fisheries; the Rio Declaration; and the Convention on Biological Diversity as examples of such instruments. The ACAP Preamble also indicates that: 'Northern Hemisphere albatrosses and petrels may in future benefit from incorporation into the Agreement with a view to promoting co-ordinated conservation actions between Range States.'

INITIATIVES

United Nations Conference on the Human Environment 1972

The United Nations Conference on the Human Environment met in Stockholm on 5–16 June 1972. This conference identified the need for concerted action to protect the world's environment and identified ocean and sea pollution as one priority area. The Declaration of United Nations Conference on the Human Environment adopted at the conference included as Principle 7:

> States shall take all possible steps to prevent pollution of the seas by substances that are liable to create hazards to human health, to harm living resources and marine life, to damage amenities or to interfere with other legitimate use of the sea.

United Nations Conference on Environment and Development

The outcomes of the United Nations Conference on Environment and Development (UNCED) – also known as the Rio Earth Summit – in 1992, most notably the Rio Declaration and Agenda 21 (particularly Chapter 17), as well as the Biodiversity Convention and the Framework Convention on Climate Change have had significant impacts in the development of oceans governance (Haward and VanderZwaag 1995). A decade and a half later, key post-Rio principles – sustainable development, integration, the precautionary principle (now more commonly seen as the precautionary approach) and intergenerational equity – have introduced new approaches and tools to the management of marine living resources and conservation of the marine environment. These approaches and tools have been important in developments in oceans governance, and are appearing in a number of national policy documents; for example in the development of the Canadian Oceans Act in 1995 and Australia's Oceans Policy in 1998 (Haward and VanderZwaag 1995; Haward 2003; Vince 2004).

World Summit on Sustainable Development

One indication of the scope and direction of these legal and policy developments can be seen in the focus given to fisheries and the marine environment at the World Summit on Sustainable Development (WSSD) held in Johannesburg in August–September 2002. WSSD outcomes include establishing a regular process under the United Nations for global reporting and assessment of the state of the marine environment, and encouraging the application of an ecosystem approach to sustainable development of the oceans by 2010. The conference agreed with establishing marine protected areas (including outside areas of national jurisdiction) consistent with international law by 2012. In relation to global fisheries the conference made commitments to maintaining or restoring depleted fish stocks to levels that can produce the maximum sustainable yield 'on an urgent basis' by 2015, and to commit to putting into effect FAO international plans of action by the agreed dates, including eliminating subsidies that contribute to IUU fishing and overcapacity (see Shotton and Haward 2005).

There are significant challenges in the shift to ecosystems-based approaches as identified in the WSSD outcomes, particularly in relation to what has traditionally been seen as a core component of the concept of high seas freedoms.

The Ocean Policy Summit

The Ocean Policy Summit (TOPS), held in Lisbon Portugal on 11–13 October 2005, had as its theme Integrated Oceans Policy: National and Regional Experiences, Prospects, and Emerging Practices. The forum attracted over 200 participants from 53 countries, with representation from United Nations agencies, the academic community, non-governmental organisations (NGOs) and industry. It was noted that: 'while most coastal countries have adopted sector-specific policies to manage ocean use, such as for fishing and oil development, it has only been since the early 1990s that some countries have started introducing an integrated approach to managing ocean and coastal areas in their jurisdiction' (TOPS 2005, p. 1).

The Ocean Policy Summit was specifically designed to provide a forum where participants learned from each other, and to 'capture emerging good practice, or at least useful observations on trends and issues' (TOPS 2005, p. 3). The summit included targeted discussion in eight themed panel sessions:

- Integrated national and regional policies: a growing worldwide phenomenon.
- Learning from the most mature cases: Canada and Australia.
- Getting started: establishment of integrated national and regional ocean policies.
- Achieving cross-sectoral harmonisation of ocean uses and agencies.
- Principles for integrated national and regional ocean governance.
- Achieving national/sub-national collaboration in national ocean policies.
- Issues in implementing national oceans policies: financial considerations, evaluation and stakeholder support.
- Enhancing regional ocean policies and national/regional linkages.

The summit focused on 'barriers to formulation and implementation of national policies; key lessons learned and how national policy formulation may be best catalyzed; whether there is a need for continued comparative learning on policy and governance, and how that need may be met and how capacity development opportunities can be enhanced' (TOPS 2005, p. 11).

These issues directly link back to our focus on governance as outlined in Chapter 1 as addressing: ways in which common priorities are determined; how consistency and coordination of policy is achieved; how appropriate policy instruments and implementation strategies are developed; and ensuring appropriate means for accountability for and evaluation of policy.

INSTITUTIONS

United Nations

The United Nations General Assembly
The UNGA provides an important forum in the development of oceans governance. UNGA resolutions have driven important initiatives related to the law of the sea, as noted above. The annual debate on the law of the sea within UNGA provides an opportunity for a review of current status of international oceans governance. The report of the Secretary-General presented to this UNGA debate is an important compilation of information.

The United Nations General Assembly provides an important forum for ongoing discussions on oceans-related issues. General Assembly Resolutions provide opportunities for states to express current concerns and help promote action. Resolution 5517 (30 October 2000), for example, requires signatories to prioritise change in their domestic policies by adhering to the legally binding measures outlined by the LOSC with a particular focus on adopting integrated approaches to the management of exclusive economic zones (see Juda 2003).

The United Nations Open-ended Informal Consultative Process on Oceans and the Law of the Sea
The UNICPOLOS was initiated in 1999 following a decision of the UNGA to facilitate the annual review of 'developments in oceans affairs and the law the sea'. Meetings of the UNICPOLOS have been held annually since 2000 with the eighth meeting held in June 2007 at the UN headquarters in New York. Each meeting addresses a theme or related topics, with the 2007 meeting covering marine genetic resources. Past topics have included: protection and preservation of the marine environment; capacity building; regional cooperation and coordination of integrated oceans management; safety of navigation; protecting vulnerable marine ecosystems; new sustainable uses of the oceans; marine biodiversity of the seabed beyond national jurisdiction; fisheries and their contribution to sustainable development; marine debris; ecosystems approaches and oceans management. Meetings of the UNICPOLOS are open to all 'States Members of the United Nations, States members of the specialized agencies, all parties to UNCLOS, entities that have received a standing invitation to participate as observers in the work of the General Assembly pursuant to its relevant resolutions and intergovernmental organisations with competence in oceans affairs as well as major groups, as identified in Agenda 21' (DOALOS 2007).

The United Nations Environment Program (UNEP)

UNEP, headquartered in Nairobi, Kenya, provides significant capacity for developing regional strategies and supporting national actions through the Regional Seas Programme. This programme has been an important catalyst for ocean and coastal management in the Indian Ocean Region. The Regional Seas Programme was established in 1974, following the 1972 United Nations Conference on the Human Environment held in Stockholm. The focus of the programme is to develop 'sound environmental management to be coordinated and implemented by countries sharing a common body of water' (UNEP 2007).

The Regional Seas Programme covers 13 marine regions involving more than 140 countries:

- the Black Sea;
- the Wider Caribbean;
- East Africa;
- South-East Asia;
- the ROPME Sea Area (Middle East);
- the Mediterranean;
- the North-East Pacific;
- the North-West Pacific;
- the Red Sea and Gulf of Aden;
- South Asia;
- South-East Pacific;
- the Pacific; and
- West and Central Africa.

Six of these programmes are directly administered by UNEP: the Caribbean, East Asia, East Africa, the Mediterranean, the North-West Pacific; and West Africa regions. For the other programmes 'another (regional) organization hosts and/or provides the Secretariat. In addition, their financial and budgetary services (Trust Funds) are managed by the programme itself' (UNEP 2007). At the centre of the programme is an Action Plan, bolstered by an intergovernmental agreement, and detailed protocols dealing with particular environmental problems (Stokke and Thommessen 2003). In most cases the Action Plan is underpinned by a strong legal framework in the form of a regional convention and associated protocols on specific problems (UNEP 2007).

The United Nations Educational, Scientific and Cultural Organization
UNESCO hosts the International Oceanographic Commission (IOC) that provides a coordinating role for a range of international programmes. It directly contributed to the discussion of ocean governance through hosting the Global Conference on Oceans and Coasts at Rio+10 in late 2001. Most recently the IOC has been involved in developing 'the new tsunami warning system in the Indian Ocean' (TOPS 2005, p. 3), and IOC representatives took part in TOPS. The IOC has a thematic programme within its science stream related to oceans and provides support to the implementation of the World Summit on Sustainable Development (WSSD) goals.

Global Environment Facility
GEF is a joint initiative of the United Nations Development Programme, the United Nations Environment Programme and the World Bank. The GEF has a mandate to protect the environment or ecosystem health and has one programme area related to international waters. The GEF International Waters program:

> targets transboundary water systems, such as river basins with water flowing from one country to another, groundwater resources shared by several countries, or marine ecosystems bounded by more than one nation. Some of the issues addressed are:

> - transboundary water pollution;
> - over-extraction of groundwater resources;
> - unsustainable exploitation of fisheries;
> - protection of fisheries habitats;
> - invasive species; and
> - balancing competing uses of water resources. (GEF 2007)

The GEF is a significant source of funds for sustainable fisheries and is likely to be a major institution in international programmes over the next decades, and it is designed to play 'a catalytic role in helping nations making full use of policy, legal, and institutional reforms and investments necessary to address these complex concerns about transboundary water resources' (GEF 2007).

Commission on Sustainable Development
The CSD was established to ensure effective follow-up to 1992 United Nations Conference on Environment and Development (UNCED). The CSD reports to the United Nations Economic and Social Council (ECOSOC). It reviews progress in the implementation of UNCED agreements. It also

elaborates policy guidance and options for future areas of concern in the achievement of sustainable development. It is committed to promoting dialogue and partnership building for sustainable development with governments, the international community and major groups. The CSD considered Chapter 17 of Agenda 21, the broad chapter covering recommendations over oceans and coasts, in 1996 and in 1997. Oceans and seas were a sectoral theme of the CSD in 1999 and in 2002. In April 2004 CSD-12 served as a preparatory meeting for the ten-year review of the Barbados Programme of Action for the Sustainable Development of Small Island Developing States (SIDS). The CSD's future work plan lists oceans and seas, marine resources, SIDS and disaster management and vulnerability as a thematic focus of its session in 2014–15. The CSD's active involvement in oceans matters, the focus of the UN through the 1998 International Year of the Ocean, and the increasing focus of the United Nations General Assembly (UNGA) on oceans matters has raised the CSD's profile on international oceans governance.

Food and Agriculture Organization

The FAO is the specialist body in the United Nations system responsible for fisheries matters and has vast technical resources and data on global fisheries. Its role in facilitating and supporting the development of both hard law and soft law instruments has been noted earlier. The FAO provides significant capacity building, and technical training in fisheries management. FAO has also increased its work programme on marine environmental issues since UNCED in 1992 and has embodied post-UNCED principles of sustainable development in its operations. It is working closely with the World Bank and other UN agencies on fishery and marine-related matters. It has also taken the lead in promoting responsible fishing with the release of the non-binding, but increasingly influential Code of Conduct for Responsible Fisheries.

International Maritime Organization

The IMO was established under an international convention in 1948, with the IMO first meeting in 1959. The IMO is a specialised agency of the United Nations with headquarters in London comprising 167 member states and three associate members with the primary task to provide a regulate shipping. This has broadened to include safety, marine environmental protection and security, encapsulated by the mission statement: 'Safe, secure and efficient shipping on clean oceans' (IMO 2007). As noted earlier, the IMO provides a coordinating role in the international implementation of a wide range of measures to reduce ship-sourced marine pollution.

The IMO oversees a range of international conventions that govern ship operations: the safety of life at sea through the Safety of Life at Sea (SOLAS) Convention; MARPOL providing a regime to prevent pollution of the sea by ships, the London Convention and Protocol on dumping at sea; and the convention that sets standards for training for seafarers. The IMO has also established conventions related to dealing with accidents and disasters at sea, including search and rescue and oil pollution preparedness and responses. In addition the IMO administers international conventions related to compensation and liability for pollution and loss at sea. The IMO provides capacity building through technical support and training with high-level educational institutions established in Europe and has developed a Global Programme for the Protection of the Marine Environment.

The World Bank
The World Bank has an increasing influence in ocean governance. It is an important institution in relation to fisheries development through direct funding of fisheries projects or indirectly through regional development banks. Increasingly, however, the World Bank is focusing on the consequences of unsustainable development. The World Bank views depletion of fish stocks as one of a number of pressing environmental problems that threaten the global commons, as identified in the *World Development Report 1999–2000* (World Bank 1999). It identifies the most important causes of overfishing as national subsidies, overcapacity in the fishing industry and government's inability to enforce fishing limits in their economic zones.

In order to address these issues and to respond to growing international concern over unsustainable fishing practices, the World Bank and the FAO have established a partnership, PROFISH, that held its first forum in March 2007. 'The PROFISH Forum is an inclusive and informal umbrella for the exchange of information on sustainable fisheries particularly with respect to the role, execution and performance of development assistance' (World Bank 2007). The World Bank and its regional development banks are shifting away from 'industry development' approaches to fisheries that focused on building up fishing fleets to a focus on sustainable development that includes greater focus on the management of fishing capacity.

The International Council for Exploration of the Sea
The International Council for Exploration of the Sea (ICES) claims to be 'the oldest intergovernmental organisation in the world concerned with marine and fisheries science' (ICES 2007) and coordinates and promotes marine research in the North Atlantic, Baltic Sea and North Sea. The ICES comprises 20 member countries and six affiliated member countries, with

the World Wide Fund for Nature (WWF) and BirdLife International non-governmental organisations having observer status. The ICES supports a major and influential marine science journal and contributes to management advice and policy development, primarily in the North Atlantic region, but with broader influence.

NON-STATE ACTORS

Non-state actors play a number of roles in international oceans governance. In their traditional roles as interest groups they are catalysts for action, politicising issues and mobilising support for action. They also provide increasingly important support for international instruments and institutions, providing information and data, aiding compliance and enforcement.

International non-governmental organisations are focusing on fisheries issues and increasing their influence in international fora. Marine issues are, of course, not new to the environmental agenda, nor to the work of NGOs. Anti-whaling and sealing campaigns were led by NGO activism. These campaigns have included direct action with associated media coverage. At the same time NGOs have also been active in pursuing goals and objectives set by the current international agenda of sustainability and responsible fishing. In these areas they have become important stakeholders in international fisheries policy and management. Groups such as the WWF and Greenpeace run major international campaigns on oceans-related issues, from toxic waste transport to unsustainable fishing practices.

Non-governmental organisations are at the table at international meetings, with either as full participants or with observer status. The broadening of stakeholder involvement in international oceans governance post-UNCED has been profound. Organisations such as TRAFFIC and ISOFISH (the International Southern Oceans Longline Fisheries Information Clearing House linking conservation groups and licensed fishing companies), focusing on trade in fisheries products, have played important roles in the fight against IUU fishing. The WWF has campaigned against the negative effects of fisheries subsidies on capacity and unsustainable harvesting, and on the impact of the worlds distant-water fishing fleets. ISOFISH and Greenpeace have provided coverage of illegal fishing and trade in Patagonian toothfish.

The World Conservation Union
The World Conservation Union was established in October 1948 as the International Union for the Protection of Nature (or IUPN) following an international conference in France. The name 'International Union for the

Conservation of Nature and Natural Resources' was used from 1956, and 'World Conservation Union' from 1990. The title 'International Union for the Conservation of Nature and Natural Resources' and abbreviation IUCN is still, however, commonly used.

The World Conservation Union continues to improve scientific understanding of what natural ecosystems provide to humans. But the Union also seeks to ensure this knowledge is used in practical ways by bringing together scientists, policy-makers, business leaders and NGOs to impact upon the way the world values and uses nature (IUCN 2007).

Global Forum on Oceans, Coasts and Islands

The Global Forum was initiated in 2001 and established formally at WSSD in 2002. It serves as a 'multi-stakeholder forum for cross-sectoral discussion, policy analyses, and mobilization of knowledge and other resources to achieve the full implementation of international agreements related to oceans, coasts and Small Island Developing States (SIDS)' (Global Forum 2005, p. 1). The Global Forum comprises a steering Committee of more than 80 members, with the International Coastal and Ocean Organization providing administrative support.

Its major goals are to:

- Work as a catalyst to mobilize knowledge, resources, and organizational action to advance the global oceans agenda and to promote integrated oceans management;
- Foster a mutually-supportive global network of ocean policy leaders with the capacity to implement integrated oceans management;
- Raise the international profile of oceans, coasts, and SIDS in relevant global, regional, and sub-regional fora;
- Mobilize public awareness on global issues related to oceans, coasts, and islands, and promote information sharing and dissemination; and
- Work together with governments, international and intergovernmental organizations, nongovernmental organizations, and others to effectively implement, at national and regional levels, major international agreements on oceans, especially the commitments made in the Plan of Implementation of the WSSD, commitments from Agenda 21, and other related agreements. (Global Forum 2007)

The Global Forum was a major actor in the organisation of the Ocean Policy Summit in Lisbon in 2005. It has worked with funding from the Nippon Foundation to establish a Task Force on National Oceans Policies examining experiences in integrated oceans governance in over 20 countries and four regions around the world.

In late 2006 the Global Forum developed a major ten-year plan (2006–16) 'to chart strategic activities which could be undertaken together with governments, the United Nations, NGOs, industry, and scientific groups to advance the global oceans agenda' (Global Forum 2007).

CONCLUSION

A number of commentators have examined the development of regimes governing the oceans (see Johnston and VanderZwaag 2000). While the 'bulk of this ocean law has been created during the last three decades' (Joyner 2000, p. 200), it is noteworthy that the scope of this ocean law has also broadened. The expansion of activities of institutions such as the FAO and IMO, and work by the IOC and Global Forum building on the post-UNCED and WSSD focus on oceans, has provided important institutional support. Initiatives such as TOPS provide invaluable opportunities to disseminate knowledge and experience on oceans governance, including lessons (both positive and negative) on policy development and the use of new policy tools and approaches. While there are challenges in embedding principles and practices developed from international instruments and initiatives, there are promising opportunities at the regional and national levels.

3. Regional initiatives in oceans governance

The previous chapter has emphasised increased international attention to oceans governance from the 1980s. The discussion on oceans issues within international fora has been an important catalyst for the development of legal and policy responses, including, as noted in the preceding chapter, both 'hard' and 'soft' law initiatives. Oceans governance has also been addressed at the regional or supra-national level. This chapter focuses on initiatives in differing regional arrangements; highlighting in particular actions undertaken and initiatives established by the Asia-Pacific Economic Cooperation (APEC) forum, the European Union, and the Organisation for Economic Co-operation and Development (OECD). The chapter also discusses oceans governance initiatives in the Caribbean (an example of regional initiatives supported by the United Nations Environment Programme's Regional Seas programme), the Pacific (with the first attempt at a regional oceans policy framework) and oceans management in the Arctic and the Antarctic.

ASIA-PACIFIC ECONOMIC COOPERATION (APEC)

APEC originated through an initiative co-sponsored by Australia and the Republic of Korea as a forum for promotion of growth and economic development in the Asia-Pacific. APEC also enables discussion on regional and international issues and facilitates links to other forums and arrangements. APEC began in 1989 and in 2008 has 22 members, with a focus on economies, not states. Current APEC member economies are Australia, Brunei Darussalam, Canada, Chile, China, Hong Kong China, Indonesia, Japan, Korea, Malaysia, Mexico, New Zealand, Papua New Guinea, Peru, The Philippines, Russia, Singapore, Chinese Taipei, Thailand, the USA and Viet Nam.

APEC emphasises public–private sector linkages, improving corporate governance, and is committed to the reduction of barriers to trade and investment. APEC, unlike the World Trade Organization's focus on rules-based deliberations, encourages consultation and consensus centred on 'Three Pillars':

- trade and investment liberalisation;
- business facilitation; and
- economic and technical cooperation.

These pillars are reinforced in the APEC Bogor Declaration of 1994, committing to 'free and open trade and investment'. APEC has an annual Leaders and Ministers Meeting, supported by senior officials meetings. It has 11 specialist working groups with 'lead shepherds' responsible for coordinating the work programmes of these groups, and is supported by a Secretariat based in Singapore.

APEC has encouraged and facilitated the linking of the region's economies through technical exchanges and capacity building and providing information and learning in areas such as oceans management and governance. Its broad membership, including economies such as Chinese Taipei (Taiwan), enables interaction that cannot take place within other international forums. APEC has, however, been criticised for the dominance of developed market economies and its focus and agenda on trade liberalisation.

Australia, Canada and New Zealand have been an active participants in discussions on trade-and market-based approaches to oceans governance being championed through APEC's Marine Resource Conservation (MRC) Working Group (Bache et al. 2003). APEC's MRC Working Group established an oceans policy initiative in 2000–04 that provided opportunities for collaboration and capacity building amongst APEC economies on developing integrated approaches to oceans management. This initiative was led by Canada and Australia and also involved the work of the Australian Canada Ocean Research Network (ACORN), a network of legal, politics and policy studies academics from universities in Australia and Canada interested in oceans policy and governance. ACORN was established in 1992 and was engaged in relevant policy developments in both Australia and Canada in the 1990s, discussed in detail in subsequent chapters (Haward and VanderZwaag 1995; Rothwell and VanderZwaag 2006).

APEC initiated its focus on oceans governance in 1996, with the APEC leaders giving commitments to address the environment and ensure sustainable development of the oceans that bounded the region. The APEC leaders recognised that the health of the marine environment was critical to the continuing economic well-being of all APEC economies (Laughlin 2003).

The APEC Sustainable Development Ministerial Meeting held in the Philippines in 1996 'directed APEC to focus on three issues: sustainability of the marine environment, sustainable cities and cleaner production' (Laughlin 2003, p. 10). As Laughlin notes, it was recognised that oceans transcend sectoral APEC working groups and must be addressed in a cross-sectoral, integrated manner.

APEC's Strategy for the Sustainability of the Marine Environment developed out of this commitment. This strategy had three key objectives:

- integrated approaches to coastal management;
- prevention, reduction and control of marine pollution; and
- sustainable management of marine resources (Laughlin 2003, pp. 1–2).

The Strategy for the Sustainability of the Marine Environment centred on the use of research and exchange of information and technology and expertise, capacity building, training and education, and public and private sector participation and partnerships.

In 1998 APEC's commitment to oceans issues saw a high-level oceans conference convened in Honolulu in 1998, as part of the International Year of the Ocean. The Honolulu Declaration reinforced APEC's commitment to 'economic, social and environmental value of healthy marine, coastal and Small Island ecosystems' (cited by Laughlin 2003, p. 2). The first APEC oceans-related Ministerial Meeting was held in Seoul in 2002. The Seoul Declaration provides a commitment to ecosystem-based management and the need to implement such approaches in an integrated and cross-sectoral manner (Laughlin 2003, p. 2).

The second APEC oceans-related Ministerial Meeting was held in Bali, Indonesia, in September 2005. This meeting saw Ministers reaffirm their commitment to progress the 2000 Seoul Oceans Declaration (APEC 2005) and led to the adoption of the Bali Plan of Action Towards Healthy Oceans and Coasts for Sustainable Growth and Prosperity for the Asia-Pacific Community. APEC Ministers committed to:

work domestically, regionally and internationally, in the near to mid term (2006–2009) towards:

I. ensuring the sustainable management of the marine environment and its resources;
II. providing for sustainable economic benefits from the oceans; and,
III. enabling sustainable development of coastal communities. (APEC 2005)

Regional fisheries management is enhanced by the operation of the APEC Fisheries Working Group (APEC FWG). While the APEC FWG is not a management body per se it clearly has an important actual and potential role in the region and is supported by a number of officials and academics who saw a number of benefits in such meetings. These benefits include opportunities to discuss management arrangements, improve understanding of approaches and improve policy capacity for Asian countries. This has been enhanced by the responsibilities of 'lead shepherds' in providing greater opportunities to enhance cooperation between developed and developing fisheries nations in the region. To this end greater focus on technical exchanges within the ambit of the APEC FWG was seen as a desirable outcome, and greater efforts to engage the developing fisheries nations of the forum were encouraged. It was suggested that workshop sessions be considered as part of the annual APEC FWG meeting given that the benefits of such exchanges would be significant for very little additional costs to member economies.

APEC economies display considerable diversity yet all have significant interest in their maritime zones. Management of these maritime areas also reflects considerable diversity, with an equally diverse range of institutional arrangements, agency responsibilities and legislation. This diversity also extends to the extent to which the issues and problems related to oceans management and governance are identified and acted upon, or whether specific responses through legislation or policy responses are developed to tackle them. It is not surprising that there is a continuum of institutional responses to issues of oceans governance within APEC. This continuum ranges from highly developed institutional and legislative responses to more limited action on emerging issues.

While information on the approaches adopted in different economies is beneficial for potential 'lesson drawing' it is important to note that even when there are management arrangements in place, effective policy implementation may be affected by a range of factors. These factors include, inter alia, the level of inter-agency coordination and cooperation, jurisdiction and available resources. It is important to note, too, that such diversity in institutional structures and legislation provides considerable scope for developing appropriate responses suitable for each economy and supporting the effective development and implementation of risk management frameworks to address introduced marine pests.

EUROPEAN UNION

The European Union (EU) has major maritime interests and has been active in international discussions on oceans governance. As well as taking part in developing major initiatives such as the EU Marine Strategy and the European Maritime Policy (see below), EU member states are also active in responding to the challenges of oceans governance, and have developed national policy documents or legislation. Twenty of the 25 constituent states of the EU have coastlines, and with a total coastline of over 65 000 kilometres in length. Maritime areas account for over 40 per cent of the region's gross national product (Juda 2007, p. 260).

A key element in governance within the European Union is the question of the competence of the European Union institutions to enact provisions binding on member states. The question of competence is important and, common to federal systems such as Australia, Canada and the USA, where sub-national units of government are actively engaged in implementation of policy, this shapes patterns of intergovernmental interaction as a key component of governance. This interaction reflects what Chapman called the 'federal factor' (Chapman 1990), shaping what may be termed 'regulatory federalism' (Kelemen 2002). Given that the European Union's member states retain considerable interests in policy areas such as the marine environment, and that effective implementation of policy relies on intergovernmental cooperation (the core of regulatory federalism (see Kelemen 2002), such processes can mediate among the difficulties arising from attempts to assert jurisdictional paramountcy by Strasbourg (the seat of the European parliament) or Brussels (the home of the European Commission). In addition actions by the European Union related to governance of the region's oceans and coasts also necessarily interacts with the work of regional institutions and instruments such as that of the OSPAR Commission (see below). Regulatory federalism, according to Kelemen, makes two claims:

First, the division of power between federal and state governments generates a similar *politics of competence* in all federal systems. As the two levels of government interact strategically, the division of regulatory competence moves through a similar series of stages and reaches a similar outcome: federal governments take on a large role in policy making and state governments control most implementation. Second, differences in the concentration of power within the structure of the federal government explains differences in the *politics of discretion* ... the degree of discretion granted to state governments in their role as agents of the federal government. (Kelemen 2002, p. 134)

This approach reintroduces the concepts of 'vertical' and 'horizontal' governance discussed in Chapter 1 that, in simple terms, address the relationships between and within central and sub-national governments, and how such arrangements affect policy implementation. A centralised administrative system that delegates activities will have a different focus to a system that devolves responsibility to sub-national government. Such a crude dichotomy masks a range of possibilities but draws attention to alternative institutional approaches to policy implementation and regulatory actions. In relation to vertical divisions of power Kelemen notes the key differences between 'Westminster-style parliamentary federal systems' and 'separation-of-powers federal systems', where the latter 'encourage the federal judiciary to play a powerful role in regulation ... that reduces the discretion of states in implementing federal regulations' (Kelemen 2002, p. 134).

Despite, or in fact because of, its importance the European marine domain is under pressure:

the environmental integrity of European waters is seriously endangered, and a list of identified threats contains the same element that have been noted in other areas of the world, such as:

- overfishing;
- alien species introductions;
- port and other coastal development;
- sand and gravel extraction;
- oil and hazardous substance discharges and spills;
- land-based pollution;
- eutrophication; and
- the effects of climate change. (Juda 2007, pp. 260–61)

The EU's identification of the marine environment as one of a set of 'priority environmental problems' reflects similar concerns raised in other regions and within a number of nation states. These concerns have clearly 'pushed the governance of oceans and coasts onto the public policy agenda across the globe' (Juda 2007, p. 261).

The EU is a major fishing power at the global level but it now sources only about 50 per cent of its fish consumption from within the exclusive economic zones (EEZs) of member states, with some 25 per cent of the fish consumed in EU landed by its distant water fleets operating in the South Atlantic, Indian and Pacific Oceans. Overfishing of northern hemisphere stocks has forced fleet owners from the northern hemisphere to begin to look for other seafood supplies for their fleets. These activities, and fishing within EU waters, are managed under the Common Fisheries Policy, developed to coordinate fisheries within the European Union. Concern over the state of the environment in Europe led to the European Parliament and the EU Council adopting the Sixth Community Environment Action Programme of 2002 (ibid. p. 261). The marine environment was one of seven policy areas for which 'thematic strategies' were to be developed (Juda 2007), and in the case of the marine environment the objective centred on 'the conservation, restoration and sustainable use of marine environments, coasts and wetlands' (Juda 2007, p. 262). This initiative focused attention on the need to concentrate on environmental considerations within the Common Fisheries Policy, and to develop more integrated approaches to coastal and marine management (Juda 2007).

Fisheries in the European Union – Background

Currently EU fleets are active throughout the Atlantic as well as the western and southern parts of the Indian Ocean and in the Pacific. Such wide activity is facilitated by a network of fisheries agreements with other, mostly African, countries, but with increasing interest in developing access agreements with Pacific Island countries. While fisheries agreements were initially designed to reduce pressure on stocks in EU waters, such agreements are viewed as a short-term solution to the structural problem of overcapacity.

Most of the EU purse seine freezer tuna fishing fleet is French and Spanish, and the longline fleet is mostly Spanish. Apart from some units in the eastern Pacific, these two fleets now fish in the waters of the Atlantic and Indian oceans in coastal state waters or on the high seas. Spain is the only EU country that engages in fishing activity in all the waters of the world. The most important zone for the EU in percentage terms is the north-east Atlantic, which accounts for 74 per cent of catches. Added to catches in the Mediterranean the figure rises to almost 90 per cent.

The number of fishing vessels in Europe has shown a long-term decrease. In some cases, for example the United Kingdom and France, fleets have been dramatically reduced. Such decreases in fleet size can be explained by vessel decommissioning policies established by the EU, although the number of large vessels has also decreased in Iceland and Norway, which are not members of the EU. Many of the member states have had long traditions of distant-water fishing. Apart from the Spanish, and to some extent the Dutch, that era has passed. The British and German distant-water fleets, for example, have disappeared.

The Common Fisheries Policy (CFP)

The Common Fisheries Policy (CFP) was established in 1983. Prior to this fisheries had been considered as part of the agricultural policy framework embedded in the Treaty of Rome, with specific regulations developed for fisheries in 1970. The development of the law of the sea in the 1970s, particularly in the customary acceptance of extended areas of fisheries jurisdiction, and extension to states' territorial seas, means that a more formal policy instrument was needed. The first moves towards the CFP began in 1976, and involved significant negotiations that led to the conclusion of the CFP in 1983. The CFP has been subject to regular revisions, with the most recent revision in 2002 being the most significant, with detailed information on background to the revisions, key components and implementation plan included in what is termed the 'Roadmap' (European Commission 2002).

The CFP 'was created to manage a common resource and to meet the obligation set in the original Community Treaties. Because fish are a natural and mobile resource they are considered as common property'. The CFP was developed in accordance with the principle that a common policy creates 'common rules adopted at Community level and implemented in all Member States' (Europa 2008).

The CFP address four areas:

- conservation of fish stocks;
- structures (such as vessels, port facilities and fish processing plants);
- the common organisation of the market; and
- external fisheries policy which includes fishing agreements with non-Community members and negotiations in international organisations.

The CFP uses two types of instruments to conserve fish stocks: setting total allowable catches – upper limits for total amount of fish that can be landed from particular areas; and utilising gear restrictions, closures and size limits (Daw and Gray 2005). The CFP also includes measures that attempt to control capacity of the EU fleets (Daw and Gray 2005, p. 189). These structural adjustment arrangements were known as the Multi-Annual Guidance Programme (MAGP). In its later forms the MAGP was designed to establish mechanisms for reduction of fishing effort. This programme required member states to reduce fishing efforts in certain segments of the fleets, in line with binding objectives.

MAGP IV, for example, ran from the period 1997 to 2001 and required member states to achieve a 30 per cent reduction in fishing effort targeted at 'depleted stocks' and 20 per cent for overfished stocks in order to match 'available resources'. Other fleet segments are prohibited from increasing fishing effort. The member states could choose whether they would achieve these targets by decommissioning fishing tonnage or by shortening the existing fleets' fishing times at sea. Some pressure was felt by EU states with the largest fishing fleets continuing to press for continuation of the previous fishing agreement volumes in order to continue to supply their domestic markets, to utilise domestic processing capacities and to keep fishermen dependent on distant-water catches employed. Reductions in fleets and capacity have been facilitated by the use of subsidies (Financial Instrument for Fisheries Guidance – FIFG) to link fishing capacity with available resources. This should, however, take better account of 'technology creep', where new technology creates increases in the fishing capacity of vessels of the same tonnage (Bergin and Haward 2000).

The CFP has been strongly criticised over failing to achieve its conservation objective. Overfishing of major stocks in areas like the North Sea and the Mediterranean has been a cause of growing concern in the 1990s and 2000s. Most commercial species in the North Sea are heavily exploited. Stock such as herring and cod have been close to the point of collapse; plaice stocks are at a low level; North sea mackerel has declined over the years and is still at a relatively low level; the stability of fish stocks such as haddock is still uncertain. Within the north-east Atlantic all fin-fish stocks are being exploited at or above maximum limits. The structural adjustment packages associated with MAGP IV have also been criticised, as not leading to desired reductions in capacity.

The problems facing the EU fisheries are serious and on 9 March 2006 the Commission adopted a Communication *Improvement of the Economic Situation in the Fishing Industry* (see European Commission 2006). As Commissioner Joe Borg (Member of the European Commission responsible for Fisheries and Maritime Affairs) noted in a speech on 19 May 2006:

> This communication aimed to help the fishing industry to overcome the difficulties generated by high oil prices in the short term. We have sought to offer possibilities for rescuing and restructuring fishing firms by helping them to become profitable in a world where oil prices will remain high, and also by using Community funds. But beyond the rescue and restructuring it is important to define ways to structurally improve the situation of the sector, and to create an environment that will lead to a healthy fishing sector in the long term. (Borg 2006)

Reviews of the Common Fisheries Policy 1992 and 2002

A key part of the CFP was the provision for reviews of the policy. These reviews have taken place in 1992 and 2002. The first review of the CFP:

> showed that if there are too many vessels for the available resources, technical measures and control alone cannot prevent overfishing. The amount of fishing has to be regulated too. In order to make the common fisheries policy more effective the link between its component parts was reinforced. Control measures were also developed to ensure that rules are respected throughout the industry. New technologies are being used to transmit data to the authorities and to monitor larger vessels through satellite tracking systems. (Europa 2008)

The 2002 review highlighted that 'more effective conservation and management of fisheries resources is a clear priority' (European Commission 2002, p. 7). The Roadmap document provides a detailed analysis of the issues facing the CFP, noting significant changes in both the internal and external policy environment in which the CFP operates.

Future of the CFP

The CFP is subject to significant criticism (see Daw and Gray 2005; Gray and Hatchard 2003). Overfishing of stocks has led to concern over the limitations of management capacity and ability of management systems to incorporate appropriate scientific advice. There is still significant overcapacity in European fleets. Effective decommissioning is not taking place in distant-water fleets, despite considerable efforts. In addition the EU is under increasing pressure in the negotiation of access agreement with third countries. In the event that third-country agreements end, a prospect that may occur over the next ten years, the question remains over where these European vessels will operate. Most of these vessels never have fished in European waters and were purpose built for distant-water operations. These vessels could therefore go elsewhere and/or enter into private sector joint ventures. Political pressure for some kind of structural adjustment arrangement (fleet withdrawals, aid for ship owners and crews) may soon develop – a scenario identified in the 2006 European Commission's Communication (European Commission 2006).

The European Union and Oceans Governance

The first decade of the twenty-first century has seen the EU provide a concerted focus on oceans governance. This effort has included, as noted above, a reform agenda for the CFP but it also saw the EU focus on developing policy responses to incorporate emerging concerns over the state of the region's oceans and seas. These initiatives included a Marine Strategy Directive in 2005, and the European Union Maritime Policy launched in October 2007.

The Marine Strategy Directive

The Marine Strategy Directive was released in October 2005, and 'detailed the obligations of member states to develop a Marine Strategy and implement it for its internal waters' (Juda 2007, p. 267). Each member state was to undertake a 'comprehensive assessment of the environmental conditions' of its marine area, identify 'the impacts of human use' and undertake an 'economic and social analysis of the use of these areas' (Juda 2007, p. 267). Commissioner Borg commented in mid-2007 that 'the aim of the directive is to ensure that all EU marine waters are environmentally healthy by 2021 so that Europeans are able to benefit from seas and oceans that are safe, clean and rich in biodiversity' (Dimas and Borg 2007).

The directive established three regions: The Baltic, the North-East Atlantic Ocean, and the Mediterranean, with the latter regions further subdivided into four sub-regions each. Once member states had established programmes to implement the directive (as approved by the European Commission), progress towards implementation would also be reviewed by the Commission (Juda 2007).

While it was clear from the statements of EU Commissioners that it was the view of the EC that 'the Marine Strategy will constitute the environmental pillar of the integrated Maritime Policy' (Dimas and Borg 2007), this nexus was seen as downplaying a focus on ecosystem protection or rehabilitation. For one commentator the linking of the Marine Strategy Directive into the broader Maritime Policy initiative would mean that: 'environmental concerns, consequently, would become one of a variety of considerations rather than the overriding priority as some environmental groups might desire to be the case' (Juda 2007, p. 272). The Marine Strategy Directive also has direct links to EU member states' engagement with the OSPAR Convention (see below).

European Union Maritime Policy

In June 2006 the European Commission adopted a Green Paper *Towards a Future Maritime Policy for the Union: A European Vision for the Oceans and Seas* (Green Paper 2006). A year-long consultation was then begun that concluded in June 2007. The Green Paper provided a 'rationale' for 'a debate about a future Maritime Policy for the EU that treats the oceans and seas in a holistic way' (Green Paper 2006, p. 4). This discussion paper emphasises the need for an alternative to current practice, and has clearly been influenced by work undertaken by Canada and Australia:

> Principles of good governance suggest the need for a European maritime policy that embraces all aspects of the oceans and seas. This policy should be integrated, inter-sectoral and multidisciplinary, and not a mere collection of vertical sectoral policies. It should look at the oceans and seas based on sound knowledge of how they work and how the sustainability of their environment and ecosystems may be preserved. (Green Paper 2006, p. 5)

The Green Paper addressed 'a very broad range of what have traditionally been regarded as separate activities and policy areas' (Green Paper 2006). In proposing a focus on integrated management of oceans, and on governance arrangements to facilitate this, the EU followed policy initiatives from Australia, Canada and the USA.

> The Green Paper did not propose immediate action but rather highlighted a number of areas where integrated effort might either provide benefits for a number of individual sectoral policy areas or help to resolve conflicts between them. It posed a number of questions ranging from the fundamental 'Should the EU have an integrated maritime policy?' to more detailed issues. (Europa 2007)

Following the release of the Green Paper a year-long consultation period was undertaken, concluding at the end of June 2007. The report of this consultation, together with other relevant material forming what was termed 'the integrated EU maritime policy package', was presented to member states by the European Commission on 10 October 2007.

What's in a Name? The EU Maritime Policy

It is too soon to judge the impact or effectiveness of the EU Maritime Policy. One interesting aspect of this policy framework is its name. As Juda has noted, the term 'maritime' in countries such as the USA and Australia has a specific meaning, tending to focus on issues such as ports and harbours, shipping, transportation and other sectorally oriented activities, including naval interests (Juda 2007). As a result Australia, Canada and the USA have used the term 'oceans policy' rather than 'maritime policy' as part of an attempt to focus on integrated oceans management. In Australia, Canada and the USA maritime interests and activities are recognised as significant but are incorporated in broader policy and governance arrangements.

An Integrated Maritime Policy for the European Union

The European Commission released its Communication *An Integrated Maritime Policy for the European Union* on 10 October 2007 (European Commission 2007). This document, noting that 'the seas are Europe's lifeblood' and that 'Europe's well being is ... inextricably linked with the sea', emphasises that the policy was 'based in the clear recognition that all matters relating to Europe's oceans and seas are interlinked. And that sea-related polices must develop in a joined-up way if we are to reap the desired results' (European Commission 2007, pp. 1–3). The Communication provides the 'foundation for a governance framework and cross-sectoral tools necessary' for implementation of the EU Integrated Maritime Policy.

The governance framework focuses on the application on an integrated approach at 'every level', including the use of 'horizontal and cross-cutting policy tools', recognising that the initiative will 'require a sound financial basis', and take 'into account the results of preparatory actions' (European Commission 2007, p. 4). The Commission will invite the development of national integrated maritime policies, and proposes to develop a set of guidelines in 2008 to guide the development of these national policies, taking into account the key EU principle of subsidiarity (European Commission 2007, p. 15). The Commission will report annually on EU and member states' actions from 2009. The development of maritime spatial planning 'is seen as a fundamental tool for the sustainable development of marine areas and coastal regions, and for the restoration of Europe's seas to environmental health' (European Commission 2007, p. 4). The focus on maritime spatial planning will be fostered by the development of a 'roadmap' in 2008 to facilitate such planning by member states.

The development of the EU's maritime policy provides a link with the earlier initiatives by Australia and Canada in their development of national oceans policy process, as discussed in subsequent chapters. The EU maritime policy follows similar directions in a focus on improving oceans management by removing constraints posed by sectoral management models and improving environmental sustainability of activities. As in the case of Australia and the USA, where oceans policy affects interests of state governments, implementation of the Integrated Maritime Policy will lead to significant interaction between the EC and member states. There is likely to be considerable interaction within member states as they respond to the governance framework developed in the October 2007 communication. This is already emerging within the United Kingdom, with the Scottish parliament indicating its interest in developing a separate marine or oceans policy for its waters, independent of work undertaken by the United Kingdom.

UNITED NATIONS ENVIRONMENT PROGRAMME'S REGIONAL SEAS PROGRAMME

The UNEP Regional Seas Programme (RSP), described briefly in Chapter 2, has been an important framework for development of regional ocean governance initiatives. A review of the Regional Seas Programme in 2003 saw a new strategic focus established to 'identify actions to be implemented during 2004–07 to enhance the RSP at the global level, while continuing the implementation of the action programmes of the individual RSPs as agreed upon by their governing bodies' (UNEP 2007).

The programme's strategic elements or directions were to:

- Increase the Regional Seas Programme's contribution to sustainable development through the enhancement of local, national, regional and global partnerships with relevant social, economic and environmental stakeholders.
- Enhance sustainability and effectiveness of the Regional Seas Programme through increasing country ownership, translating regional seas conventions and protocols into national legislation, promoting compliance and enforcement mechanisms.
- Enhance the Regional Seas Programme's visibility and political impact in global and regional policy setting.
- Support knowledge-based policy-making, development and implementation of relevant environmental legislation, improve knowledge on the state of the marine environment.
- Increase the use of Regional Seas Programme as a platform for developing common regional objectives, promoting synergies and coordinated regional implementation of relevant instruments.
- Promote the development of a universal vision and integrated management, based on ecosystem approaches, of priorities and concerns related to the coastal and marine environment (UNEP 2007).

In regions such as the Caribbean (Fanning et al. 2007a; Fanning et al. 2007b) and off East Africa and in South Asia, the UNEP Regional Seas Programme has been an important catalyst for ocean and coastal management and provides significant capacity for developing regional strategies and supporting national actions (Haward forthcoming).

THE ORGANISATION FOR ECONOMIC CO-OPERATION AND DEVELOPMENT (OECD)

The Organisation for Economic Co-operation and Development (OECD) was established in 1961 as a successor institution to the Organisation for European Economic Co-operation (OEEC). The OEEC was formed to administer the Marshall Plan that provided aid and reconstruction assistance to Western European countries after the Second Word War. The OECD has 30 members; twenty countries signed the convention establishing the OECD – with this instrument entering into force in 1961 – and ten countries subsequently joining the organisation (OECD 2007). OECD member states are Australia, Austria, Belgium, Canada, the Czech Republic, Denmark, Finland, France, Germany, Greece, Hungary, Iceland, Ireland, Italy, Japan, Korea, Luxembourg, Mexico, the Netherlands, New Zealand, Norway, Poland, Portugal, Slovak Republic, Spain, Sweden, Switzerland, Turkey, the United Kingdom and the United States of America.

The OECD has been active in providing advice and analysis on fisheries matters and has been active in initiatives to combat illegal, unregulated and unreported (IUU) fishing. The OECD provides important capacity building in relation to the development of policy instruments directed at ocean governance. The OECD also provides an important opportunity for bilateral linkages and exchanges of information. For non-European member states it also provides opportunities to interact with European countries outside the institutional framework established by the European Commission.

OSPAR: PROTECTING THE MARINE ENVIRONMENT OF THE NORTH-EAST ATLANTIC

The OSPAR Convention of 1992 (the Convention for the Protection of the Marine Environment of the North-East Atlantic) was established through the amalgamation and updating of the 1972 Oslo Convention on Dumping Waste at Sea and the 1974 Paris Convention on Land-Based Sources of Marine Pollution. States party to the OSPAR Convention added an annex on biodiversity and ecosystems that was adopted in 1998 'to cover non-polluting human activities that can adversely affect the sea' (OSPAR 2006). Fifteen European states are members of the OSPAR Commission: Belgium, Denmark, Finland, France, Germany, Iceland, Ireland, Luxembourg, the Netherlands, Norway, Portugal, Spain, Sweden, Switzerland and the United Kingdom. The European Commission, representing the European Union, also attends meetings. The OSPAR Commission Secretariat is headquartered in London.

The development of OSPAR instruments has been described as a story of 'evolution from a state of water and marine pollution "anarchy" to domestic and international "governance"' (Skjærseth 2006, p. 158). The Paris Convention allowed the EU to join as a 'contracting member', and this provided impetus for EU action on water policy within its environmental policy framework (Skjærseth 2006, p. 158). The question of competence of the EU in this area was under challenge, as 'the environmental policy of the EU did not gain a firm legal basis until the Single European Act was adopted in 1986' (Skjærseth 2006, p. 158; see also Kellow and Zito 2002).

The OSPAR Commission emphasises cooperation amongst member states, with measures developed on the basis of the best available scientific advice (OSPAR 2006). Collaborative work plans are developed, with 'lead countries' taking responsibility for developing particular proposals. These proposals are examined by all member states prior to gaining formal approval at the annual meeting of the Commission. In addition to member states and the EU a wide range of accredited observer organisations attend OSPAR Commission meetings. These observers include non-governmental groups, who can table documents at the meeting. OSPAR, too, has a memorandum of understanding with the International Council for the Exploration of the Sea (ICES), 'the specialist international body for marine science in the North Atlantic' (OSPAR 2006).

OSPAR's work has direct relevance for the EU, particular as the latter develops its Marine Strategy and Maritime Policy. While there has been considerable achievement made through the 'synergistic relationship between these institutions [that] has been enhanced by means of conscious institutional design' (Skjærseth 2006, p. 158), the development of the International North Sea Conferences has also enhanced the effectiveness of governance of the north-east Atlantic marine environment. The conferences, and their 'soft law declarations', 'became linked to OSPAR and the EU water policy ... and were deliberately designed to speed up decision making processes in these bodies' (Skjærseth 2006, pp. 158–9).

OSPAR has undertaken pioneering work on the marine environment, with over 30 years experience in the analysis of threats to the marine environment. It completed its Quality Status Report on the North East Atlantic in 2000. This report 'was based on six years scientific work on monitoring and assessment, supported by monitoring over a much longer period' (OSPAR 2006). In 2005 it completed scientific assessments of the results of monitoring over the previous decade, noting substantial reductions in inputs of heavy metals to the marine environment, significant reductions in inputs of nitrogen and phosphorus, and a statistically significant downward trend in direct atmospheric inputs if all contaminates were monitored (OSPAR 2006).

While OSPAR has had extensive experience in managing the marine environment of the north-east Atlantic the development of the EU's Marine Strategy and Maritime Policy will have some impact on its future work plan. The Marine Strategy has the potential to cut across the work of OSPAR, with member states of OSPAR and the EU having to address similar issues for both organisations. It is possible that member states may find EU policy commitments coming into direct competition with the work of OSPAR. The OSPAR Commission notes, however, that its 'proven record of success makes it a vital partner in further efforts to improve the protection of all the European seas' (OSPAR 2006). This reinforces the point made by Skjærseth:

> Overlapping institutions covering the North Sea and the wider North-East Atlantic have proved mutually beneficial by fulfilling different functions all of which are needed to manage marine pollution effectively. ... The result of institutional interplay in this policy field is evident in the significant overall reductions achieved in the emission of regulated organic substances, pesticides, heavy metals, nutrients, and dumping and incineration at sea. (Skjærseth 2006, p. 157)

THE CARIBBEAN

The Caribbean is 'one of the geopolitically complex regions in the world' (Fanning et al. 2007a, p. 435). Despite these complexities an innovative oceans governance framework is being developed, based on the Caribbean large marine ecosystem (LME). This project funded by the Global Environmental Facility has focused on the management of shared living marine resources, fundamentally important for artisanal or subsistence-based fisheries and for the region's economy. As noted above, the Caribbean has a UNEP administered Regional Seas Programme that has provided a base for the development of regional management.

The Caribbean Large Marine Ecosystem (CLME) Project focuses on developing effective resources management based on 'sound natural and social sciences' (Fanning et al. 2007a, p. 436), yet recognising weakness in linkages between governments and capacity within each government. These particular features make top-down models of management inappropriate, and clearly ineffective. By adopting a 'policy cycle approach' and recognising the multi-scale and multilevel nature of decision-making in the region, the CLME Project provides a mix of horizontal and vertical governance that should also increase capacity at all levels through the policy and management learning that takes place (Fanning et al. 2007b). This project introduces an interesting regional model that addresses some of the major challenges in oceans governance, providing an effective framework for multilevel decision-making, integrating vertical and horizontal dimensions.

THE PACIFIC

The interests of the Pacific Island countries (PICs) are defined by the ocean surrounding them. The Pacific region comprises 'approximately 200 high island and approximately 2,500 low islands and atolls' (Wright et al. 2006, p. 740) with a total land area of less than 0.6 million km^2 but generating an area of maritime jurisdiction of an estimated 30.6 million km^2 (Wright et al. 2006, p. 740). These micro–states are environmentally and economically vulnerable dependent on coastal and ocean resources for both subsistence and the development of export income (Cordonnery 2005).

The tuna fishery in the west-central Pacific ocean is the largest and most productive in the world, yielding catches of around 1 million tonnes of tuna annually, with a landed value in excess of US$1 billion per year (Cordonnery 2005; Bergin and Haward 1996). These catches represent around one-third of all tuna landed worldwide, 60 per cent of tuna for canning, and 30 per cent of the sashimi-grade tuna imported into Japan (Bergin and Haward 1996). Over 30 states and entities are involved in the fishery that spans over 30 million km^2 of ocean. Tuna represents one-third of all exports in the west-central Pacific and provides employment for an estimated 30 000–40 000 islanders. For many of the islands it represents the only significant source of income and the basis for future economic development: 'given the limited economic development options available, the importance of tuna resources and their exploitation to the economic security and sustainable development of the PICs are considerable and cannot be overstated' (Cordonnery 2005, p. 2).

The PICs concern with ensuring appropriate management of ocean resources within their EEZs and adjacent high seas areas has fostered the development of extensive regional cooperation, with the development of a number of institutions, instruments, programmes and policies. This has led to a comprehensive and collaborative regional framework that is 'globally unique' (Wright et al. 2006, p. 740):

> This framework is based on political cooperation, support for environmental initiatives of common interest, harmonised approaches to resource management, economic development, policy matters, technical back-stopping, security, capacity building, education and social issues of shared concern. (Wright et al. 2006, p. 740)

This framework has included the development of the Pacific Islands Regional Oceans Policy following a request from the Pacific Islands Forum in 1999 (Cordonnery 2005). The Pacific Islands Forum (founded as the South Pacific Forum in August 1971, with its name changed to the Pacific Islands Forum in October 2000) comprises 16 independent and self-governing states in the Pacific. The Forum's membership has increased from the original seven founding members (Australia, the Cook Islands, Fiji, Nauru, New Zealand, Tonga and Western Samoa – now Samoa) to include also the Federated States of Micronesia, Kiribati, Niue, the Republic of the Marshall Islands, Palau, Papua New Guinea, the Solomon Islands, Tuvalu and Vanuatu. New Caledonia and French Polynesia, previously forum observers, were granted associate membership in 2006. Current forum observers include Tokelau (2005), Wallis and Futuna (2006), the Commonwealth (2006) and the Asia Development Bank (2006), with Timor Leste as special observer (2002) (see Pacific Islands Forum 2008).

The Pacific Islands Forum is the primary regional organisation providing a means to coordinate actions within the Pacific. The Secretary-General of the Forum, based in Fiji, is also permanent Chair of the Council of Regional Organisations in the Pacific (CROP) which brings together 11 main regional organisations in the Pacific region, including the Secretariat of the Pacific Community, and the Pacific Regional Environment Programme (SPREP).

The Pacific Community was founded in 1947 as the South Pacific Commission by six developed countries with an interest in the region: Australia, France, the Netherlands, New Zealand, the United Kingdom and the United States. The Netherlands and the United Kingdom have since withdrawn from membership. The Pacific Community consists of the island countries as well those having territories in the region (New Zealand, the UK, the US and France). It is a non-political organisation with its secretariat (the SPC) providing advice on technical aspects of social and economic development, and has a major focus on fisheries research and development through its Marine Resources Division (MRD).

The Oceanic Fisheries Programme of the MRD works in close cooperation with Forum Fisheries Agency (FFA). There is common membership of the governing councils of FFA and the Pacific Community, which coordinate policy aspects, and by a memorandum of understanding and regular inter-agency colloquia, to coordinate aspects of their work programmes. The Oceanic Fisheries Programme maintains a mechanism for collaboration with distant-water fishing nations scientists and data sources through the annual Standing Committee on Tuna and Billfish and facilitates widespread contribution to a common pool of politically cleared data for research purposes.

The Pacific Regional Environment Programme (SPREP) is a regional organisation based in Apia, Samoa, established by the governments and administrations of the Pacific region to look after its environment. It has grown from a small programme attached to the South Pacific Commission in the 1980s into the Pacific region's major intergovernmental organisation charged with protecting and managing the environment and natural resources (SPREP 2007).

The Forum Fisheries Agency is comprised of an executive, the Forum Fisheries Committee (FFC), and a Secretariat, based in Honiara in the Solomon Islands (Herr 1990). The FFC delegates from each of the 16 member countries and provides direction to the Secretariat in terms of work plans as well as acting as a major forum for discussion of fisheries-related issues by FFA member countries. The FFA only deals with tuna and tuna-related species. The Secretariat provides a wide range of technical and policy-related advice, bilaterally, sub-regionally and to FFC as a whole. Areas of specialisation include legal issues, monitoring, control and surveillance, economics and marketing. The FFA is not a management body, and it does not purport to have the ability to implement comprehensive management arrangements throughout the WCP, but provides important coordination and capacity building roles for the PICs, and provides a mechanism for intergovernmental consultation between members that include Australia and New Zealand.

The Pacific Islands Regional Oceans Policy (PIROP) 'was the first attempt to adopt such a policy framework on a regional scale' (Cordonnery 2005, p. 1). This soft law policy framework focused on the sustainable development of the region's oceans and its oceanic resources. It was developed to provide the basis for national oceans policies and to 'harmonise national and regional actions' (Cordonnery 2005) in its implementation. Implementation of the PIROP is ongoing. A meeting of regional leaders in early 2004 focused on practical means to move the policy forward.

The PIROP was envisaged as a template for the PICs to adopt and adapt and facilitate the development of national policy, reflecting the range of interests, priorities and capacity within the region. The policy has five guiding principles:

- improving understanding of the oceans;
- sustainably developing and managing the use of ocean resources;
- maintaining the heath of the ocean;
- promoting the peaceful use of the ocean; and
- creating partnerships and promoting cooperation (see Cordonnery 2005).

Implementing a regional framework such as the PIROP, moving from paper commitments to an effective, if only hortatory, regional guidance instrument, will be difficult (Cordonnery 2005). Political will and commitment will be needed, as well as cooperation between PICs to ensure the aspirations of the PIROP are met. The deep-seated regional framework in the Pacific is important here. While this framework is complex (Wright et al. 2006, p. 759) it provides important support for the implementation of international instruments. The long-standing commitment to cooperation, as reflected in the complex institutional structure for ocean and marine management in the Pacific, provides great opportunities, although this may also mean implementation is necessarily inconsistent and patchy (Wright et al. 2006).

THE ANTARCTIC

Antarctica has long held the imagination. Ptolemy in AD 150 postulated that a land mass would be found in the south, leading to the consideration of Terra Australis Incognita – 'unknown south land' on maps and charts. Often these maps and charts showed imaginary beasts and fearsome creatures living at the end of the world. The 'end' or 'edge' of the world began to be explored by the first European navigators, Da Gama, Magellan and Drake in the sixteen century, although none actually saw or reported Antarctica. The late eighteenth century, with the voyages of Yves Kerguelen Tremarec and Captain James Cook, helped expand knowledge of this region. It was the late nineteenth and early twentieth centuries, when Antarctica was the focus of interest and activity, a period that was later termed the 'Heroic Era', that saw the two drivers of exploration and science become closely linked.

The Heroic Era has ongoing influence in Antarctic geo-politics (Dodds 1997). Exploration and discovery are recognised elements of claims to sovereignty and it is significant that all Antarctic claimant states use exploration and discovery as a basis of their Antarctic interests. It is interesting, too, that the first claims to Antarctic territory were made in the Heroic Era, prior to the First World War. Proclamations of Antarctic Territory gave rise to potential (and actual) competing claims and helped shape Antarctic geo-politics for the twentieth century. The question of territorial claims and sovereignty was the critical element of what was termed the 'Antarctic problem' in the 1940s. States like Australia, which had territorial claims (in addition to Australia the 'claimant states' are France, New Zealand, Chile, Argentina, Great Britain and Norway), wished to maintain the status of their claims. This position was opposed by the United

States and the Soviet Union which did not recognise territorial claims made by the claimant states but had reserved the right to make claims in the future.

The development of the Antarctic Treaty was a significant diplomatic effort, balancing the aspirations and interests of a number of different actors. Formal negotiations lasted 18 months from June 1958 and included 60 preparatory meetings and a formal diplomatic Conference on Antarctica that began on 15 October 1959 and concluded with the Antarctic Treaty open for signature on 1 December 1959. The claimant states wished to maintain the status of their claims. New Zealand indicated some support for internationalisation of the continent under the United Nations, while the option of condominium was also investigated. The Chilean delegate, Escudero, provided a modus vivendi to resolve the differences between claimants and others – through effectively 'freezing' existing and any further territorial claims, while allowing states to recognise claims. This, together with significant diplomatic efforts by the Australian delegation, was critical in ensuring the Union of Soviet Socialist Republics (USSR)'s support for the Antarctic Treaty.

The first meeting of Antarctic Treaty parties (the first Antarctic Treaty Consultative Meeting or ATCM) was held in Canberra on 10–14 July 1961. Addressing the first ATCM the Australian Prime Minister Robert Menzies noted the intense negotiations that had accompanied the drafting of the Antarctic Treaty and commented on the way in which the parties had accommodated different views and interests within this instrument for the pursuit of peaceful scientific exploration. The Antarctic Treaty forms the basis of an extensive and continually evolving regime governing the Antarctic and Southern Ocean. This regime – the Antarctic Treaty System (ATS) and the institutions associated with it – comprises instruments and arrangements dealing with marine living resources and environmental protection. Antarctic Treaty parties have also addressed emergent issues such as tourism, shipping and biological prospecting, amongst other matters. The success of this regime over almost 50 years provides the opportunity for significant research into the relationship between national interests and the establishment and functioning of international instruments and regimes.

The ATS includes the Antarctic Treaty (1959) and the following subsidiary and related instruments:

- Convention for the Conservation of Antarctic Seals – CCAS (1972).
- Convention on the Conservation of Antarctic Marine Living Resources – CCAMLR (1980).
- Protocol on Environmental Protection to the Antarctic Treaty – Madrid Protocol (1991).

It also includes the following institutions:

- Antarctic Treaty Consultative Meetings (ATCMs);
- Scientific Committee on Antarctic Research (SCAR);
- Committee for Environment Protection (CEP);
- Standing Committee on Antarctic Logistics and Operations (SCALOP);
- Council of Managers of National Antarctic Programs (COMNAP)
- the CCAMLR Secretariat; and
- the Antarctic Treaty Secretariat.

The Commission for the Conservation of Antarctic Marine Living Resources is an international organisation established in 1982 through the entry into force of the Convention on the Conservation of Antarctic Marine Living Resources. This convention, and the work of its Commission, applies to Antarctic marine living resources in an area bounded to the north by a line which approximates the position of the Antarctic Circumpolar Front and to the south by the Antarctic continent. The CCAMLR Commission and its Scientific Committee (SC-CCAMLR) is charged with using an ecosystem approach to the conservation of Antarctic marine living resources. This has meant that populations of seabirds and their interactions with other species in the ecosystem have been the focus of considerable study. CCAMLR pioneered the ecosystem approach now incorporated into contemporary fisheries arrangements and oceans policy.

Membership of the Commission is available to contracting parties and states that have acceded to the convention. In the case of the latter, membership of the Commission is gained following notification of a state's willingness to become a member, and its acceptance of conservation measures that are in force. There are currently 25 members of the Commission: Argentina, Australia, Belgium, Brazil, Chile, China, the European Community, France, Germany, India, Italy, Japan, the Republic of Korea, Namibia, New Zealand, Norway, Poland, the Russian Federation, South Africa, Spain, Sweden, Ukraine, the United Kingdom, the United States of America and Uruguay. States party to the convention, but not members of the Commission, are: Bulgaria, Canada, Cook Islands, Finland, Greece, Mauritius, the Netherlands, Peru and Vanuatu.

The CCAMLR operates on a consensus model of decision-making. This approach has been criticised by some non-governmental organisations as leading to weaker outcomes. Some criticism has also been levelled in the past at the CCAMLR's concern with managing single-species finfish rather than utilising an ecosystem approach. In its early years the CCAMLR did experience difficulties with developing an agreed approach to resource management and in obtaining data on resource stocks and use. Overcoming obstruction from the former Soviet Union meant that the CCAMLR was able to focus more attention on multi-species and ecosystem aspects of the Scientific Committee's work.

The Commission and Scientific Committee, supported by a Secretariat, are established under Articles VII, XIV and XVIII, respectively, of the CCAMLR. Article XVI enables the Commission to establish 'such subsidiary bodies as are necessary for the performance of its functions'. Three working groups provide advice to SC-CCAMLR. These are the Working Group on Ecosystem Monitoring and Management, WG-EMM; the Working Group on Fisheries Monitoring (originally Fish Stock Assessment), WG-FSA; and the ad hoc Working Group on Seabird and Mammal Interactions with Fisheries.

The European Commission (EC) is a party to the CCAMLR and represents the interests of its member states as it has competence over fishing for all member states of the European Union. Individual member states of the EC are also contracting parties (Belgium, France, Germany, Italy, Sweden and the United Kingdom). The United Kingdom and France also have sovereign territories in the sub-Antarctic. In 1999 the EC's application for a fisheries permit for Portugal (a non-member) was opposed by a number of member states. Opposition to Portugal's application centred on the problems of adequate flag-state control and the question of the EC's competence. The issue led to ongoing discussions and was resolved with the Portuguese application being withdrawn. The relationship between the EC and its member states is an ongoing dynamic within the Commission.

THE ARCTIC

Polar exploration, after the opening up of Africa, became one of the last great challenges. The Arctic – and the lure of the North-West Passage – was the first to attract interest, with some heroic and equally tragic results. Sir John Franklin disappeared trying to find the North-West Passage, a possible shorter trade route from Europe to the Asia. The Arctic, an area of significant geopolitical rivalry in the Cold War, differed significantly from the Antarctic in that a regional focus to management did not develop until the 1980s. This is solely due to the presence of sovereign states bordering the Arctic Ocean. The Arctic, too, supports indigenous communities, and has large-scale and varied resource exploitation from mining, oil and gas extraction and significant fisheries activities. The Arctic, as implied, has also a strong military focus and has major shipping and air transport routes. In contrast the Antarctic has none of these, except for the controlled exploitation of fish stocks in the Southern Ocean and a growing tourism industry (Haward and Jabour 2007).

The thawing of the Cold War provided an impetus for increased collaboration amongst Arctic states. This collaboration was facilitated by increasing concern over environmental degradation, transboundary movement of pollutants and concerns over the impact of climate change on the Arctic region. Eight Arctic countries adopted the Arctic Environmental Protection Strategy in 1991 and in 1996 the Arctic Council was established under the Ottawa Declaration. The Ottawa Declaration provided a mandate to undertake a broad programme of work under the ambit of sustainable development and environmental protection in the Arctic (Arctic Council 2008). The member states of the Arctic Council are Canada, Denmark, Finland, Iceland, Norway, the Russian Federation, Sweden and the United States of America:

> Arctic Council Ministerial Meetings are held biannually in the country holding the chairmanship ... Meetings of Senior Arctic officials are held every six months in the host country. (Arctic Council 2008)

Environment assessment and monitoring has been a major focus of the Arctic Council's work programme. This has involved extensive collaboration between governments and indigenous peoples of the region. This work has included assessment of the impact of climate change. While the Antarctic can be seen as an exemplar of the science–policy interface, science is still important in guiding Arctic decision-making (Haward and Jabour 2007). The Arctic, however, unlike the Antarctic, does not have a coherent regional management regime despite its population, resource exploitation and prominent strategic profile (Haward and Jabour 2007).

CONCLUSION

The range of regional initiatives in oceans governance discussed above indicates the scale, scope and diversity of such activity. Regional action has gained impetus from two related drivers: the increased attention to integrated oceans management in international forums, institutions and instruments (discussed in the preceding chapter); and developments from within nation states as members of regional forums. While progress in these regional initiatives is, not surprisingly, uneven, analysis of regional institutions and arrangements directs attention to opportunities for capacity building, information exchange (policy transfer) and policy learning amongst member states. We have already identified these elements, and the tools that they are centred on, as key aspects of oceans governance.

4. Australia

Australia has responsibility for the fourth-largest maritime jurisdiction in the world, with an exclusive economic zone (EEZ) and continental shelf of approximately 18.5 million km² in area, extending from tropical to Antarctic waters (see Figure 4.1). This area is almost twice the size of the Australian land mass. The Australian marine domain supports a number of commercially lucrative fisheries, significant offshore oil and gas production areas and globally important marine environments. As an island continent the ocean provides Australia with resources and vital links to the rest of the world, yet until recently the nation has lacked any notion of an oceans policy, instead managing this vast domain through a range of sectorally oriented, oceans-related policies.

The policies and management of Australia's ocean and coastal areas have been shaped by the historical development of the nation, domestic politics and the influence of developments in international oceans governance. Australia has taken a high-profile lead in developing marine protected area management in the 1970s, supporting stronger initiatives against marine pollution in the 1980s, and taking significant action against illegal, unreported or unregulated (IUU) fishing in the 1990s (Haward 2003, 2004). Australia's international actions have been matched by the development of oceans governance initiatives including a national Oceans Policy framework (Bergin and Haward 1999; Haward 2001; Vince 2003, 2004, 2006).

This chapter provides an overview of the political and constitutional base for Australian oceans management. We discuss the interestingly named Offshore Constitutional Settlement that, in providing a political settlement to long-running jurisdictional battles over the offshore, reinforced jurisdictional boundaries and entrenched a sectoral base to oceans management. This provides the context for legislation and policy development for the management of Australia's marine resources and coasts. We examine the development and implementation of Australia's Oceans Policy, introduced in late 1998, which attempted set out for the first time a comprehensive, integrated, national approach to ecosystem-based oceans management. While the Oceans Policy aimed to implement 'integrated and ecosystems based planning for all of Australia's marine jurisdictions' (Commonwealth of Australia 1998a, p. 4) the influence of 'offshore federalism' and the way in which the Commonwealth developed the oceans policy meant that these aspirations were thwarted. Australia's experience, often promoted as an example for lesson-drawing by others, or as an example of a 'more mature case' in oceans policy development, reinforces the utility of a governance lens focusing on process and practices of policy development and implementation involving a range of instruments and approaches, interests and stakeholders.

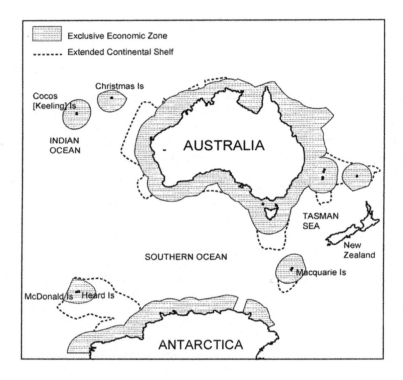

Figure 4.1 Australia – maritime jurisdiction

THE AUSTRALIAN CONSTITUTION, JURISDICTION AND THE OFFSHORE

The Australian Constitution separated jurisdictional responsibilities between the Commonwealth and the states. Following federation on 1 January 1901 the states were, and continue to be, responsible for activities relating to the administration of ocean and marine resources, whilst the Commonwealth powers outlined in the Constitution are limited to regulating 'fisheries beyond territorial limits' (Section 51 (x)) and 'external affairs' (Section 51 (xxix)). Discussions during the Constitutional Conventions in the 1980s did focus on the wording 'fisheries beyond territorial limits', and although this construction is confusing, and made little sense in context of the then current customary law of the sea, it did ensure that states retained their control over established fisheries.

As the Commonwealth became more involved in offshore activities throughout the twentieth century, as the following section on fisheries illustrates, the states disputed the validity of the phrase 'territorial limits' whenever the opportunity arose. This led to major High Court cases that either directly, or indirectly, raised issues related to territorial limits and jurisdictional boundaries of the states and the Commonwealth. These cases included Bonser v La Macchia in 1969 and Raptis v South Australia in 1977 dealing with fisheries, and Robinson v Western Australian Museum in 1977, dealing with historic offshore wrecks and salvage of artefacts.

The first intergovernmental debates over the offshore resources began during the 1940s when the Commonwealth began to pursue its maritime interests. The discovery of hydrocarbon reserves in the Gippsland Basin area of the Bass Strait by Broken Hill Propriety Company Ltd, and Esso Exploration and Production Australia Inc., prompted the Commonwealth to take further interest in the offshore (Cullen 1990). The Commonwealth became involved in offshore matters as a result of the financial incentives it provided to stimulate offshore exploration. This led to discussions between the Commonwealth and the states with regard to revenue sharing. The Commonwealth taxation concessions and financial incentives were aimed at increasing investor confidence in offshore oil products and were successful in doing so. Whilst investor confidence was high, unresolved jurisdictional disputes over the offshore were put on hold. The successful gas and oil strikes in the Gippsland Basin raised problems of legal uncertainty over title to offshore resources and stimulated tensions between the Commonwealth and the states.

Both Commonwealth and state governments disagreed on which activities beyond territorial limits they should regulate. The Commonwealth insisted on resolving the offshore disputes with the states for two main reasons. First, the Commonwealth wanted to clarify the issue of constitutional power in the territorial sea. Second, the United Nations Convention on the Continental Shelf entered into force in 1964 and it gave the Commonwealth the opportunity to extend its role in offshore policy developments. Interestingly, neither the states nor Commonwealth wanted a constitutional challenge over the offshore, but they were attracted by the 'potential economic return' from these resources (Haward 1992, p. 102) and while 'keen to set aside jurisdictional questions' neither abandoned claims to constitutional power (Rothwell and Haward 1996, p. 71).

Commonwealth and state disputes reached a high point in the late 1960s and early 1970s, when the Commonwealth asserted its jurisdiction from the low water mark in the Seas and Submerged Lands Act 1973. The states' legal argument to retract the Commonwealth legislation was based on the provisions of the Petroleum Agreement. They claimed that the actions of the Commonwealth did not comply with the agreement and therefore should be reversed (Haward 1992, p. 142). The states decided to challenge the validity of Section 51 (xxix) that was used by the Commonwealth as a 'constitutional anchor' for the Seas and Submerged Lands Act (Rothwell and Haward 1996, p. 33). They took their dispute against the Commonwealth to the High Court in the 1975 'Seas and Submerged Lands' case (New South Wales v The Commonwealth) where the majority of the Court found that the Commonwealth had sovereign rights from the low water mark and beyond:

> The Court decided (5:2) in the Seas and Submerged Lands Case that the Commonwealth government enjoyed sovereignty over internal waters and the territorial seas and (unanimously) sovereign rights over the continental shelf. (Cullen 1996, p. 132)

The High Court upheld Section 51 (xxix) of the Constitution and found that the ruling was valid when based on two international conventions – the 1958 Convention on the Territorial Sea and Contiguous Zone and the 1958 Convention on the Continental Shelf (Rothwell and Kaye 2001, p. 279). Australian political history has a number of examples which show that in cases where Commonwealth legislation is challenged by the states, the High Court rules in favour of the Commonwealth in accordance with the latter's powers under Section 51 (xxix) of the Constitution. The High Court ruling reinforced that the jurisdictional limits of the states stopped at the low water mark and that 'the states only retained control over waters considered to be internal waters of a state at federation ... and also offshore fishing subject to extraterritorial limitations' (Rothwell and Kaye 2001, p. 280). Nonetheless, the states continued to search for avenues to regain control over their offshore jurisdiction.

During this period the Commonwealth also acted to address concerns over mining activities in the Great Barrier Reef region. The Queensland government encouraged offshore oil and gas exploration in the Great Barrier Reef region, despite its ecological uniqueness. The Commonwealth and Queensland disputed who should control activities concerning the reef. Queensland argued that all activities were under state jurisdiction since the

Reef was located within territorial waters. The Commonwealth, however, used international ratified agreements and their external affairs powers to gain legislative control over the Great Barrier Reef. In 1975, the Commonwealth enacted the Great Barrier Reef Marine Park Act, which established the Marine Park and the Great Barrier Reef Marine Park Authority (GBRMPA). The aim of the GBRMPA was to protect and advocate wise use of the Marine Park, whilst incorporating economic development, involvement with the community and minimal regulation (Sainsbury et al. 1997, p. 27). During the development of the Great Barrier Reef Marine Park, intergovernmental tensions were already fuelled by the decisions of the Seas and Submerged Lands case. The Commonwealth's involvement in Queensland coastal issues only furthered the intergovernmental tensions.

These tensions were reduced following the development of what was termed the Offshore Constitutional Settlement (OCS) in 1979 (see below). The main objective of the OCS was to overcome the intergovernmental difficulties that had arisen from the Seas and Submerged Lands case that determined that the Commonwealth held constitutional power offshore from the low water mark. The Commonwealth sought primarily to give the states a greater legal and administrative role from the low water mark, whilst maintaining control of waters beyond territorial limits. While the OCS has become a major framework for oceans policy development and resource management in Australia it 'was not entirely constitutional in character, nor a settlement in total' (Davis 1996, p. 27), with jurisdictional issues continuing to shape oceans policy.

FISHERIES

In the colonial period prior to federation, and continuing for several decades, the majority of fishing activities were located inshore, and offshore fishing was undertaken close to the coast. Although fishing beyond territorial limits for sedentary species had already commenced, the extent of future use of the offshore was not anticipated (Campbell 1960, p. 256). Interest in further developing the Australian fishing industry emerged during a conference between the Commonwealth and states in 1907. The national conferences in 1927 and 1929 also focused on the extent of Commonwealth involvement in fisheries beyond territorial limits. During 1929, too, a Royal Commission report on the Constitution found that major trawl fisheries were operating up to twenty miles off the New South Wales coast and deep-sea fisheries had been discovered in the Great Australian Bight (Harrison 1991). The Commission recommended that the Constitution should be altered to give full power over Australian fisheries to the Commonwealth. A suggestion that a Commonwealth agency be developed to manage fisheries, raised at the 1929 conference, was ignored.

The Commonwealth's Beaches, Fishing Grounds and Sea Routes Protection Act was passed in 1932; however, this legislation had little impact on Commonwealth activities in fisheries and was primarily concerned with regulating dumping waste at sea (Harrison 1982). Similarly, the Commonwealth's Whaling Act 1935 only dealt with the regulation of whaling in Australian waters. The impact of the Second World War focused the attention of the Commonwealth on other policy matters. During the 1946 Premiers' Conference the first Commonwealth fisheries authority was developed and was allocated to the Commonwealth Department of Commerce and Agriculture.

A proposal for fisheries legislation first arose during the Commonwealth and State Fisheries Conference in 1947. The Commonwealth stressed that it wanted to help the states and not take over their responsibilities. The legislation was not introduced for a number of years until the state and Commonwealth governments had agreed on their respective roles. The states did resist the legislation that followed, however, the Commonwealth passed the Fisheries Act 1952 and it became the 'first legislative base for formal intergovernmental relations offshore' (Haward 1991b, p. 111). Although it passed through the Senate in 1952, the Commonwealth Fisheries and Pearl Fisheries Acts were not proclaimed until 1955 when the major intergovernmental issues were resolved.

The Fisheries and Pearl Fisheries Acts reinforced the notion that the Commonwealth had jurisdictional responsibilities beyond territorial limits. It can be argued that the Commonwealth chose not to legislate on fisheries until 1952 as it had reasonable faith in state policy (Herr and Davis 1982). The Pearl Fisheries Act demonstrated Australia's independence from Britain in policy-making with regard to sedentary fisheries issues in Australian waters and resulted in a sense of 'national ownership' of ocean and marine living resources. The Fisheries Act, on the other hand, was a response to the pressure exerted on the Commonwealth from the states who were concerned about the fishing activities beyond the territorial limits (Byrne 1985, p. 1).

The Commonwealth did finally take action on fisheries matters beyond territorial limits through the Continental Shelf (Living Natural Resources) Act 1968. The Act was enacted for two distinct purposes. First, it ensured that the ratified principles from the 1958 Convention of the Continental Shelf were translated into domestic policy. The Commonwealth sought to uphold international agreements while it legislated on domestic issues. Second, it brought the continental shelf under 'Commonwealth jurisdiction for the purposes of conserving fish resources' (Evans 1998, p. 93) and by doing so, it replaced the Pearl Fisheries Act 1952. During the Premiers' Conference in 1979, a new fisheries agreement was reached and the Offshore Constitutional Settlement was launched (see details below). The Commonwealth's Fisheries Act 1952 was to be finally repealed in 1991 by the Fisheries Legislation (Consequential Provisions) Act, and the Fisheries Management Act 1991 (Bergin et al. 1996, p. 176).

The Development of Commonwealth Fisheries Administration

A decision to establish a Commonwealth Fisheries Agency was agreed upon during the Premiers' Conference in 1946. Initially, the states were not in favour of the decision. Two factors, however, influenced the states to agree to the use of the Commonwealth's powers over fisheries beyond territorial waters. First, fishing activities were expanding beyond the three nautical mile limit and deep-sea trawl fisheries were being developed. Second, international interests in high seas fisheries were increasing. The fishing industry in Australia had developed in an ad hoc manner with divisions across jurisdictions and also within the industry. Haward (1998) argued that:

> a major influence on the development of fisheries policy, and the management of particular fisheries is the diversified and decentralised nature of the Australian fishing industry. The sectoral split within the industry is the most obvious example of this.

The Australian Fisheries Council (AFC) and a number of Commonwealth-state advisory committees were established during the Premiers' Conference in 1960. The establishment of the AFC has been labelled as 'a major landmark' (Herr and Davis 1986, p. 684) and 'a positive move towards the coordination of fisheries management in Australia' (Byrne 1985, p. 1). The AFC comprised state and Commonwealth ministers, and although the AFC increased Commonwealth involvement in fisheries matters, the day-to-day fishery management practices continued to be controlled by the states.

The first meeting of the AFC did not occur until 1968, and this delay reflected the level of intergovernmental difficulties in ocean-related policies during this period. The advisory committees were comprised of senior managers and scientists from Commonwealth and state agencies and were set up under the umbrella of the AFC. The aim of these committees was 'to coordinate Commonwealth, state and Territory control over fishing' (Byrne 1985, p. 1), but failed to prevent diversion and conflict between states, and between the Commonwealth and the states.

This prompted the Commonwealth to become more active in fisheries management and by the mid-1970s the states had formed advisory committees 'with strong industry representation to advise the respective agencies and/or government on fisheries matters' (Byrne 1985, p. 2). The states encouraged the fishing industry to avoid consultation with the Commonwealth, and as a result, many of the fisheries that transcended the 3 mile limit were left unmanaged. The Australian Fishing Industry Council (AFIC), a national industry organisation, was also established in 1968 (Haward 1992, p. 90). The AFIC focused on intergovernmental cooperation, similarly to the AFC, and was endorsed by the Commonwealth Department of Primary Industries. Herr and Davis argue that this departmental support was 'unusual' as the Commonwealth was taking 'deliberate steps to foster the growth of the national industry body, in part to help legitimate the growing use of Commonwealth fisheries powers' (Herr and Davis 1986, p. 684). The states had little support for another Commonwealth agency and this became the source of some internal frictions between fishermen and industry officials. The AFIC's difficulties were further extended by the lack of funding and, as a result, the AFIC was not a powerful player in fisheries management.

During 1983 an Interim Fishing Industry Panel was formed and was chaired by the Minister for Primary Industry to oversee the implementation of the fisheries package that was decided upon during the Offshore Constitutional Settlement (Bain 1984, p. 15). Shortly after, the National Fishing Industry Council (NFIC) replaced the AFIC following the Australian Fisheries Conference held in February 1985. The aim of the conference was to establish an effective, independent and representative voice for the Australian fishing industry. The conference recommended that the National Fisherman's Association, National Marketers and Processors Association, and Association of National Industry Associations be represented by the NFIC (later known as the Australian Seafood Industry Council). The Fishing Industry Policy Council of Australia, on the other hand, was to provide a forum for the Minister of Primary Industry and the Australian Fisheries Service with fishing industry officials.

The Commonwealth found that the existing fisheries agencies were not adequately equipped to deal with the rapid growth in the industry. As a consequence the Australian Fisheries Management Authority (AFMA) and the Fishing Industry Policy Council of Australia (FIPCA) were established in 1992 through the Fisheries Management and Fisheries Administration Acts 1991. The FIPCA was to be responsible for advising the Commonwealth Minister on fisheries-related issues, however, it was never instituted. Interestingly, the Commonwealth Fisheries Policy Review released in 2003 proposed a similar policy forum.

The AFMA is responsible for the day-to-day management of Commonwealth fisheries and consults with the Management Advisory Committees (MACs) over fisheries management (AFMA 2007). The Department of Agriculture, Fisheries and Forestry (DAFF) is responsible for broader fisheries policy, international negotiations and strategic issues (DAFF 2007). The level of industry growth is demonstrated through the Australian Bureau of Agricultural and Resource Economics (ABARE) statistics which estimated that in 1991–92 the value of the Australian fishing industry was approximately A$1.7 billion and in 2005–06 the value increased to approximately A$2.13 billion (ABARE 2007).

The Fisheries Management Act 1991 required AFMA to establish a system of statutory fishing rights in Commonwealth-controlled fisheries. This encouraged a shift from input to output management controls with the introduction of transferable quotas in Commonwealth and in some state-controlled fisheries. Economic instruments have also increased in salience through policy to recover costs of management from participants in fisheries through licence fees and levies. The 1993–94 Commonwealth budget emphasised a commitment that users should pay for management services in proportion to benefits received, and from 1994–95 industry has been responsible for payments of 100 per cent of attributable costs of management of Commonwealth fisheries.

Emphasis on improving the sustainability of fisheries is mandated by legislative requirements that focus on principles of ecologically sustainable development. Developments in broader government policies, primarily through the implementation of Australia's Oceans Policy, reinforce the requirement that fisheries policy and management needed to reorient towards an ecosystem-based approach. The development of the Environment Protection and Biodiversity Conservation Act 1999 (EPBC Act) and its entry into force in 2000 saw the introduction of 'strategic assessment' of fisheries where fisheries are assessed against a standard set of environmental indicators. The strategic assessments for Australian fisheries, paralleled a more strategic, science-based approach to setting total allowable catch and/or effort levels in Commonwealth fisheries. Intervention by the Australian government through a 'Ministerial Direction' aimed to constrain overfishing and recover overfished stocks (Skivington 2006). In addition, the Australian government announced in late 2005 a $220 million structural adjustment package 'Securing our Fishing Future'. This 'package will help secure Commonwealth fish stocks and sustainable, profitable future for the fishing industry' (ibid. p. 7). The Ministerial Direction's focus is on ensuring even more concerted efforts are made in maintaining, rebuilding and developing sustainable fisheries in Australia. The structural adjustment package provides for the first time a means of reducing actual and latent capacity and effort.

OFFSHORE OIL AND GAS

Prior to the 1960s, the Commonwealth had little interest and was 'clearly inexperienced' in the management of offshore oil and petroleum resources and 'displayed little inclination to move in this direction' (Evans 1998, p. 55). The individual states during the early 1960s, sought to legislate and control offshore exploration by applying onshore mining and petroleum legislation to the offshore activities (Reid 1980, p. 59). The legality of these arrangements was questioned by the Commonwealth but not challenged. At the time the Commonwealth acknowledged that the states could continue regulating offshore activities due to their background in offshore management practices in fisheries.

The negotiations over the offshore between governments and industry stakeholders began in 1962 and concluded in 1967 with the enactment of the Australian offshore petroleum agreement (Lang and Crommelin 1979, p. 227). The agreement set the foundations for offshore petroleum activities by outlining the legal, political and industrial parameters for intergovernmental interaction with regard to offshore oil petroleum and mining. It was agreed upon by all governments and vested control of all offshore mining and petroleum activities with the states. The states made it clear that they were the dominant administrators of offshore petroleum and mining activities and argued that they were entitled to more royalties than the Commonwealth. The determination to avoid a constitutional challenge of both the states and Commonwealth was highlighted in the Preamble of the agreement which read:

> The Governments of the Commonwealth and of the states have decided, in the national interest, that, without raising questions concerning, and without derogating from, their respective constitutional powers, they should cooperate for the purposes of ensuring the legal effectiveness of authorities to explore for, or to exploit, the petroleum resources of those submerged lands. (Commonwealth of Australia 1967, p. 714)

The offshore petroleum settlement consisted of two components. The first was the Petroleum Agreement and legislative measures and 'was described in the 1970s as the most complex and innovative inter-governmental agreement yet negotiated' (Haward 1992, p. 115). Despite this, it has been argued that the agreement only postponed constitutional issues and did little to resolve them (Reid 1980, p. 60). The second component of the settlement included Commonwealth and state legislation. Supporting the Petroleum Agreement was the chief Commonwealth statute, the Petroleum (Submerged) Lands Act 1967, and related legislation, the Petroleum (Submerged Lands) Royalty, Exploration Permit Fees, Production Licence Fees, Pipeline Licence Fees, Registration Fees, and Ashmore and Cartier Islands Acts 1967 (Lang and Crommelin 1979, p. 227).

The states' legislation mirrored the Commonwealth to the extent that they only dealt with the offshore waters within their territorial boundaries. The Commonwealth legislation, on the other hand, applied to the whole offshore area. Consequently, any amendments to either Commonwealth or state legislation could only happen with unanimous consent. The Commonwealth and state legislation did not directly distinguish between the territorial sea and the continental shelf although numerous discussions were held on this topic.

THE OFFSHORE CONSTITUTIONAL SETTLEMENT

The outcome of the Seas and Submerged Lands case provided a dilemma for the Fraser Government. Elected to power with massive support after an election triggered by the dismissal of Prime Minister Whitlam by the Governor-General, Fraser had campaigned for a more cooperative model of federalism in contrast to the 'coercive' federalism of Whitlam (Sawer 1977). At the same time it was not going to acquiesce to all state government demands over the offshore. The Commonwealth quickly realised that the High Court's decision in upholding Commonwealth power over the offshore provided a complicated fractious situation for stakeholders and all governments involved. The Commonwealth and states entered detailed negotiations along with the Standing Committee of Commonwealth and State Attorneys-General at the Premiers' Conferences in October 1977, 1978 and June 1979. The negotiations resulted in the 1979 Offshore Constitutional Settlement (OCS) that came into force in 1983 (Haward 1989).

The OCS was designed to include 'complementary' Commonwealth and the state legislation rather than the 'mirror' legislation of the 1967 Petroleum Agreement. The OCS made provisions for the states to regain their jurisdiction from the low water mark to the 3 mile territorial limit. Despite this, the Commonwealth continued to have control over the policy agenda during the OCS negotiations. The OCS did not reduce Commonwealth involvement but supported it in oceans and marine resource policy decision-making. As a result, the OCS was implemented in a complex, and overlapping administrative manner (Haward 1992, p. 196). The Commonwealth government introduced a package of 14 bills to the House of

Representatives on 23 April 1980. Following the understandably slower passage of legislation through the states (necessary for the complementary nature of the legislative design) the OCS was completed with the assent to the Coastal Waters State Title Act in February 1983 (Haward 1989).

The development and implementation of the OCS was unique in that it addressed each sector's issues separately within its 'agreed arrangements'. The agreed arrangements comprised: a legislative package; an offshore petroleum package; an offshore fisheries package; a Great Barrier Reef package; and new ancillary arrangements. Previous approaches to ocean and marine resource management were organic in design where 'the arrangement in which each component was established as an integral part of the larger settlement' (Haward 1992, p. 199). The sectoral approach used to implement the OCS along with the embedded jurisdictional divide resulted in a segregated oceans management regime.

The Legislative Package

The legislative components of the OCS were made up of complementary legislation, the Coastal Waters (State Powers) and the Coastal Waters (State Title) Acts 1980. The State Powers Act extended the legislative powers of the states from the low water mark. The low water mark excludes the pre-federation internal waters that are within the constitutional boundaries of the state, such as Sydney Harbour. The State Title Act made provisions for state territory to include the seabed beneath the territorial sea. This legislation was also the first to be passed under Section 51 (xxxviii) of the Constitution that gives power to the Commonwealth to make laws provided it occurs with the agreement 'of the Parliaments of all the States directly concerned.'

The Offshore 'Petroleum Package'

The offshore petroleum package established that the Commonwealth was to continue regulating activities beyond territorial limits. The day-to-day management, on the other hand, was to be administered by the states through a joint authority arrangement. The joint authorities were comprised of the relevant Commonwealth minister and state ministers to 'decide the major issues under the legislation including the award, renewal, variation, suspension and cancellation of titles and conditions of titles' (Starkey 1987, p. 25). It was agreed that the royalty payments to the states, which the Commonwealth established in the 1960s, were to continue with close consultation between Commonwealth and state officials and the Standing Committees of the Australian Minerals and Energy Council (Davis 1996, p. 28). The Common Mining Code established by the 1967 Petroleum

Agreement was not retained as it was found to be not 'practicable' (Hunt 1989, p. 108).

The Fisheries Package

The OCS fisheries package, although incomplete, outlined new arrangements for fisheries management between the Commonwealth and the states. The delay in completing the package was a result of the long negotiation process over the classification of fisheries. The package aimed to introduce flexibility to fisheries management through provisions for individual fisheries and joint authorities where intergovernmental cooperation was required. Despite this, there was limited progress in the establishment of joint authorities due to disputes over their functions.

The package outlined the Commonwealth's fishing responsibilities that included retaining control over the Australian Fishing Zone (AFZ) and transboundary stocks such as the southern bluefin tuna. Section 4 (1) of the Fisheries Amendment Act 1978 specified that the AFZ includes:

> waters adjacent to Australia commencing at baselines and extending 200 nautical miles seaward, provided that such waters are 'proclaimed waters' under Section 7 (1) and not 'excepted waters' (under section 7 (A)).

The states, conversely, regained their original jurisdiction over territorial waters up to the 3 mile limit and were allocated control of fisheries to the boundary of the AFZ. The OCS focused primarily on the offshore fisheries disputes, and following this, the AFZ was declared. This influenced the implementation of the fisheries package and the extended zone was announced in November 1979. Nevertheless, the fishing arrangements outlined in the Fisheries Act 1980 did not enter into force until 1986.

The implementation of the fisheries package emphasised many facets of intergovernmental relations. The states and the Commonwealth identified the need for a uniform approach to fisheries management and to establish guidelines against stock decline, but the states, in order to protect their own interests, did not agree to all Commonwealth suggestions. The states found the joint authority approach facilitated by the OCS was adding to, rather than reducing, the existing complexities in fisheries management. A provision in the OCS Agreed Arrangements further extended the power of the Commonwealth by stipulating that 'in the event of disagreement within a fisheries authority, the views of the Commonwealth Minister will prevail'.

The Great Barrier Reef Package

The Great Barrier Reef package in the OCS applied not only to the reef area but also to other marine protected areas. The package reinforced the Great Barrier Reef Marine Park Act 1975 and the joint consultative arrangements between the Commonwealth and the state of Queensland with regard to the marine region. The OCS package led to the proclamation of the first zone of the Marine Park and the establishment of the Great Barrier Reef Ministerial Council (Haward 1991b, p. 120).

The Great Barrier Reef Marine Park Act and OCS arrangements established provisions for the Great Barrier Reef to be managed by Queensland government officials who report to the GBRMPA. The Ministerial Council's role was to facilitate intergovernmental relations with regard to the Great Barrier Reef Marine Park. This OCS package also provided for state management of other marine parks within territorial limits and Commonwealth management of the parks that were located beyond territorial limits.

AUSTRALIA AND THE LAW OF THE SEA

Australia ratified the Law of the Sea Convention on 5 October 1994 (Rothwell and Haward 1996, p. 30). Australia's conservative approach to policy-making in this area did solve the domestic offshore disputes at the time. It 'led to a number of significant policy decisions, which all involve bringing Australian law into line with certain provisions from the Law of the Sea Convention' (Burmester 1995, p. 51). Australia has taken an orthodox, cautious approach to the implementation of ocean policies and this is reflected in its negotiations over the OCS and other marine policies. For example, in late 1990 Australia was one of the last signatories to extend its territorial sea from 3 nautical miles to 12. Up until then it had raised straight baselines on provisions from the 1958 Convention on the Territorial Sea. The proclamation, which was given domestic effect through the Commonwealth's Sea and Submerged Lands Act 1973, included all Australian territories, external territories and islands that are part of state territories.

Australia's intention to declare an EEZ was announced in 1991 and was formally proclaimed following ratification of the Law of the Sea Convention (LOSC) in 1994. Australia's EEZ is the third-largest in the world and the LOSC provides Australia with the sovereign rights over living and non-living resources within its boundaries. The Commonwealth did maintain that the continental shelf regime and Australian Fishing Zone (proclaimed in

1979) should be kept completely separate to the EEZ. Although the fishing zone and the EEZ are identical in area the definitions were kept separate to avoid unnecessary amendments to legislation. The new contiguous zone and the EEZ were applied through the Commonwealth's Maritime Legislation Amendment Act 1994.

MARINE ENVIRONMENTAL MANAGEMENT

Action on oceans and coastal policy during the 1980s and 1990s had implications for intergovernmental relations and oceans policy development in Australia. The focus on the offshore by all governments in previous decades was replaced by a focus on global, national and local environmental concerns. Increasing public concern over degraded beaches and waterways dominated political discussions, and increased Commonwealth activism. Despite the 'settlement' of the jurisdictional issues through the OCS, Commonwealth and state relations in oceans and coastal issues throughout the 1990s continued to be difficult. At the same time, however, a number of significant Commonwealth initiatives were developed that dealt with marine environmental management. These included Ocean Rescue 2000; The Intergovernmental Agreement on the Environment; the National Ecologically Sustainable Development Strategy; and the Commonwealth's Coastal Policy.

Ocean Rescue 2000

The Commonwealth's strong interest in the management and protection of Australia's oceans and coasts was reflected in the decade-long Ocean Rescue 2000 (OR 2000) programme. It was established by the Labor government in 1991 and administered by the Commonwealth Department of Environment, Sport and Territories (DEST). Its main support structure included the GBRMPA and the Australian Nature Conservation Agency (ANCA), both agencies within the DEST portfolio. OR 2000 aimed to promote the conservation and sustainable use of Australia's marine and coastal environments by building upon existing government programmes and complementing initiatives such as Landcare, the Biological Diversity Strategy and coastal strategies.

The main elements of the programme included the creation of a national network of marine protected areas (MPAs) in Australia and an Australian Marine Conservation Plan to guide the use and management of ocean resources. The Australian and New Zealand Environment and Conservation Council (ANZECC) established an Advisory Committee on Marine

Protected Areas that included key OR 2000 agencies to facilitate the development of a national representative system of MPAs. Other aspects of the OR 2000 programme included a national marine education programme and the establishment of the Marine and Coastal Community Network.

During February 1995, the State of the Marine Environment Report (SOMER) (see Zann 1997) was released as a part of the OR 2000 programme. The SOMER was the first comprehensive scientific description of the state of Australia's marine environment (Tarte 1995, p. 1). It covered the region from estuaries and seashores up to the edge of the 200 mile exclusive economic zone. The SOMER also discussed MPAs in detail, as they were the major reason for the establishment of the OR 2000 programme (Zann 1997).

The Intergovernmental Agreement on the Environment

The Commonwealth, states and the Local Government Association entered into negotiations for what became known as the Intergovernmental Agreement on the Environment (IGAE). Negotiations were initiated in the first Special Premiers' Conference in 1990 and continued in other meetings throughout the following year. Although the Commonwealth and state governments supported the development of the agreement, environmental groups such as the Australian Conservation Foundation (ACF) argued that state negotiations were unnecessary since the Commonwealth had the power to enforce most environmental controls. The ACF's concerns were taken into consideration but they did not impede the completion of the intergovernmental agreement. At least 12 drafts of the IGAE were prepared within the year up to November 1991. The release of the IGAE on 25 February 1992 coincided with the release by the newly appointed Prime Minister, Paul Keating, of his government's *One Nation* policy statement.

The IGAE came into effect in May 1992 as 'a major watershed in Commonwealth–State relations over the environment, and has particular relevance in terms of institutional arrangements concerning aspects of ocean management' (Haward 1996, p. 26). The IGAE aimed to facilitate a cooperative approach for environmental management whilst improving relations and decision-making processes between the Commonwealth, state and local governments. Accordingly, the agreement outlined the environmental responsibilities of each sphere of government. The states and territories are recognised as having responsibility over the majority of issues within their boundaries. The agreement also made provision for the involvement of the Commonwealth government in areas where it has demonstrated responsibilities and interests. The IGAE included guidelines for marine and coastal management and referred to the importance of preserving biodiversity. The IGAE outlined the need for marine protected areas and measures to control introduced pests within the marine environment.

Ecologically Sustainable Development

Following the release of the *Our Common Future* document by the World Commission on Environment and Development in 1987, Australian Prime Minister Robert Hawke released a major statement on the environment in July 1989. Following consultation with industry, union and environmental organisations the Commonwealth released a discussion paper, *Ecologically Sustainable Development*, in June 1990.

The National Ecologically Sustainable Development Strategy (NESDS) was completed in December 1992 (ESDSC 1992), despite a difficult political environment; government focusing on economic issues, a change of leadership in the Australian Labor Party and the appointment of a new Prime Minister. The strategy's guiding principles are that 'decision making processes should effectively integrate both long and short term economic, environmental, social and equity considerations' (ESDSC 1992, p. 8) Chapter 16 of the NESDS is devoted to changes within government institutions while Chapter 17 specifically concentrated on coastal zone management and the development of policies that coincide with ESD principles. In essence the strategy encouraged a holistic, integrated approach to environmental management.

Coastal Zone Management

Australia's population, although relatively small in ratio to the area of land, was, and continues to be, heavily concentrated on the coastal zone. It is estimated that the coastal zone supports 86 per cent of Australia's population. During the 1970s population impacts on the coastal environment led to calls for a national approach to coastal management. In 1974 the first recommendation for such a policy approach was made in the report from the Committee of Inquiry into the National Estate (Hope 1975) presented to the Commonwealth government. In 1978, the House of Representatives Standing Committee on Environment and Conservation (HORSCEC) was requested to investigate the uses, development and management of Australia's coastal zone.

Although coastal management was a recognised item on the political agenda, offshore resources issues were given priority with the consequence that coastal issues did not receive adequate attention until the late 1980s. The OCS provided a cooperative framework for Commonwealth and state management as the states retained responsibility from the low water mark to the 3 mile offshore boundary. Therefore, the states and the Northern Territory had near complete jurisdiction over the coastal zone within their boundaries. There were some areas, however, where the Commonwealth had direct responsibilities for the coastal zone and these included 'land containing defence establishments, lighthouses or other reserves, and the regulation of foreign investment in development projects through the Foreign Investment Review Board' (Haward 1990).

The Commonwealth announced in 1992 that it was formulating a national coastal policy but the funding for this policy was not confirmed until several years later. The government announced during the 1995–96 Commonwealth budget that a A$53 million package was included for improving the management of Australia's coastal zone. Following this announcement a working group was established to formulate a national coastal policy. Despite these announcements there were a number of criticisms to the government's decision. First, the Commonwealth chose not to develop a Coastal Management Act and not to establish a National Coastal Management Agency (Australian Democrats 1994). Second, it was argued that another working group was not required, and thus the proposal was a waste of funds. The government was reminded by the Australian Democrats that around A$100 million in total had been spent on coastal inquiries since 1970. Nonetheless, the Interdepartmental Working Group was established and proceeded to complete Living on the Coast: The Commonwealth Coastal Policy (Commonwealth of Australia 1995). The Coastal Policy was launched by the then Federal Minister for the Environment, Senator Faulkner, in May 1995.

The summary of the Coastal Policy states that the main aim of the policy 'is to promote ecologically sustainable use of Australia's coastal zone'. It also specifies that the main objectives are sustainable resource use, resource conservation, public participation, knowledge and understanding, and the use of principles to guide decision- making. The states and local governments are required to match the funding provided by the government as a way of continually financing the policy. The Australian Conservation Foundation (ACF) and the Wilderness Society supported the release of the policy. The Australian Democrats, however, argued that it was 'short sighted and failed to provide enough money to fix problems of sewerage outfalls and overcrowding on the coasts' (McLean 1995, p. 4). The National Coastal Action Program (NCAP) was also released in 1995 as the implementation component of the Coastal Policy. It outlined the framework of the policy, the boundaries for state and Commonwealth responsibilities in coastal management, community participation, sustainable use of the coastal areas and Australia's international responsibilities (Environment Australia 1997).

The election of the Howard Government in March 1996 saw major reviews of many policy areas. The new government did, however, make significant commitments to oceans and coastal policy. The NCAP was endorsed by the following government in the Investing in our Natural Heritage statement made by the Minister for the Environment, Senator Robert Hill in August 1996. Ocean Rescue 2000's establishment of a National Representative System of Marine Protected Areas received continual support within the NCAP. The Commonwealth government's main initiative was a suite of programmes under the auspices of the Coasts and Clean Seas initiative of the Natural Heritage Trust, established by the Howard government from funding provided following the partial sale of Telstra, Australia's telecommunication carrier (Foster and Haward 2003, p. 551).

In 2002 the Commonwealth government made commitment to develop, in conjunction with the states, a National Coastal Policy that will 'conserve and restore coastal and estuarine biodiversity, encourage ecologically sustainable use of coastal and estuarine resources and bring about much needed coordination and planning for the coastal zone' (Kemp 2002).

State Coastal Policies

The states and the Northern Territory have extensive responsibility in coastal policy development and management of the coastal zone.   The 1993 Resource Assessment Commission Coastal Zone Inquiry emphasised that the states and the Northern Territory, and local governments, are responsible for 95 per cent of expenditure on coastal zone management activities. One of the main priorities for the states is regulating local government control over coastal areas. The approval for developments in coastal areas has a marked impact on the coastal environment; however, such projects provide important sources of revenue for local government. Even though such approvals are often constrained by the structure of planning, and the extent to which local government is given autonomy in these decisions, these activities result have a major influence on the coastal zone's amenity and environment values.

All states and the Northern Territory underwent major reforms to their coastal policies during the mid-1990s. The states initially divided into two groups based on their implementation strategies and as a consequence, experienced varying degrees of Commonwealth influence on their policy principles and objectives. The Commonwealth worked with each state and established a memorandum of understanding (MOU) according to specific circumstances. South Australia and Queensland decided to focus on the allocation of funding due to the non-legally binding nature of the MOU with the Commonwealth over coastal policy. Victoria and Western Australia incorporated components of the MOUs into their existing programmes that already had funding provisions for their recently implemented community coastal groups. They had also revised and upgraded their coastal advisory systems that formed the basis for assessment of most project proposals in the states at regional and state levels, and accordingly avoided the setting up of new projects under the NCAP.

The implementation of the administrative arrangements outlined in the MOUs has proved to be difficult. The first meeting of the Intergovernmental Coastal Reference Group was delayed until May 1996, 'and it was only after sustained pressure from the states that the Commonwealth agreed to convene the first meeting' (Kay and Lester 1997, p. 282). The MOUs were revised in 1997 and 1998 to include the Coasts and Clean Seas programmes under the Commonwealth's Natural Heritage Trust. Moreover, an Intergovernmental Coastal Reference Group was established to provide all governments with an exchange of information on coastal management practices. Tasmania, New South Wales and Western Australia began the review processes on the management of their coastal zones in 1994 and were closely followed by the other states of Australia. Victoria, South Australia and Queensland were unique in their approaches by either establishing or amending existing legislation for managing their coastal zones. Victoria had first-hand experience in coastal management, as the first ever attempt at successfully managing a part of Australia's coastal zone was in 1966 when the Port Philip Authority was created to manage Port Philip Bay (Kay and Lester 1997, p. 270).

The Australian Local Government Association developed a Local Government Coastal Management Policy in 1997. This policy recognizes that local government has primary planning authority for coastal development and land use as well as responsibility for community education and on-ground community works. As local government has been described as underequipped to deal with the increasing complexities of integrated coastal zone management (Haward 1995), adequate resources and capacity are needed to ensure effective local planning and management.

AUSTRALIA'S OCEANS POLICY

The development and implementation of Australia's Oceans Policy placed Australia as a world leader in this approach to oceans governance (Vince 2005, 2006). The policy was initiated on 8 December 1995 when Prime Minister Keating announced that the Commonwealth government had agreed to the development of an 'integrated oceans strategy' that would deal with the management of Australia's marine resources (Keating 1995). The Department of Prime Minister and Cabinet assumed responsibility for developing the policy; however, little progress was achieved as the federal election dominated the political agenda. The Keating government was defeated in March 1996 and the Howard government announced that it would continue the development of an oceans policy primarily with the intention of it being an 'environmental protection policy' (Bateman 1997). The responsibility for oceans policy development was transferred to the Department of Environment, Sport and Territories (DEST). In mid-1996, the DEST established an intergovernmental committee to assist with the preparation of the policy that included members from major Commonwealth agencies involved in marine affairs (Wescott 2000, p. 862).

Prime Minister Howard announced the development of the Oceans Policy and launched a consultation paper titled Australia's Oceans – New Horizons (Commonwealth of Australia 1997b) for public comment on 3 March 1997. In September 1997 the Minister for Environment and Heritage established the Ministerial Advisory Group on Oceans Policy (MAGOP) consisting of 18 members that represented various key interest groups. The MAGOP's role was to provide advice to the Minister on the views of the broad range of stakeholders of the policy and any other issues the Group thought relevant to the development of the policy. It is also suggested that the MAGOP was established to gain the support of non-governmental organisations (NGOs) during the oceans policy process as well as to promote public awareness (Vince 2003).

In order to stimulate responses to the consultation paper, the Commonwealth government requested that the Marine and Coastal Community Network (MCCN) inform the community of the development of Australia's Oceans Policy. The public consultation period ended in April 1997 with a commitment to another round of public consultation scheduled later that year followed by the final policy paper by the end of 1997 (Wescott 2000, p. 863). Environment Australia organised several workshops and face-to-face interviews to gather a broader understanding of stakeholders' views. Again, the Commonwealth turned to NGOs and a national workshop convened by the Australian Committee for the World Conservation Union (ACIUCN) was held during 15–17 May 1997 to provide a broader community input on the development of the oceans policy. The main recommendation from the Workshop was support for the Commonwealth along with the continued and enhanced involvement of local and state governments in the development of the Oceans Policy (ACIUN 1998, p. 3). Vince (2006, p. 425) argues that the 'Commonwealth deliberately allowed NGOs to participate in the decision making process as a strategic advantage – where friends are kept close, and in this case, "enemies" kept closer'.

The states reacted positively to the New Horizons paper and were involved in discussions with the Commonwealth until July 1998. The consultation paper claimed that 'the States and Northern Territory have embraced this [New Horizons] initiative and joined with the Commonwealth in the cooperative development of the Oceans Policy' (Commonwealth of Australia 1998a, p. 10). At the time, the states and territories agreed that there was a need for a better base to care for, use and understand Australia's marine resources and that the 'oceans are too vulnerable to the tyranny of small decisions' (Commonwealth of Australia 1998a, p. 10). They were, nevertheless, concerned with the policy's institutional arrangements, financial commitments and obligations. Considering the past difficulties with the Commonwealth over offshore jurisdictional arrangements, the states' concerns were warranted. Some discussions were held between the Commonwealth and the states on institutional arrangements and financial commitments; however, by September 1998, Senator Hill indicated that Environment Australia was to complete the final document – without the states. The drafting of the final policy document within Environment Australia emphasised that the policy was a Commonwealth initiative.

The development of the Oceans Policy was carefully organised so that the final document would be released during 1998, the International Year of the Ocean. Preceding the release of the Oceans Policy, four background papers and seven issues papers were released for public consultation, and these consultations analysed in the drafting of the Oceans Policy. The Oceans Policy documents accompanied by background and issues papers extended and updated the biophysical, environmental, social, cultural and legal examination of Australia's ocean domain first undertaken by the SOMER. Sectoral interests were represented in the consultation and development process through the relevant Commonwealth agencies and through representation of key interests within the MAGOP.

The Commonwealth government released the national Oceans Policy on 23 December 1998 in two volumes: *Australia's Oceans Policy*, and *Specific Sectoral Measures* (Commonwealth of Australia 1998b, 1998c). The two documents provided a broad range of initiatives and actions. Analysis of the *Specific Sectoral Measures* document has identified 390 commitments across five broad areas. TFG International, commissioned to provide a review of the implementation of the Oceans Policy in August 2002, (see below), identified 157 'key initiatives' within the Oceans Policy (TFG International 2002, p. 26). The difference in the two figures can be explained simply, as many of the 390 commitments outlined in the Sectoral Measures document were linked together. While a number of these commitments and initiatives were new and innovative, many of the sectoral level commitments were developed independently and then linked to the Oceans Policy.

The Oceans Policy was introduced by an opening message from Prime Minister John Howard. He stated that 'with the release of Australia's Oceans Policy we again demonstrate our world leadership by implementing a coherent, strategic planning and management framework capable of dealing with the complex issues confronting the long term future of our oceans' (Commonwealth of Australia 1998b, p. 1). The document outlined that the development of Regional Marine Plans (RMPs) would be the core of the Oceans Policy and all Commonwealth agencies would be bound to those plans (Vince 2006).

New institutions and structures to aid of the 'whole of government approach' to implementation of the policy were outlined. The new institutions included the National Oceans Ministerial Board, Nation Oceans Office (NOO), Regional Marine Plan Steering Committees and the National Oceans Advisory Group (NOAG) (see Vince 2003). The NOO was given primary responsibility for development of the Regional Marine Plans, and is also responsible for monitoring the implementation of the 390 initiatives announced in the Oceans Policy. The NOO was initially planned 'to be housed in Environment Australia' (Commonwealth of Australia 1998b, p. 16) but was later designated as a separate executive agency under the Public Service Act 1999 that came into effect in early December 1999. This meant that the Director of the National Oceans Office reported directly to the Minister for Environment and Heritage, and through the Minister to the National Oceans Ministerial Board. This arrangement, and the decision to locate the NOO in Hobart, was to pose its own challenges, as noted in the 2002 review of the Oceans Policy (TFG International 2002). The decision to locate the NOO in Hobart, rather than in Canberra, arose as a result of negotiations with then Independent Senator for Tasmania, Brian Harradine, and the Howard government. Harradine at the time held 'the balance of power' in the Australian Senate, with his support necessary for government legislation to pass the upper house, a necessary condition for its eventual enactment into law.

The Australian and New Zealand Environment and Conservation Council (ANZECC) was tasked with the role of facilitating intergovernmental (cross-jurisdictional) coordination for the Oceans Policy. The Council was made up of Environment Ministers from all states, the Commonwealth and Territories as well as New Zealand's Environment Minister. Members of the Ministerial Board who are also part of ANZECC and other relevant Commonwealth–state ministerial councils were to 'ensure that linkages are made on issues of mutual interest' (Commonwealth of Australia 1998a, p. 17). The ANZECC's main responsibility was to assist Commonwealth and state consultations on the implementation of the Oceans Policy. Additionally to consulting on intergovernmental issues, the Council discussed transboundary issues that relate to the environment and ocean resources (Hundloe 1998, pp. 87–91).

The Australian states did not formally involve themselves with the Oceans Policy when it was released; however, they continued to participate in decisions made within the policy community through the ANZECC. The state participation through ANZECC was limited as the ANZECC responsibilities are restricted to environmental matters. Broader marine issues that deal with fisheries or oil and gas proved difficult to address through the ANZECC forum (Haward and Herr 2000). In 2001, the ANZECC was replaced by the Natural Resource Management Ministerial Council (NRMMC) as part of broader reform to intergovernmental institutions. The NRMMC's function is to monitor, evaluate and report on natural resource management, including marine and coastal issues in Australia (Environment Australia 2003).

Marine Science and Technology

Whilst the Oceans Policy was being developed, the Commonwealth continued with its commitment to develop a comprehensive review of Australia's marine science and technology. The *Marine Science and Technology Plan – Draft for Consultation* was a companion to *Australia's Oceans Policy – An Issues Paper* and was released on 10 June 1998 (Michaelis 1998).

Australia's Marine Science and Technology Plan (Commonwealth of Australia 1999) was released on 25 June 1999 by the Minister for Industry, Science and Resources, Senator Nick Minchin. The Plan was developed by an expert working group in the Department of Industry, Science and Resources, well away from the Marine Group in Environment Australia (now the Department of Environment, Water, Heritage and the Arts) that developed the Oceans Policy. Reichelt and McEwan commented that:

> in particular, the [Oceans] Policy provides both the themes and the structure to bridge and integrate the actions and jurisdictions of the Commonwealth and the seven state/Territory governments concerned and to link them from the ministerial to the working level, while the [Marine Science and Technology] Plan helps to better define the responsibilities and tasks of the Commonwealth agencies who will provide the scientific and technical implementation. (Reichelt and McEwan 1999, p. 712)

Senior government ministers noted that the Plan 'reinforces the importance of the regional marine planning concept at the core of the Government's Oceans Policy' (Minchin 1999). The Marine Science and

Technology Plan focused on the problems and opportunities for marine science and technology in supporting the Oceans Policy. It outlined three interdependent programmes: understanding the marine environment; using and caring for the marine environment; and infrastructure for understanding and using the marine environment. In summary, Australia's Marine Science and Technology Plan outlined the then immediate priorities identified within the programmes that underpinned the implementation of the policy.

Implementation of Australia's Oceans Policy

The first regional marine plan was developed for the south-east marine region, covering 2 million km² of ocean including waters off the states of Victoria, Tasmania, southern New South Wales and eastern South Australia (Vince 2006). The South-East Regional Marine Plan process comprised four phases of development that included: the scoping or definition of the Plan; determining the economic, social, environmental and cultural characteristics of the region via assessments; developing potential options; and analysing those options in order to implement the Plan.

The process to develop the SERMP was launched at a two-day Oceans Forum in Hobart in April 2000. The SERMP, as the first RMP, was the 'blueprint' for the process in Australia. The south-east is perceived to be one of the more complex maritime regions with the inclusion of four states and the Commonwealth in major sectors such as fisheries and oil and gas production. The SERMP evolved over time. Initially it was expected to be primarily a plan that would identify gaps and direct future oceans-related policy and management within the region. The SERMP evolved into an ecosystem-based decision-making process, or framework for making management and policy decisions at the regional level whilst identifying specific issues that need to be addressed. This reorientation from plan to process was in part a response to concerns expressed by Commonwealth agencies over progress in developing the SERMP. On 21 February 2003 a workshop was held by the National Oceans Office (NOO) in Canberra with all board agencies to discuss the way forward and to ensure that agencies were satisfied with the SERMP agenda.

The SERMP process was expected to produce three products in June–July 2003 that would adequately cover the concerns and hesitations of the Board agencies. These products were:

- a post-budget assessment of the ongoing role of the National Oceans Office in light of the Oceans Policy review and a document of achievements to date;

- a governance framework document highlighting implementation strategies; and
- an action plan or strategy for the south-east, which was more programme related.

The Chair of the National Oceans Ministerial Board and Minister for the Environment and Heritage, the Hon Dr David Kemp, released the draft SERMP on 18 July 2003. The Draft South-east Regional Marine Plan was seen as the 'action plan' for implementing Australia's Oceans Policy in the south-east marine region. The Draft SERMP was released with an *Oceans Policy: Principles and Processes* companion document outlining the Integrated Oceans Process for improving cross-sectoral integration of oceans management, effectively defining the governance framework and implementation strategies. Whilst the NOO worked hard at addressing these issues, there still remained a certain level of uncertainty about its ongoing role.

Prior to the release of the Draft SERMP a consortium of environmental groups released a report, *Oceans Eleven*, in March 2003 (Smyth et al. 2003). *Oceans Eleven* argued that although there was widespread support from the stakeholders for the Oceans Policy, 'five years on movement from policy to action has stalled' (Smyth et al. 2003, p. 6). The report argued for a stronger legislative base for policy development, establishment of a national oceans authority and adoption of 'eleven steps to ecosystem based regional marine planning' (Smyth et al. 2003, p. 8). In a formal submission commenting on the draft SERMP the conservation sector argues that a 'comparison [of] ... desired outcome with what is delivered by the Draft SERMP ... reveals that the Draft SERMP delivers few if any' of these outcomes (Conservation Sector 2004, p. 4).

The South-east RMP was completed in May 2004 and, like the Draft SERMP, met with a mixed response. The challenges in developing a 'world's first' plan, translating the commitments announced in the Oceans Policy into practice was broadly recognised. Some 'disappointment' was expressed with the Plan (ACF 2004) for not providing strong enough commitments in key areas. This response from environmental groups may have reflected the differing expectations of stakeholders. The focus on the SERMP as an framework did not meet expectations or the 'concept that some have of a more definitive plan that mandates particular outcomes and zones spatial areas for particular uses' (TFG International 2002, p. 3). The SERMP reflects contemporary governance issues, the recognition of the mix of policy instruments available, the inclusion, explicitly, of stakeholder interests as well as government obligations.

Review of the Oceans Policy

As noted above 'performance assessment and reporting' was included in the Oceans Policy documents released in December 1998. In August 2002 a review of the Oceans Policy was commissioned prior to the completion of the SERMP. The review addressed three themes: progress with the implementation of the policy to date including progress with regional marine planning; value for money with the funding spend to date; and effectiveness of institutional/governance arrangements in supporting and implementing the policy (TFG International 2002, p. 1).

The review concluded that that the initial implementation schedule for regional marine planning was 'very ambitious' (TFG International 2002, p. 2), but at the same time noted that there was 'uncertainty about what will be delivered, how it will work and whether it will add value' (ibid.). The review noted the 'major impediments' affecting implementation including that the Oceans Policy 'did not represent an agreed position with the States and Territories and it has not been subsequently endorsed by them' (TFG International 2002, p. 8). The Review considered ways to improve coordination between the Commonwealth and the states and territories. It noted that while 'complex interactions and interrelationships between legislation is one of the major impediments to implementation' (TFG International 2002, p. 10), the lack of a legislative base to the Oceans Policy was explicable, and 'reflects both the complicated interactions and interrelationships between existing legislation and the sensible focus on pursuing a co-operative approach to developing a framework for integrated marine planning' (ibid.).

In relation to progressing key aspects of the Oceans Policy the review found that of 157 key initiatives within the Oceans Policy 136 (or 87 per cent) were 'completed', 'proceeding' or a 'continuing activity'. The review also explored options for the future direction of the National Oceans Office. These options included maintaining the office's independent status, or locating it as a 'separate and distinct office within an existing department, but with primary location in Hobart, with staff in Canberra and other centres'. The third option was to relocate the National Oceans Office to Canberra and have a small number of staff in Hobart and in other centres (TFG International 2002, pp. 13–14).

The assessment of 'value for money' included analysis made by the accounting and finance firm KPMG. This concluded that the 'National Oceans Office has delivered satisfactory value for money against Government's original expectations, although it has taken some 12 months longer than originally anticipated' (TFG International 2002, p. 13). The

KPMG analysis also provided the costing of implementing the three options identified by TFG for the future direction of the National Oceans Office.

Outcomes of the Review of Oceans Policy

In 2005 a restructuring of the Australian oceans institutions occurred. The NOO lost its executive agency status, as these institutional models lost favour with the government, and was located within the Marine Division of the Department of Environment and Heritage (Department of Environment and Heritage 2005), with this Department renamed and restructured as the Department of Environment and Water Resources in early 2007. The Department was further restructured in late 2007, following the Australian Federal election, as the Department of the Environment, Water, Heritage and the Arts. The Minister for the Environment has responsibility for the NOO and reports to Cabinet on its progress. The National Oceans Ministerial Board was also dissolved and replaced by the Oceans Board of Management, while the NOAG was retained as an advisory body and as a forum to facilitate cross-sectoral discussion.

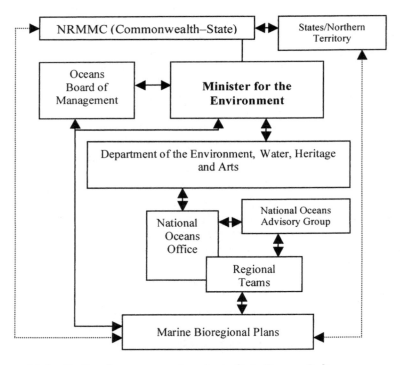

Figure 4.2 Institutional arrangements – Australia's Oceans Policy

Table 4.1 Marine bioregional planning

Components	Focus
Planning elements	Regional profile
	Development of sustainability and conservation objectives
	Development of integrated marine conservation strategy
	Establishment of tools for monitoring and review
Planning process	Information and data gathering
	Assessing risks to biodiversity
	Setting desired outcomes in relation to strategic values
	Developing alternatives and evaluation
	Establishing performance assessment tools
Marine bioregional planning – outputs	Regional profile
	Draft plan
	Final plan
Marine bioregional planning – outcomes	Identification of conservation values
	Regional risk assessment (existing and emerging pressure)
	Development of objectives and indicators for conservation values
	Development of an integrated marine conservation strategy
	Monitoring state of marine environment and assessing performance of conservation measures

In October 2005, following the restructuring of the NOO, Senator Ian Campbell, then Environment Minister, announced that RMPs will be established under section 176 of the Environment Protection and Biodiversity Conservation Act 1999 (EPBC Act). This would provide some consistency across different regional marine plans and provide a legislative basis for their implementation. Under the Act the marine bioregional plans will also provide the platform for the National Representative System of

Marine Protected Areas. The SEMP was to be reviewed and if necessary adjusted to conform to a marine bioregional plan

The use of Section 176 of the EPBC Act addressed criticism of the lack a legislative base to the Oceans Policy, but does not go as far as instituting an Oceans Act as is the case in Canada (see ACF 2006; Vince 2005; Foster et al. 2005). In 2006–07 the Australian Conservation Foundation began advocating the development of an Australian Oceans Act (ACF 2006), although the Commonwealth government regards the linking of the Oceans Policy to the EPBC Act as providing a sufficient legislative anchor.

CONCLUSION

Australian oceans governance is influenced greatly by the particular pattern of offshore jurisdiction that has developed over the past century. The introduction of the Oceans Policy in 1998 has provided opportunities for innovative, regionally-based approaches to ocean management, yet the failure to fully 'solve the problem that motivated its establishment' (Underdal 2002, p. 40) – integration across sectors and jurisdictions – raises some significant questions over the effectiveness of this policy framework. Despite this relatively negative and admittedly simplistic assessment, the Oceans Policy process has had other, more positive, impacts.

The development of a regional marine planning process has provided greater understanding of Australia's ocean domain. It has indicated both the opportunities and challenges inherent in marine planning and the implementation of an integrated Oceans Policy. The Oceans Policy has fostered a number of initiatives including marine protected areas and the development of broader-based environmental assessments of Australian fisheries. This latter initiative was, however, also fostered through implementation of the Environment Protection and Biodiversity Conservation Act 1999.

The period 1998–2007 has seen increasing attention to institutional arrangements and policy outcomes affecting the governance of the world's seas and oceans. Governance is linked to institutional capacity and to effectiveness of public organisations, drawing attention to tools and approaches underpinning effective and efficient institutional arrangements. Australia has over 100 laws and policy instruments addressing aspects of the management of the marine environment. Many of these instruments incorporate principles such as sustainable development as well as reflecting a broader government reform agenda that saw government moving to more market-oriented and/or collaborative forms of governance.

5. Canada[1]

Canada has a vast ocean domain, bordering three oceans with the longest coastline in the world (see Figure 5.1). As a federation Canada, like Australia and the United States of America, has an oceans regime that historically has been fraught with conflict between its sub-national (provincial) and central governments. This has occurred despite a very different constitutional basis for the division of powers between governments in Canada than in either Australia or the USA. Even though Canada, like Australia, has a Westminster-style parliamentary political system, the Canadian Constitution provides greater authority and jurisdiction for the federal government when dealing with oceans and marine-related affairs. Despite significant federal primacy in oceans matters, Canada does share similar issues in oceans governance to those that face other coastal states. The development of strong sector-based legislative and regulatory arrangements in Canada has been a major factor in influencing the development of oceans governance, and as with other states establishing arrangements that better integrate oceans management remains a current challenge.

CANADIAN OCEANS POLICY: INTERNATIONAL INFLUENCES AND DOMESTIC DRIVERS

Canada has been proactive in the management of its oceans and often a source of policy learning for others, first in relation to the Arctic, where it asserted national interests in response to transit activities of USA vessels in the North-West Passage in the 1970s, and more recently in 2007 in response to Russian 'claims' to the Arctic Oceans. Canada, too, has been proactive in projecting a 'radical' coastal state position in the 1990s in relation to fisheries within its exclusive economic zone (EEZ), and particularly in

---

[1] Some material in this chapter was originally published in Haward (1991a). We thank *Australasian Canadian Studies* and its editor Sonia Mycak for permission to reproduce this material.

relation to management of fish stocks that 'straddle' the boundary of the EEZ and the high seas.

In 1977 Canada declared its 200 nautical mile EEZ. This declaration was done in part to address excessive fishing pressure applied by vessels from the European Economic Community on the stocks of the Grand Banks, a fishing area within Canada's 200 nautical mile EEZ (VanderZwaag 1992).

Figure 5.1 Canada – maritime jurisdiction

Canada was following emerging practice from the deliberations at the United Nations Third Conference on the Law of the Sea (UNCLOS III) and as a result distant-water fishing nations that were previously only limited by the territorial sea were forced outside the limits of the new EEZ.

Canada played a major role at the UNCLOS III and as McRae and Munro noted it went to this conference

> with clear and detailed jurisdictional objectives related to such matters as Arctic Waters, fisheries and the continental shelf and deep seabed. By and large these objectives were achieved. By the time the conference was over Canada had

extended its fisheries jurisdiction to 200 miles, had secured its interests in respect of the continental shelf and marine pollution in the Arctic and other waters, and had become a central player in the continuing negotiations to implement a regime for the deep seabed. Moreover, within a few years of the conclusion of the 1982 Convention, steps had been taken to resolve the maritime boundary problem with the United States in the Gulf of Maine area and to consolidate the Canadian claim to sovereignty over Arctic waters. (McRae and Munro 1989, pp. vii–viii)

In 1982, the Law of the Sea Convention (LOSC) was concluded. As discussed in Chapter 2 the LOSC provided a framework to protect the marine environment and to delineate national maritime rights (Chircop 1996). Canada did not ratify the convention until November 2003. Despite its general activism in issues related to the law of the sea (see below) one reason for Canada's reluctance to ratify the convention was its concerns over the difficulties of managing straddling stocks, a key feature of a crisis it was experiencing in its fisheries in the late 1980s and early 1990s. Prior to the United Nations Conference on Environment and Development (UNCED) held in Rio de Janerio in June 1992, Canada had convened a meeting in St Johns, Newfoundland in January 1992 for like-minded states to discuss high seas fisheries. Canada had also taken part in the Cancun conference on responsible fishing in May 1992.

Canada's concern over the straddling stocks problem led it to press for commitments at the UNCED for a United Nations-sponsored conference on the matter, a clearly identified lacunae in the LOSC (Miles and Burke 1989). While the subject matter of the conference was broadened to address issues affecting the management of highly migratory fish species (matters of interest to Australia, New Zealand and the USA in particular) as well as straddling stocks, Canada took a high profile in the meetings, utilising the conference to publicise and promote its conflict with the European Union over its vessels fishing 'straddling' stocks, in this case turbot (Greenland halibut) on the Grand Banks. The Conference on the Conservation and Management of Straddling Fish Stocks and Highly Migratory Fish Stocks took place over six sessions in New York from 1993 to December 1995. As noted in Chapter 2 the conference resulted in negotiation of a binding 'hard law' instrument nested within the broader provisions of the LOSC, the 1995 Agreement for the Implementation of the Provisions of the Law of the Sea Convention relating to the Conservation and Management of Straddling Fish Stocks and Highly Migratory Fish Stocks (the UN Fish Stocks Agreement or UNFSA).

Canada has also taken a leading role in the Asia-Pacific Economic Cooperation (APEC) forum in promoting integrated oceans management and ecosystem-based oceans management. The APEC initiative, co-led by Australia, saw a major commitment through APEC's Marine Resources

Conservation Working Group (MRC-WG) building on the APEC ministerial declaration related to oceans (see Chapter 2). The work in APEC built on long-standing Canadian activities in capacity building in the Asia-Pacific region related to ocean matters, at both the formal level through the Canadian International Development Assistance (CIDA) programme from the Canadian Ministry for Foreign Affairs and International Trade and, perhaps more importantly, through 'second track' initiatives such as the Southeast Asian Programme in Oceans Law, Policy and Management (SEAPOL) and the Council for Security Cooperation in the Asia-Pacific (CSCAP). As noted in Chapter 4, Canada, along with Australia, also supported the research on ocean policy and governance undertaken by the Australia–Canada Ocean Research Network (ACORN) (Kriwoken et al. 1996; Haward 2001; Rothwell and VanderZwaag 2006).

Canada has also developed innovative legislative and policy instruments and approaches to domestic oceans governance. Canada has had a number of 'oceans policies' and a legislative framework established through the Oceans Act that entered force in 1997. This innovative legislative effort had its antecedents in legislative and policy development from the preceding two decades. Canada undertook a review of its ocean management responsibilities in the 1970s, initially spurred on by the voyage of the USS *Manhattan* (an ice-breaking tanker) through the North-West Passage in September 1969. This voyage was seen by Canada as a direct challenge to its claims over the Arctic and led to its extending its territorial sea and the enactment of the Arctic Waters Pollution Prevention Act in 1970. In 1973 the Minister of State for Science and Technology announced a 'national oceans policy' (Crowley and Bourgeois 1989, p. 254). Crowley and Bourgeois note that:

> the policy was based on two premises. First, Canada must develop and control within its own borders the essential elements needed to exploit offshore resources. Second, it must increase its knowledge to operate both on and below ice-covered waters and in the process, assert sovereignty in Arctic waters (Crowley and Bourgeois 1989, p. 254).

The voyage of the US Coast Guard vessel *Polar Sea* through the North-West Passage in May 1985 reignited Canadian concern over perceived challenges to its sovereignty. In this case the Canadian response included the development of new law (Crowley and Bourgeois 1989, pp. 254–62). In 1979 the enactment of the Fisheries and Oceans Act focused responsibility 'for policy and program co-ordination' related to broad oceans management and governance, as well as the more traditional and sectoral focus in fisheries management within the Department of Fisheries and Oceans (Auditor General of Canada 2005a, p. 8). These contending functions were to pose governance challenges in their own right in the 1990s and 2000s (see following discussion).

Proposals to explore and develop offshore oil and gas resources was in Canada, as in the USA and Australia, to loom large over discussions over oceans management. This question focused first on the question of jurisdiction, and then over the share of offshore oil and gas revenues between federal and provincial governments (particularly in the Atlantic region). While jurisdiction in the waters of British Columbia was addressed in the mid 1960s by an advisory opinion from the Canadian Supreme Court in response to a reference to this question, the issue of jurisdiction offshore was less clear off Canada's Atlantic coast, and particularly in relation to the waters offshore from Newfoundland. As discussed below, the status of Newfoundland's offshore waters were subject to debate as the province entered the Canadian federation in 1949. While the question of jurisdiction in the Atlantic regions was settled (see below), debates over the share of offshore revenues became a major issue in 2007, when the federal and Nova Scotian governments renegotiated financial transfer arrangements (*Globe and Mail* 10 October 2007).

The focus of the 1970s policy on offshore resources development, and securing sovereignty, parallels experiences in other states such as Australia and the USA where legislative and administrative efforts were focused on developing the newly accessible (through rapid technological and engineering developments) oil and gas resources from increasingly deep waters or otherwise extreme environments. It was in the 1980s that emergent paradigms such as 'sustainable development', together with concern over the ecological health and environmental quality of the coastal and ocean areas, encouraged a reappraisal of oceans policy.

THE QUESTION OF OFFSHORE OIL AND GAS

In 1967, following concern over the doubtful legal status of exploration titles to offshore Canada, given the ongoing political and legal challenges over offshore jurisdiction in the United States of America (see Chapter 7) a reference was given to the Canadian Supreme Court to consider jurisdiction beyond the then 3 mile territorial sea, and between the low water mark to the 3 mile limit for areas offshore from the province of British Columbia. In both cases the court in the BC Offshore Reference found 'jurisdiction to lie with the federal government' (Hunt 1989, p. 9). Despite resolving the issue of jurisdiction in Pacific Canada and establishing a legal precedent for federal management, provincial interest in the management of oil and gas continued to dominate intergovernmental negotiations for the next 40 years.

Complaints from the oil and gas industry that uncertainty over jurisdiction 'would make it difficult to proceed' with full development of these resources (Hunt 1989, p. 5) led to an attempt to introduce an intergovernmental agreement between the Canadian government and each of the Atlantic provinces in 1977. This Memorandum of Understanding proposed, like the 1967 Petroleum Agreement in Australia, to set aside the question of jurisdiction. The 1977 Memorandum of Understanding was signed by the Canadian Prime Minister and the premiers of Nova Scotia, New Brunswick and Prince Edward Island; however, it was never implemented as a newly elected provincial government in Nova Scotia renounced the agreement (Hunt 1989). Importantly, and establishing a position of asserting its independent rights offshore that persisted through to 2007, Newfoundland had refused to take part in the negotiations. As Hunt commented: 'without the involvement of Nova Scotia and Newfoundland, the provinces whose offshore areas were of principal interest to the industry, the 1977 Understanding faded away' (Hunt 1989, p. 6).

Newfoundland maintained its claim for jurisdiction over the continental shelf and offshore resources surrounding the province. This claim was based on: first, the manner under which Newfoundland entered the Canadian federation in 1949; and second, that prior to this, as a self-governing dominion, Newfoundland had gained sovereignty over the offshore areas as a result of the evolution of the customary international law of the sea. Newfoundland's claims were rejected by the Trudeau government although the short-lived Clark administration promised the provinces greater involvement in offshore resources management (Harrison and Kwamena 1979). Following the re-election of the Liberal Party in 1980 the Newfoundland government under Premier Peckford continued to press its claims. The intensity of the dispute increased as oil and gas companies increased drilling programmes in response to the incentives provided under the National Energy Program (NEP) in the Hibernia and Sable Island fields.

The issue of jurisdiction offshore from Newfoundland was brought to a head in the early 1980s. A union dispute over employment conditions for offshore workers triggered judicial action when this dispute gave rise to consideration of the legal status of offshore waters. Newfoundland's Premier Peckford, arguing that he had 'been forced to act' (Pollard 1985), referred two questions to the Newfoundland Court of Appeal over ownership of offshore resources. As a result of Premier Peckford's actions, the federal government felt free from the political constraints of acting unilaterally over the question of jurisdiction in Atlantic Canada. It referred the matter to the Supreme Court of Canada in what was known as the 'Hibernia Reference'. This matter was narrower in scope than the Newfoundland Reference and concerned jurisdiction over the Hibernia field (Hunt 1989). The decision in the Newfoundland Reference was brought down in February 1983 with the Newfoundland Court of Appeal holding that while Newfoundland had claims, and exercised some jurisdiction over the territorial sea, jurisdiction over the continental shelf remained with the Canadian government (Hunt 1989). The federal government's Hibernia Reference was handed down a year later in March 1984 and, following the precedent set by the British Columbia Reference of 1967, found that the Canadian government held rights over the continental shelf following the line of reasoning established in the BC Reference and the evolution of international law.

While engaged in conflict with Newfoundland the Trudeau government had continued to negotiate with Nova Scotia over the management of offshore oil and gas. The outcomes of these negotiations became known as the Nova Scotia Agreement and established joint federal provincial management. Nova Scotia was encouraged to conclude this agreement following increased interest in offshore drilling and the onshore economic benefits accruing from the National Energy Program-inspired activity. In addition, following a precedent from the BC Reference, the constitutional issues were less doubtful than those surrounding Newfoundland's claim (Doucet 1984). The federal government was encouraged to develop the agreement to provide an example of cooperative management over offshore oil and gas as a lever while Newfoundland was committed to the judicial process (Barry 1986).

The election of the Mulroney government in 1984 again altered the character of Newfoundland's relations with Ottawa. Mulroney, while in opposition, had indicated that he would, if elected, be prepared to negotiate an agreement that enabled the province to maintain involvement in the administration of offshore developments. This agreement, which was to form the basis of the Atlantic Accord, recognised that jurisdiction rested with the federal government but that the province had a major input into the support and provision of infrastructure in any developments. This arrangement arose from agreement by both federal and provincial governments that development of the Hibernia oil field may be a way of ameliorating Newfoundland's economic problems and reducing its dependence on a narrow resource base (mostly fisheries) and lack of major industry. The Atlantic Accord was signed in February 1985 and was implemented through 'mutual and parallel legislation' introduced into the Canadian and Newfoundland parliaments. The negotiating and establishment of intergovernmental agreements over oil and gas in Atlantic Canada follows the earlier experiences in Australia. One commentator claimed that the administrative regime for oil and gas under the Australian Offshore Constitutional Settlement could provide some lessons for Canada (Hunt 1989, p. 138).

With the signing of the Atlantic Accord the Nova Scotian government took the opportunity to utilise the 'favoured province clause' in the 1982 Agreement and renegotiate the administrative regime for offshore oil and gas. This agreement, negotiated by Nova Scotian Premier John Buchanan and Prime Minister Trudeau included a revenue stream, and allocation of part of the 'crown share' of oil and gas revenues for the province. The Nova Scotia Accord was signed in August 1986 and followed, in broad terms, the structure established by the Atlantic Accord. Hunt has commented on the differences between the Nova Scotia Agreement and the accord, and given the experience of negotiating the former, 'not surprisingly ... one finds a slightly higher degree of detail in the Nova Scotia Accord than in the Atlantic Accord' (Hunt 1989, p. 33). The election of the Mulroney government saw the concept of the crown share being overturned, and instead commitments to provide the province with equivalent payments for the lost crown share revenues. Despite this commentators have noted that 'more than two decades and two offshore projects later, Nova Scotia has yet to receive a single penny under this deal' (*Chronicle Herald* 11 October 2007, p. A5).

The debates over revenue sharing from the offshore areas in Atlantic Canada increased in intensity with the election in 2006 of the Conservative government led by Stephen Harper. The March 2007 federal budget broke the preceding financial arrangements that had developed under the offshore accords whereby Nova Scotia and Newfoundland would receive oil and gas revenues, and federal equalisation payments. Such payments have been critical to the Maritime Provinces from at least the 1920s. In an attempt to reform the process of providing equalisation payment to the provinces the Harper government addressed the issue of Nova Scotia and Newfoundland being able to retain offshore and gas revenue and gain equalisation payments, by forcing the provinces to chose between retaining offshore oil and gas revenues or instead adopting an enhanced equalisation formula. This action, brought down in the March 2007 federal budget, had an immediate impact.

Both the Newfoundland and the Nova Scotia governments objected to this action by the federal government. The outcome was stark; in the words of one commentator: 'the offshore-resource dispute with Newfoundland and Nova Scotia has poisoned politics in eastern Canada for the federal conservatives since the spring budget' (*Globe and Mail* 11 October 2007, p. A8). The Newfoundland provincial election saw a win to the incumbent premier, who had campaigned strongly on an anti-Ottawa platform. Earlier in 2007, in response to the budget provisions, a Nova Scotian backbench government member of the federal parliament voted against the budget and was thrown out of the party by Prime Minister Harper. The day following the Newfoundland election Prime Minister Harper and Nova Scotian Premier Rodney MacDonald announced a deal to end the dispute over the Atlantic Accord. In addition agreement was reached to mediate the long-standing dispute over the crown share revenues (*Chronicle Herald* 11 October 2007; *Globe and Mail* 11 October 2007). Pointedly Prime Minister Harper made no mention of Newfoundland's concerns.

DEVELOPMENT OF CANADA'S OCEAN POLICY

In the mid-1980s Canada, influenced by the conclusion of the UNCLOS III and the finalisation of the LOSC, undertook further appraisal of oceans policy and management. A number of difficulties with oceans and marine resource management had been identified. In response to concerns over future management of Canadian fisheries following the declaration of the Canadian EEZ, and a focus on 'Canadianisation' of fishing activities in the new zone, the federal government established two major enquiries, the first directed at the Atlantic and the second at Pacific fisheries; the Kirby Report (Task Force on Atlantic Fisheries) and the Pearse Report (Commission on Pacific Fisheries Policy) respectively. In response to concerns raised in these reports, the federal government devised a series of legislative changes. The major change was the revision of the 1970 Fisheries Act in 1985. These amendments allowed for greater government control over fishing licenses and leases. Foreign fishing was controlled under the auspices of the Coastal Fisheries Protection Act 1985 (see Haward et al. 2003).

Although lacking formal constitutional or legislative powers over fisheries management the provincial governments' role in fisheries policy under the Canadian Constitution cannot be understated. As Pross and McCorquodale noted, the Canadian Constitution deals with fisheries as it does in other areas, setting out a role for each tier of government. Some interaction is inevitable, as while the federal government manages fisheries within the 200 mile fishing zone, fish processing falls under provincial control, yet the federal government regulates the export of fish from these processing plants (Pross and McCorquodale 1987, p. 37). It is the overlap in responsibilities that led VanderZwaag to describe the Canadian fisheries management system as a ghost ship: 'everyone knows the system exists but it often lies veiled under a mysterious mist of flexibility and informality' (VanderZwaag 1983, p. 172). Fisheries remained on the constitutional agenda in Canada during the 1980s as the provinces including fisheries in negotiations over the (aborted) Meech Lake Accord (Haward 1991a).

In 1986 the Canadian Prime Minister Brian Mulroney 'asked Minister of Fisheries and Oceans, Tom Siddons, to review oceans policy, giving special attention to his legislative mandate to co-ordinate all programs and activities related to oceans' (Crowley and Bourgeois 1989, p. 254). This led to the development of an Oceans Strategy by the federal government that was announced in September 1987. Prior to this initiative Canadian oceans policy developed in an ad hoc manner, 'with varied measures and initiatives reflect[ing] Canada's traditional responsiveness or pragmatism on ocean issues' (Lee and Fraser 1989, p. 250). At the same time: 'changing conditions, both foreign and domestic have made a more comprehensive and forward-looking approach to oceans issues a necessity' (Lee and Fraser 1989, p. 250). While one view was that the limited efficacy of policy efforts in 1980s encouraged the development of the 1987 Oceans Strategy (Herriman et al. 1997), an alternative view was that this initiative was 'consistent with past approaches and buil[t] on resulting strengths' (Lee and Fraser 1989, p. 251).

The development of the Oceans Strategy involved an inventory of federal government programmes, and the establishment of an ad hoc 'Minister's Oceans Group, with a mandate to advise on the best mechanisms for industry consultation' (Crowley and Bourgeois 1989, p. 256). The Minister's Oceans Group undertook wide consultations at the same time that an 'Interdepartmental Committee on Oceans (ICO) was reactivated with a broader mandate to serve as a forum for federal departments and agencies ... and prepare new initiatives' (Crowley and Bourgeois 1989, p. 256). A 'specially convened meeting in September 1986 at Patricia Bay' brought together representatives of industry, universities and government to discuss 'issues and opportunities on the ocean frontier' (Crowley and Bourgeois 1989, p. 255). This meeting reached consensus on the need:

1. to coordinate government programs and activities;
2. to put in place mechanisms for consultation between the private sector and governments; and
3. to develop a new national oceans policy to guide government endeavours into the next decade (Crowley and Bourgeois 1989, p. 255).

Consultations also took place with provincial governments. Following federal Cabinet approval the Oceans Strategy was announced on 29 September 1987. It included broad-based Canadian government priorities including regional development and assertion of Canadian sovereignty over its oceanic domain (Crowley and Bourgeois 1989, p. 256). The strategy had a broad objective to 'secure maximum social, economic, scientific and sovereignty benefits for Canadians from Canada's oceans resources and oceans space' (Crowley and Bourgeois 1989, p. 256). This objective was to be fulfilled through four goals:

- the promotion of dynamic ocean industries, employment and economic development benefits, particularly for coastal regions;
- the creation of conditions favourable for the development of first-rate expertise and capabilities in ocean-related science, technology, and engineering;
- sound management and protection of Canada's ocean resources and the ocean environment; and
- the assertion and protection of sovereign rights over our ocean resources (Crowley and Bourgeois 1989, p. 256).

The Oceans Strategy saw development of new governance arrangements, including new institutions and programmes and policy initiatives. These arrangements included the creation of the National Marine Council, 'drawn from the major sectors and constituencies of the Canadian ocean economy, [with] the mandate to inform and advise the minister on marines issues and oceans policy' (Crowley and Bourgeois 1989, p. 257). The establishment of an industry-oriented programme for 'ocean mapping and the development of ocean information infrastructure and ocean R&D [research and development]' was proposed, jointly supported by the Department of Fisheries and Oceans (DFO) and the Department of Energy, Mines and Resources 'to facilitate activities of Canada's oceanic industries sector' (Crowley and Bourgeois 1989, pp. 257–8).

The Oceans Strategy proposed the establishment of the Oceans Industries Promotions Office with a mandate to 'improve effectiveness of government assistance programs ... and facilitating joint ventures involving the public and private sectors (including universities)' (Crowley and Bourgeois 1989, p. 259). The Oceans Strategy also encompassed the Arctic Marine Conservation Strategy, an important initiative in the development of Canada's commitment to developing governance regimes in the Arctic (see Chapter 2).

One important component of the Oceans Strategy was the 'governmental commitment to establish an appropriate legal foundation to facilitate oceans development including the consideration of a *Canada Oceans Act* to consolidate existing legislation' (VanderZwaag 1992, p. x). As recognised by Crowley and Bourgeois: 'oceans legislation, like the policies and programs that it supports, is currently contained in numerous Acts of Parliament and assigns specific responsibilities to many departments and agencies' (Crowley and Bourgeois 1989, p. 261).

CANADA'S OCEANS ACT

Canada's Oceans Act took ten years to develop from the time it was first proposed in the *Oceans Policy for Canada* released by the DFO in 1987 (DFO 1987). The 1994 report, *Opportunities from Our Oceans*, by the Committee on Oceans and Coasts of the Prime Minister's National Advisory Board on Science and Technology, recommended reviving the notion of an Oceans Act from the then dormant 1987 policy (NABST 1994). The report of the National Advisory Board on Science and Technology's Committee on Oceans and Coasts provided further impetus and resulted in sustained action on federal legislative development for oceans management. In November 1994 the Minister for Fisheries and Oceans, Brian Tobin, had presented his plan in *A Vision for Oceans Management* to support the adoption of an Oceans Act as the basis for a national oceans management strategy. One important development was a focus on sustainable development of the oceans that followed from the release of the World Commission on Environment and Development (WCED) report *Our Common Future* in 1987 (WCED 1990). As noted in Chapter 2 the WCED provided a singularly important focus for ocean management into the 1990s; as VanderZwaag commented: 'it is better to discuss the subject of ocean law and policy in terms of "sustainability" and "integration"' (VanderZwaag 1992, p. x).

Canada's Oceans Act establishes the enabling framework for cross-sectoral integrated management through the development of a national Oceans Management Strategy as outlined in Part II of the Act. Under the auspices of Part I, Sections 4 to 18 of the Oceans Act, Canada's maritime boundaries are defined in accordance with the provisions of the LOSC, having previously been defined in the 1977 Territorial Sea and Fishing Zones Act that was repealed by the Oceans Act. The Act establishes Canada's maritime zones, including elaborating the continental shelf of Canada, and identifies the baselines from which these maritime zones will be delimited.

The Oceans Act gives a leadership role to the Minister 'responsible for the oceans' and thereby assigned the Department of Fisheries and Oceans as the lead agency with regard to the stewardship of the oceans, for the development of Canada's Oceans Strategy (see below), integrated management and planning, and marine protected areas (MPAs). The Minister may also assume leadership for any other oceans-related matter under federal jurisdiction that is not currently assigned to another minister. Other departments and agencies do, however, maintain their lead roles in their respective oceans-related sectors. As such, the mandate given to the Minister under the Oceans Act does not provide the DFO with carte blanche for the exercise of its power under the Act and does not replace existing federal or provincial legislated, oceans-related mandates (Chircop and Hildebrand 2006). The Act also clarifies and consolidates federal oceans management arrangements and responsibilities.

As noted above Part II of the Oceans Act provides the legal basis for the Oceans Management Strategy. In essence this means that the Minister for Fisheries and Oceans (in collaboration with other stakeholders defined clearly in the Act) 'shall lead and facilitate the development and implementation of national strategy for the management for estuarine, coastal and marine ecosystems in waters that form part of Canada or in which Canada has sovereign rights under international law'. The national strategy 'will be based on principles of sustainable development ... integrated management ... and the precautionary approach'. The Act also directs the Minister and department towards establishing an integrated oceans management regime through the development of integrated management plans (IMPs), which are to incorporate marine protected area (MPA) designations and marine environmental quality (MEQ) guidelines for outcomes-based and adaptive management.

To advance the principles and approaches of oceans management called for in the Act, in 2000 the Minister appointed two Ministerial Oceans Ambassadors. Later that year, the Minister announced the formation of the Minister's Advisory Council on Oceans (MACO) to assist the Minister in providing leadership in the sustainable development and integrated governance of Canada's oceans (DFO 2000). MACO was to provide independent expert advice to the Minister of Fisheries and Oceans Canada on ocean issues. The MACO's input was specifically sought on the following areas:

- balancing economic, environmental and social goals for sustainable development;
- managing increasing complexity and diversity of ocean uses; and
- engaging communities and stakeholders in making decisions that affect them and creating awareness of and involvement in oceans by the public (DFO 2000).

The MACO consisted of nine Canadians invited by the Minister to sit as members for a three-year term. The members were to be selected 'on the basis of merit, oceans-related knowledge and expertise, regional and sectoral interests, and standing in their community ... from coastal communities, aboriginal organizations, academia, industry and non-governmental organizations'. A principal function was to provide an independent channel for community opinion and advice to the Minister. Much was expected of MACO, and the committee was seen as an integral part, and one of 'five specific oceans commitments' of the Department of Fisheries Oceans within the Canadian Government's 2001–03 Sustainable Development Strategy (Auditor General of Canada 2005a). While the commitment to establish the MACO was met, the Auditor General noted that: 'subsequently, however, the term for the council was not renewed. There is now no national forum where stakeholders can have input into Canada's Oceans Strategy' (Auditor General of Canada 2005a, p. 20).

The Oceans Act and Canada's Oceans Strategy (COS) were seen as important initiatives that would 'help solve problems' of deteriorating Canadian ecosystems (Auditor General 2005b, p. 7). In an important review of implementation of the Oceans Act the Canadian Auditor General found that these

> expectations have not been met. The main tools of the Oceans Act – integrated management plans and marine protected areas – have not accomplished the desired results. Fisheries and Oceans Canada has fallen far short of meeting its commitments to develop and implement these tools. (Auditor General of Canada 2005b. p. 7)

The Auditor General noted that despite these failures public expectations were again rising following the release of the Canadian Oceans Action Plan and Canada's federal Marine Protected Areas Strategy in 2005 (Auditor General of Canada 2005b. p. 7). The Auditor General's criticisms reiterated earlier concerns. An early assessment noted that the Oceans Act was: 'too general and lacking firm commitments or deadlines; failing to embrace other important guiding principles such as pollution prevention, polluter pays, public participation, community-based management, intergenerational equity, and indigenous rights; failing to achieve the level of integration promised in the Act; and allowing too much political discretion to ensure effective implementation' (Herriman et al. 1997).

The development of the Oceans Act and a focus on oceans governance occurred at a time when Canadian fisheries, particularly on the Atlantic coast, were in crisis. On each of Canada's coasts fishery conflicts arising from collapses of major fisheries marked the 1990s. These crises had a broad impact on Canadian politics. The collapse of the Atlantic cod fishery off the province of Newfoundland in the early 1990s was shattering to coastal communities and the Atlantic region's economy (Charles 1997; Harris 1998) The resultant 'cod crisis' also served as a catalyst for a reassessment of management tools and policies used to govern Canada's fisheries, through the work of the Task Force on Incomes and Adjustment in the Atlantic Fishery, and its report *Charting a New Course: Towards the Fishery of the Future: Report of the Task Force on Incomes and Adjustment in the Atlantic*

Fishery (Task Force on Incomes and Adjustment in the Atlantic Fishery 1993).

Concern over salmon stocks on the West Coast in the 1990s, too, led to considerable federal–provincial conflict. In this case the conflict was driven by concerns over declines in salmon stocks and the renegotiation of the Pacific Salmon Treaty with the United States. The federal government had the constitutional authority for the treaty negotiations over the salmon fishery but the government of British Columbia and local fishers considered that the federal government did not give adequate consideration to their fisheries interests in these negotiations. On the Pacific Coast, as in Atlantic Canada, conflict between the federal government and other stakeholders dominated much of the 1990s, with this conflict termed 'salmon wars' (Brown 2005).

In July 2002 the Minister for Fisheries and Oceans, Robert Thibault, released Canada's Oceans Strategy (COS). The COS, which builds upon the framework established by the Oceans Act, provides an 'integrated approach to ocean management, coordination of policies and programs across governments, and an ecosystem approach' (DFO 2002, p. v). The COS 'provides an overall strategic approach to oceans management, [and] has been developed based on the lessons learned and issues identified through this work' (DFO 2002, p. iii) in implementing oceans management initiatives. Canada's Oceans Strategy uses similar language to Australia's Oceans Policy and establishes a framework based on Agenda 21 principles of sustainable development, integrated management and the precautionary approach.

Despite some concern over the length of time taken to release this strategy the release of Canada's Oceans Strategy (COS) was seen as a welcome development, although the lack of new funding associated with the initiative was noted by a number of stakeholder groups. The COS had three main policy objectives:

- the understanding and protection of the marine environment;
- to support sustainable economic opportunities; and
- to show international leadership in oceans management (DFO 2002, p. v).

The COS notes explicitly that 'oceans governance ... is much more than a federal government responsibility. It is a collective responsibility shared by all' (DFO 2002, p. v). The 'core commitments' for oceans governance under the COS were to:
- work collaboratively within the federal government, and among levels of government;

- share responsibility for achieving common objectives; and
- engage Canadians in oceans-related decisions in which they have a stake (DFO 2002, p. v).

The COS included three regional-scale 'integrated management initiatives at work' (DFO 2002, p. 28). These initiatives were:

- the Beaufort Sea Integrated Planning Initiative (BSIMPI) in the Arctic Ocean;
- the Eastern Scotian Shelf Integrated Management (ESSIM) Initiative in the Atlantic; and
- the Central Coastal of British Columbia Initiative.

The Eastern Scotian Shelf Integrated Management (ESSIM) Initiative is an example of one approach the Department of Fisheries and Oceans Canada (DFO) has adopted to operationalise integrated oceans management (Foster et al. 2005). The ESSIM Initiative is made up of two main components: the cross-jurisdictional, cross-sectoral institutional arrangements (the ESSIM Forum), and the development of an integrated plan for oceans management in the ESSIM area. Canada has taken a 'learning-by-doing' approach to integrated management, with the ESSIM Initiative informing and advising subsequent national policy development; hence the process is evolving with time and experience.

CANADA AS A MODEL: SHARING EXPERIENCES AND LESSONS

Canada's successes as well as its policy failures and difficulties were important lessons in the development of Australia's Oceans Policy (see Chapter 4). The Canadian experience demonstrated to the Australian oceans policy community that legislation in the form of an Oceans Act would not necessarily solve the difficulties of ocean and marine resource management. Consequently, Australia's approach has been to use existing legislation as the legal framework for its Oceans Policy. Australia did, however, emulate the Canadian model where the Minister responsible for oceans has a coordination and consultation role in the implementation of the Oceans Act through the COS and then the Oceans Action Plan (OAP).

The advice of Canadian officials was sought by Environment Australia during the development of Australia's Oceans Policy. Canadian officials participated in the oceans policy development process, and members of both governments have taken advantage of the opportunities provided by regular officer level exchanges. Officers from Fisheries and Oceans Canada (DFO) have regularly visited Australia's National Oceans Office (NOO), particularly those that are involved in the APEC Integrated Oceans Management initiative. These formal and often informal communications between Canadian and Australian officials have been invaluable for both countries (see Vince 2008). Canadian officials have observed the development and implementation of Australia's National Representative System of Marine Protected Areas and the Regional Marine Planning process (Vince 2006).

Representatives of the Office of the Auditor General of Canada also visited Australia in 2004 and the information gathered was utilized in the 2005 Report of the Commissioner of the Environment and Sustainable Development (Auditor General of Canada 2005a, 2005b). The Appendix to the review of Canada's Oceans Management Strategy in the report is titled 'Lessons Learned from International Experiences' with the opening paragraph stating that most efforts were concentrated on the Australian experience as 'Australia is viewed as the world leader in the development and implementation of a modern oceans-management approach' (Auditor General of Canada 2005b). A strong theme in the Report is for the DFO to learn from Australia's attempts at implementing a cross-sectoral and cross-jurisdictional approach to oceans governance.

GETTING IT TOGETHER? THE OCEANS ACTION PLAN

The COS involved a planning structure that draws from past Canadian practice as well as observations from Australian experience. The ongoing development and work led to the release of Canada's Oceans Action Plan in May 2005, which outlines the first phase of implementation of the Plan (DFO 2005a). The Action Plan gained government support in December 2004 and this support was bolstered by the provision of funding. As noted by the Auditor General's review: 'the February 2005 Budget provided $28.4 million over two years to implement Phase 1 of the Plan' (Auditor General of Canada 2005a, p. 10). The Oceans Action Plan was announced in October 2004 during the speech from the throne at the opening of the new parliament. The announcement was immediately welcomed but interest groups were 'looking for more detail and funding in the [forthcoming] budget' (CPAWS 2004, p. 1). The budget commitment for the Oceans Action Plan (OAP) immediately set it apart from previous initiatives, yet as noted it builds on Canada's decade-long policy development process. The OAP aimed to address the challenges identified in the implementation of the

COS. It 'articulates a government wide approach ... as the overarching umbrella for coordinating and implementing oceans activities and the framework to sustainably develop and manage our oceans' (DFO 2005a, p. 5). This rhetoric was to be delivered 'through a phased approach to implementation' of initiatives directed at 'four inter-connected pillars':

- International Leadership, Sovereignty and Security;
- Integrated Oceans Management for Sustainable Development;
- Health of the Oceans; and
- Ocean Science and Technology (DFO 2005a, p. 5).

The OAP elaborated initiatives for each of these pillars for Phase 1, yet these were in the main couched in very general terms. The OAP did, however, include a discussion of 'oceans management tools' in initiatives directed at the Integrated Oceans Management for Sustainable Development pillar. Five priority areas for integrated management planning were also identified: Placentia Bay and the Grand Banks off Newfoundland and Labrador, and the Gulf of St Lawrence in addition to the three areas identified in the COS – the Eastern Scotian Shelf, 'the most mature of the integrated management planning initiatives established under the *Oceans Act*', the Beaufort Sea and Pacific North Coast. The oceans management tools include ecosystems overview and assessment reports, identification of ecologically significant areas, seabed mapping and ecosystem objectives (DFO 2005a, pp. 13–15).

Oceans-related activities received additional funding with a federal government announcement in October 2007. These activities were supported by a budget of $2.5 million over three years in addition to $19 million over two years allocated in the May 2007 federal budget (DFO 2007). The Minister for Fisheries and Oceans stated that:

This new funding will strengthen our ability to prevent, detect and reduce pollution, increase protection for ecologically significant marine areas through nine new marine protected areas, and enhance cooperation with domestic and international partners for more integrated oceans management. The Government of Canada will also be increasing its research and protection activities in Canada's Arctic waters. (DFO 2007, p.1)

REVIEWING CANADA'S OCEAN MANAGEMENT STRATEGY

The Report of the Commissioner of the Environment and Sustainable Development to the House of Commons (Auditor General of Canada 2005b) delivered in September 2005 provided an important review of the Oceans Act. The Commissioner of the Environment and Sustainable Development is appointed by the Canadian Auditor General and is responsible for assisting the Auditor General in performing duties that relate to the environment and sustainable development. This review found that 'implementing the *Oceans Act* and subsequent oceans strategy has not been a government priority' (Auditor General of Canada 2005b, p. 2). It also noted: that the Department of Fisheries and Oceans had difficulty in developing and implementing a workable approach to integrated oceans management; the parliament had not been given the financial or performance information it needed to hold the department accountable for its Oceans Act responsibilities; and the department had not met its commitment to report periodically on the state of the oceans (Auditor General of Canada 2005a, p. 2).

The Auditor General report stated that no new funding was provided for the implementation of the Oceans Management Strategy released in 2005 or Canada's Oceans Strategy. As a result (not surprisingly) over eight years to 2005 the Department of Fisheries and Oceans 'has redirected about $100 million from its other operations to fund its activities in support of the [Oceans] Act and the Strategy. These activities included establishing an ocean organisation with roughly 110 employees in Ottawa and in the Department's six regions' (Auditor General of Canada 2005a, p. 6).

The review of the Canada's Ocean Management Strategy recognised that 'barriers to implementation exist' (Auditor General of Canada 2005b, p. 10). These barriers include:

- the complexities associated with the interdepartmental committee process for integrating the views of different departments and agencies;
- the lack of clarity over the role for Fisheries and Oceans Canada, including the role of the Minister in relation to competing legislative and administrative objectives;
- a lack of performance expectations related to short-term outputs for Canada's Oceans Action Plan; and
- ensuring adequate funding to achieve results (Auditor General of Canada 2005b, pp. 10–11).

The Auditor General recommended that Fisheries and Oceans Canada should seek to 'have the Oceans Action Plan recognized and managed as a government horizontal initiative' (Auditor General of Canada 2005a, p. 11), with the Department response indicating that 'phase 1 of the Ocean Action Plan represents the first commitment of funds across the government that aligns with the horizontal nature of oceans issues' (Auditor General of

Canada 2005a, p. 11). The inherent tensions arising from the contending 'fisheries' and 'oceans' mandates of the Department of Fisheries and Oceans was identified as an ongoing challenge in governance. As noted by the Auditor General's review:

> Is the Department through its Oceans Directorate, properly structured to play this leadership role? Can a department that has historically dedicated most of its resources to managing one of the key ocean-sector industries – the fishery – transform itself to represent and integrate a broader oceans interest? *These are difficult questions that must be answered.* (Auditor General of Canada 2005b, p. 10, emphasis added)

ENGAGING THE COMMUNITY: NEW FORMS OF OCEANS GOVERNANCE?

The concept of community-based management has become increasingly popular across Canada in a wide variety of natural resource sectors, including fisheries and forestry. In the fishery sector, community-based management may be found on all three of Canada's coasts, and including first-nation groups. On the Pacific coast, a number of community-based fishery and coastal management initiatives have been developed. A particularly innovative example is that of the West Coast Vancouver Island Aquatic Management Board (Foster and Haward 2003) which evolved from a grass-roots local initiative into a regional management body involving federal, provincial, municipal and first-nation representatives as well as local citizen members. The West Coast Vancouver Island Aquatic Management Board (WCVIAMB) provides a model or pilot project for emerging forms of community-based management.

The West Coast of Vancouver Island Aquatic Management Project is an area-based, principle-driven management project establishing the WCVIAMB to undertake integrated aquatic management in the region. The development of the WCVIAMB was in response to localized pressure on governments to enhance the community's role in decision-making processes, as well as the increasing demand for integrated and localized management, as outlined in Canada's Oceans Act 1997. Another major concern was that first-nation people's interests were not being adequately addressed in management decisions.

The WCVIAMB consists of 16 members: eight government and eight non-government representatives. These include federal, provincial, regional and first-nation government representatives and eight non-government members that represent the diverse uses and geography of the area. Non-governmental representatives are nominated by coastal communities or those with a vested interest in aquatic resource management and are jointly appointed by the participating governments. Non-governmental members are not chosen on the basis of representing any particular interest group, rather on the basis of their commitment to the Board's objectives and for their knowledge and expertise in the region.

There are two main functions of the Board. The first is an issues response procedure whereby the Board responds to issues raised by the Board members, the public or interest groups by making recommendations to the appropriate statutory authority. The other main function involves strategic planning development, whereby the Board focuses on the principles, objectives and evaluation framework outlined in the Board's Terms of Reference to develop a strategic plan for the region from which operational plans are then developed and implemented by specific departments or agencies (Foster and Haward 2003). The Board is experimental in design, and therefore incorporates adaptive management as a fundamental function of its 'learning-by-doing' approach. As such, an evaluation mechanism is attached to each strategy and target developed to determine whether goals are being met and milestones achieved.

CONCLUSION

Canada has been a leading light in international, regional and national initiatives in oceans governance. In developing its Oceans Act Canada provided a legislative framework that in the subsequent decade has seen further initiatives aimed at implementing sustainable development and integrated management of its maritime domain. This has not been an easy task, as implementation of such arrangements (in effect introducing horizontal governance) challenges existing arrangements, most notably those of sectoral agencies with clearly defined responsibilities. Although Canada has been less affected by jurisdictional issues surrounding oceans management than Australia or the USA, it has its own challenges in implementing oceans policies or strategies. While Canada has a vast maritime jurisdiction it appears that implementing oceans policies has not been a consistent priority for successive federal governments. Insufficient funding has constrained implementation. Recent announcements have, however, addressed funding issues.

Canada's national oceans governance initiatives have promise. The Integrated Management Initiatives, including the development of a plan in the Eastern Scotian Shelf, are important in moving oceans policy and governance 'beyond the buzzwords' (Chircop and Hildebrand 2006). The development of community-based management approaches in fisheries and in local oceans management provide models for assessment, and show promise as vehicles for implementing integrated approaches. Canada's work on its national MPA system will be an important contribution to commitments to ecosystem-based management and the implementation of a global representative system of MPAs made at the World Summit on Sustainable Development.

6. New Zealand

New Zealand comprises a number of islands, dominated by the main North and South islands. Its jurisdiction spans over 3 million km^2 of ocean (Mansell 2004, p. 3), following its declaration of an exclusive economic zone (EEZ) in 1978 (see Figure 6.1). New Zealand ratified the Law of the Sea Convention (LOSC) in July 1996, with this ratification taking effect on 18 August 1996. New Zealand has an extensive coastline, in excess of 15 000 km in length, with this maritime domain encompassing a 'coastal environment ... of rich diversity within relatively low-productivity seas' (Rennie 1993, p. 151). As Peart has noted: 'the oceans are thought to contain between one-third and three-quarters of New Zealand's indigenous species and are an international hotspot for some of these' (Peart 2005, p. xx).

This domain is the source of significant cultural and historical value, as well as a resource for the Maori (New Zealand's indigenous people) and Pakeha (non-indigenous Europeans). The proximity of the coast to New Zealanders, 'with no town further than 120 kilometers from the coast [means] it is natural that it should hold many ... special places; places of particular significance culturally, the whai tapu of the Maori, and similar windows to the Pakeha's much shorter past' (Rennie 1993, p. 151). Peart makes the telling comment that: 'the oceans are very important to Maori culture and significantly contribute to New Zealanders' way of life and well-being' (Peart 2005, p. xx). This attachment to the oceans and coasts has helped shape New Zealand's response to oceans governance.

New Zealand has undertaken a relatively stormy 'voyage' in relation to creating a national oceans policy (Mansell 2004). A policy development process was established with Cabinet imprimatur that recognised, explicitly, Maori interests and relationships with the ocean as an important policy consideration. This process, as is discussed in the following sections, was noteworthy for its bottom-up focus on stakeholder and community engagement, overseen by an advisory committee chaired by a former New Zealand Governor-General. New Zealand's Oceans Policy was to be released in late 2003; however, in July of that year the process stalled. Issues regarding the ownership of the foreshore and seabed that had emerged in ongoing disputes between Maori and the Crown needed to be resolved.

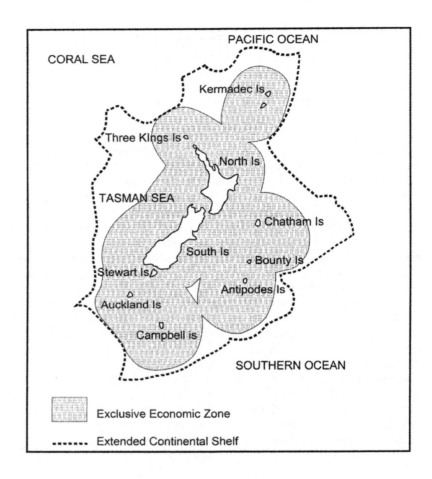

Figure 6.1 New Zealand – maritime jurisdiction

This matter was reignited following a Court of Appeal decision 'which ruled that Maori are entitled to seek exclusive title over the foreshore and seabed in the Maori Land Court' (Mansell 2004, p. 7). A government decision to legislate to overcome the consequences of this decision with the Foreshore and Seabed Act 2004 which received Royal Assent on 24 November 2004, impacted on the oceans policy process. It was not until November 2005 that the Minister for the Environment announced that work on New Zealand's Oceans Policy had recommenced (Ministry for the Environment 2007b).

New Zealand has been promoted as a model for oceans governance, despite, or perhaps because of, the particular character of the oceans policy development process (Peart 2005). It certainly provides a useful comparator to other examples of oceans policy development. New Zealand faces similar challenges in oceans management to other states yet it has a very different constitutional framework and has used different policy tools to address these challenges. As noted in Chapter 1 this provides great utility in analysis and draws out the richness of comparative analysis.

New Zealand has a unitary political system, but with a strong focus on regionalism. A unicameral parliamentary representative democracy based on the Westminster system, New Zealand has no formal written Constitution, being one of three countries in the world in this situation (Parliamentary Library 2005). New Zealand's constitutional framework is centred on New Zealand (and some United Kingdom or imperial) statutes, the prerogatives of the Crown, the principles of responsible government and parliamentary practice and precedent, as well as specific instruments including the Treaty of Waitangi of 1840 (Parliamentary Library 2005, p. 1). The Constitution Act of 1986 consolidated instruments and practices, and has been described as the 'most important New Zealand constitutional statute ... provid[ing] that no Act of the United Kingdom passed after the commencement of [the Constitution Act] shall apply to New Zealand' (Parliamentary Library 2005, p. 2).

New Zealand's governance framework is also distinguished by the influence of the Treaty of Waitangi, negotiated between the British and Maori in 1840. While there has been ongoing debate over the translations of the treaty, and over the interpretation of its key articles (see below) it nonetheless has 'acquired some permeating influence in New Zealand law' (Parliamentary Library 2003, p. 18). Of particular importance to Maori is the link to sea and resources found in Article II of the Treaty of Waitangi:

> Her Majesty the Queen of England confirms and guarantees to the Chiefs and Tribes of New Zealand and to the respective families and individuals thereof the full exclusive and undisturbed possession of their Lands and Estates Forests Fisheries and other properties which they may collectively or individually possess so long as it is their wish and desire to retain the same in their possession; but the Chiefs of the United Tribes and the individual Chiefs yield to Her Majesty the exclusive right of Preemption over such lands as the proprietors thereof may be disposed to alienate at such prices as may be agreed upon between the respective Proprietors and persons appointed by Her Majesty to treat with them in that behalf. (Treaty of Waitangi 2007)

This article has been subject to differing interpretations, but the 'orthodox position is that the Treaty guarantees in Article II to protect the exclusive possession and rangatiratanga [customary title] over lands, forests, fisheries

... are not enforceable in New Zealand law unless provided for in statute' (Parliamentary Library 2003, p. 18). At the same time, however, New Zealand Courts 'will not ascribe to parliament an intention to permit conduct inconsistent with the Treaty of Waitangi' (Parliamentary Library 2005, p. 2). The Treaty of Waitangi and Maori interests in coastal and marine environments and resources have been a significant factor in contemporary oceans governance in New Zealand.

New Zealand has 16 regions governed by regional councils, established under central government legislation, 74 authorities made up of 16 city councils, 57 district councils and the Chatham Island Council. Regional councils have administrative responsibilities in key areas that impact on coastal and marine areas such as environmental management, water quality and related river catchment management. The New Zealand system of government has resulted in an oceans regime that is free from provincial or state jurisdictional conflicts that are prevalent in Canada and Australia, yet differences between ocean resource sectors and primacy placed on indigenous peoples' interests in coastal and marine environments and resources issues have been a source of contention in the development of new Zealand oceans governance.

NEW ZEALAND FISHERIES MANAGEMENT

New Zealand followed the traditional pattern, common to other jurisdictions, of enacting sectoral-based legislation to govern the use of resources in, and protection of, the marine and coastal environment. These legislative and administrative arrangements were seen as considerable constraints on policy development and implementation, 'leading to gaps, overlaps and inefficiencies' (Parliamentary Commissioner for the Environment 1999, Preface). Prior to major legislative and policy developments in the 1980s and 1990s the most significant development in the 1970s was amendments to planning legislation, specifically the Town and Country Planning Act, in 1973 and 1977. These amendments enabled regional councils to extend planning processes to coastal areas (Rennie 1993, p. 156), and foreshadowed the increased impetus for integrated coastal zone management. The 1980s, too, saw major reforms to fisheries management. In 1983 amendments to the Fisheries Act introduced far-reaching changes:

> Prior to 1983 fisheries management had been quite haphazard and regulatory. *Ad hoc* decisions on aspects of fishing were made and sometimes reversed within a year ... The Fisheries Act consolidated the morass of regulations and added new planning and quota management approaches. (Rennie 1993, p. 156)

As part of this reform to fisheries management the introduction of the quota management system (QMS) occurred with a trial based on a developmental deep-water fishery in 1983 (Wallace and Weeber 2005, p. 516). From this initial model the QMS was introduced more broadly in inshore fisheries in 1986 (Wallace and Weeber 2005, p. 516). The New Zealand QMS was designed to address two motivations (Connor 2004, p. 181): first, the desire to reduce pressure on stocks in inshore fisheries, and second, 'the desire for a mechanisms to allow the domestic industry to capture rents and build capacity in the offshore sector' (Connor 2004, p. 181). The latter was achieved by encouraging joint ventures between New Zealand and foreign companies, leading to a rapid development in offshore and deep-water fishery skills and capacity. New Zealand interests took opportunities to purchase deep-sea trawlers from United Kingdom companies, themselves subject to increasing constraints within the European Union, for the developing orange roughy fishery in the early 1980s.

The QMS provided a major shake-out of the fishing industry, although restructuring had occurred in the wake of the reform to the Fisheries Act. This action saw the removal of part-time fishers in an attempt to reduce pressure and effort in the inshore fishery. The removal of many Maori fishers led to later claims for quota allocations (Wallace and Weeber 2005, p. 516). The QMS introduced market-based tools and approaches to what was formerly a bureaucratic model of regulatory control. The use of tradeable rights and the creation of quasi-market approaches by such 'trades' in fisheries management, for example through the QMS approaches, have clearly provided an alternative paradigm for both fishers and fisheries managers. In the 1980s and 1990s the New Zealand government was seen as a world leader in the development of this approach (OECD 2006) where they have increased the use of economic instruments, chiefly through the introduction of individual transferable quotas, fishing rights and resource rent recovery.

These market-type arrangements have encouraged the introduction of corporate models of governance in New Zealand fisheries, with quota association 'companies' taking the place of traditional associations or councils. The Orange Roughy Management Company, for example, was formed in 1991, and the Hoki Fisher Management Company was formed in 1997 (Wallace and Weeber 2005, p. 518). In its extreme form the use of tradeable rights and the creation of quasi market approaches by such 'trades' in fisheries management tackles the 'tragedy of the commons' by creating private property regimes, based on what have been termed 'privatarian' approaches to common pool resources (Haward and Wilson 2000). The development of individual transferable quotas (ITQs) creates quasi property rights, provides an opportunity to utilise market mechanisms and allows the market to determine the value of the quota or its component 'units'. Setting the total allowable catch (TAC) and determining quota and unit shares of the TAC provides a powerful tool for fisheries managers in the control of fishing effort and 'technology creep'. One effect has been to increase the direct interest and involvement of fishers in the management of their fisheries (Haward and Wilson 2000) and enhance the network nature of governance (see Chapter 1). As Ferguson has recognised, the emphasis on the tragedy of commons 'deflects analytic attention away from the actual socio-organizational arrangements able to overcome resource degradation and make common property regimes viable' (Ferguson 1997, p. 295).

The introduction of the QMS was not without controversy or its critics. The introduction of quota-based fisheries has been criticized, first, for privatising what has been a common pool resource, and second, for not adequately returning resource rents to the broader community. In New Zealand claims for the Maori access to fisheries entitlements and challenges to initial resource rental charges (Wallace and Weeber 2005, p. 519) led to court action. The dispute was settled with Maori gaining an initial 10 per cent quota allocation, 'a promise of 20 percent of future allocations and a half share in a large quota holding company, Sealords' (Wallace and Weeber 2005, p. 519).

Assessment of the QMS has focused on its achievements in relation to the aims to 'conserve inshore stocks while expanding effort into deep water fisheries' (Wallace and Weeber 2005, p. 519). As Connor notes: 'there is little doubt that the QMS successfully checked and contained expansion of the inshore fleet that were over-capitalised, and provided the means to redirect effort and existing capacity away from overfished and vulnerable stocks towards those capable of higher production levels' (Connor 2004, p. 222). There is some concern that the QMS system has led to industry 'capture' of management agencies with the interests of 'rights holders' taking priority over 'non-extractive values and use of the environment' (Wallace and Weeber 2005, p. 533). Moreover, the system could result in 'potential hazards for the future due to high concentration in ownership of catching rights' (Connor 2004, p. 221).

New Zealand also implemented major administrative reforms and legislative change affecting management of terrestrial (including coastal) environments and resources. The Resource Management Act (RMA) enacted in 1991 was the culmination of 'a massive legislative and administrative reform process as the question of "sustainable development" increased in political salience' (Haward 1995, p. 104). The reform process preceding the introduction of the RMA was unprecedented, with the proposed legislation subject to almost four years of development, formal legislative review and public consultation. The RMA achieved bipartisan political support. Initially proposed by the Labour Party (in power between 1984 and 1990), the RMA was enacted by a newly elected National Party government. The scope of the process and its outcomes were staggering; the RMA saw 700 statutory bodies in such diverse areas as harbour management trusts and drainage boards abolished, and 167 separate pieces of legislation revoked (Haward 1995, pp. 103–4).

The RMA provided the framework or architecture for development of major national resource and environmental management polices, although a major weakness was the failure to include fisheries within the RMA framework. The RMA dealt with aquaculture by providing the framework for resource consent (occupation of space) whilst the Fisheries Act 1983 gave provision for marine farming permits. Under this joint legislative approach 'marine farmers require both a resource consent from the relevant regional council (under the RMA) and a marine farming permit from the Ministry of Fisheries (granted under the Fisheries Act)' (Gibbs and Woods 2003). The coastal permits of farms that have joint permits can be reviewed under the Aquaculture Reform (Repeals and Transitional Provisions) Act 2004 (see Ministry for the Environment, Ministry of Fisheries and Department of Conservation 2006). Aquaculture is the fastest growing seafood industry in New Zealand (New Zealand Aquaculture Council 2006).

The RMA regime is 'essentially hierarchical ... local and regional plans [are] overlain by National Policy Statements and the RMA as the capstone' (Haward 1995, p. 105). Regional and local plans must be consistent with the national policy statements, although opportunities exist to tailor the lower-level plans to suit specific local conditions (Haward 1995).

NEW ZEALAND COASTAL POLICY

The New Zealand Coastal Policy Statement released in 1992 provides an opportunity to apply the RMA to an area of emerging concern to both the public and government. As in Australia, New Zealand reviews of existing coastal zone management had noted the problems of a lack of integration between legal and administrative instruments and arrangements, an inability to manage cumulative impacts in an effective manner and, as a result, outcomes shaped by what was evocatively termed in an Australian parliamentary committee report, 'the tyranny of small decisions' (see Haward 1995). The New Zealand Coastal Policy Statement was released for pubic comment on 1 October 1992. Over 600 submissions were received when submissions closed on 19 February 1993 by the Board of Inquiry appointed by the New Zealand Minister for Conservation, as required under the RMA. Public hearings were held throughout New Zealand between 5

July and 19 October 1993. The Board of Inquiry undertook an analysis of the vast amount of information gained in submissions and public hearings, completed its report and forwarded it to the Minister. The Minister is required by the RMA to 'reject, adopt or change a policy statement' (Haward 1995, p. 106). Following ministerial adoption of the policy it was forwarded to the Governor-General for formal approval, then tabled in parliament and a formal notice issued in the Government Gazette on 15 May 1994.

The Coastal Policy Statement incorporated seven principles for sustainable management of the coastal environment (Haward 1995, p. 107). These principles included: recognising that the coastal environment is available for sustainable use and development; its values should be protected; coastal management should address social, economic and cultural well being of people and communities; address reasonably foreseeable needs of future generations; address any adverse effects of activities, and to recognise the principles of the Treaty of Waitangi (Haward 1995, p. 107). The Coastal Policy and the explicit focus of the RMA provided important tools in the ongoing development of integrated approaches to resource and environmental management in New Zealand.

The 1998 International Year of the Ocean provided a further opportunity to advance the agenda. This opportunity was clearly perceived by non-governmental stakeholders. Mansell comments: 'the impetus for changes, as in Australia, came from the academic, scientific and non-governmental communities who could clearly see the opportunities and benefits that could ensue from a fully integrated management regime for the oceans' (Mansell 2004, p.5). The Environment and Conservation Organisations of Aotearoa New Zealand, a network of over 70 environmental and conservation groups, organised a conference, Seaviews, in mid-February 1998. This conference, held in Wellington:

> explored the concepts and practice of marine ecosystem management, the opportunities and obligations. All sectors with an interest in the sea were invited. The conference covered all areas – from terrestrial impacts on the sea and coastal management, through to the management of human impacts on the deep oceans. Our focus was on preferred futures, solutions, and how we get there. (Seaviews 2007)

The Seaviews conference was opened by Dame Catherine Tizard, a former New Zealand Governor-General, who was to play an important role in later policy development processes (see following). In addition to presentations and discussion on New Zealand issues, speakers from the USA and Australia provided opportunities to consider issues from these countries.

Non-governmental stakeholders continued to pursue the oceans policy agenda.

DEVELOPING AN OCEANS POLICY

Following the New Zealand election of 27 November 1999 a new Labour government took office. Early support for action on management of New Zealand's marine jurisdiction occurred with the release of the Parliamentary Commissioner for the Environment report, *Setting Course for a Sustainable Future: The Management of New Zealand's Marine Environment*, in December 1999 (Parliamentary Commissioner for the Environment 1999). This report has been seen as 'probably the most influential motivators for the New Zealand government to undertake the development of an Oceans Policy for its marine environment' (Foster 2002, p. 16; see also Foster 2003). The Commissioner's recommendation to develop an oceans policy was reflected in the observation that 'a much more cohesive government approach to marine management is urgently required' (Parliamentary Commissioner for the Environment 1999, Preface). The Commissioner commented

> We have an extraordinary plethora of legislation and agencies with marine responsibilities. There are 18 main statutes, 14 agencies and six government strategies for marine management. We have also signed up to at least 13 international conventions with marine implications. (Parliamentary Commissioner for the Environment 1999, Preface)

This situation was not unique to New Zealand. The material presented in other chapters shows similar concerns were expressed in Australia, Canada and the United States of America in respective analyses and critiques of contemporary oceans management. Similar issues were being reflected in international discussion fostered by the United Nations Conference on Environment and Development (UNCED) outcomes including Agenda 21 (see Haward and VanderZwaag 1995) and in the 'Noordwijk Guidelines' developed through the World Coast Conference organised under the auspices of the United Nations Intergovernmental Panel on Climate Change in 1993 (Haward 1995).

The key drivers of sustainable development and a more integrated approach to oceans policy and management featured as central elements in this report (Foster 2002, p. 5), which also noted the need 'for a compete reappraisal of the institutional, legal and knowledge bases with which we manage the marine environment' (Parliamentary Commissioner for the Environment 1999, p. 98; Foster 2002, p. 5). Prior to the release of the Parliamentary Commissioner for the Environment's report, a small group of three cabinet ministers in March 1999 had 'instructed officials to investigate current arrangements for the management of New Zealand's marine environment' (Mansell 2004, p. 5). As noted above there was widespread support for government action to address what were perceived as limitations in these arrangements. The Parliamentary Commissioner for the Environment recognised that a new regime for New Zealand's oceans would involve 'a strategy comprising firstly, goal and principles, and secondly, actions and policies for the future sustainable management of the marine environment' (Parliamentary Commissioner for the Environment 1999, p. 99; Foster 2002, p. 6).

In March 2000 the New Zealand Biodiversity Strategy was released. In the same month the Minister for Environment was tasked by Cabinet with responsibility for developing an Oceans Policy (Mansell 2004, p. 5). New Zealand then sent a representative to participate in the Towards a Regional Marine Plan for the South East National Oceans Forum held in Hobart, Tasmania in April 2000. Cozens argues that Australia's Oceans Policy at the time provided New Zealand with a 'point of reference, giving guidance and principles of direction, to national and local policy makers' (Cozens 2000, p. 18), the essence of policy learning between Australia and New Zealand.

July 2000 saw the formation of an ad hoc Ministerial Group of six ministers with responsibilities for economic and environmental matters affecting New Zealand's ocean domain. This Ministerial Group was chaired by the Minister of Energy, Fisheries, and Research, Science and Technology and comprised Ministers of Foreign Affairs and Trade, Conservation, Maori Affairs, Commerce, and Environment (Foster 2002, p. 17). It was asserted that: 'collectively these Ministers have responsibility for economic and environmental outcomes in relation to the marine environment and Treaty of Waitangi considerations, reflecting the need for the policy to address these considerations' (MACOP 2001, p. 10). An Oceans Policy Secretariat was also established. The secretariat was 'a group of officials who continue to work in their respective agencies and are coordinated by the Minister for the Environment's office' to oversee and support oceans policy development (Mansell 2004, p. 11; Foster 2002, pp. 17–19). In short a 'whole-of-government approach' to improve integration across sectors was sought by the New Zealand government.

The 'scope of the project was approved by Cabinet' on 18 September 2000 (Mansell 2004, p. 6; Foster 2002, p. 18), and the New Zealand government announced the development of a national Oceans Policy. This initiative was spearheaded by deliberations of the Cabinet Policy Committee in July 2000 that dealt with the proposal for an oceans policy, noted impetus for an oceans policy deriving from international and domestic drivers, and in passing included developments in Australia and Canada (Foster 2002, p. 17).

Policy development was:

> to focus on issues associated with managing the marine environment within the jurisdiction of New Zealand and the interactions between land management and the status and quality of the marine environment and inter-tidal zone, but will not address issues relating to New Zealand's management of or involvement in the Southern Oceans [sic] and the wider Pacific. (Parliamentary Commissioner for the Environment quoted in Mansell 2004, p. 10)

The relationship between the Maori, the Treaty of Waitangi and coastal and ocean areas and resources was 'a key policy consideration' (Mansell 2004, p. 10). It was recognised that the policy development process needed to ensure that Maori interests were respected, and that they were involved and engaged in 'all levels of participation' in the process. As Mansell notes, these were 'particularly poignant pleas in light of subsequent events surrounding the foreshore and seabed where these values were noticeably absent' (Mansell 2004, p. 10).

THE PROCESS AND THE POLICY

In a similar manner to the Australian Oceans Policy process, the New Zealand government proposed developing the policy in three stages:

- Define the Vision – consulting the community over the values placed on the marine environment;
- Design the Vision – designing policies to achieve the vision set out by Zealanders in the first stage; and
- Deliver the Vision – implementing the policy (MACOP 2001, p.11; Mansell 2004).

The first stage was to be facilitated by an eight-person Ministerial Advisory Committee (MAC) chaired by Dame Catherine Tizard. Dame Catherine was a former New Zealand Governor-General (13 December 1990 – 21 March 1996), the first woman to hold this vice-regal post, and prior to her appointment had extensive experience as an elected member and Mayor in local government and in a regional council.

The MAC was involved in an extensive period of consultation with New Zealanders, 'to find out what local people value about the oceans' (Ministry of Fisheries 2001). As Dame Catherine Tizard commented: 'as people of a maritime nation, with the fourth-largest exclusive economic zone in the world, even New Zealanders who don't live by the sea have a stake in the management of our oceans' (Ministry of Fisheries 2001).

The MAC noted that: 'New Zealand does not have well defined goals that give directions to decisions about the oceans and guidance when laws conflict' (MACOP 2001, p. 10). The MAC believed that the Oceans Policy provided a means to 'manage conflicts between different management regimes' (ibid., p. 11). This emphasised a departure from what could be termed a rational-technical approach, where the process of policy development resolved conflicts through the development of the best or most appropriate outcome. The limitations of such an approach are obvious. The emphasis on a solution fails to recognise that this solution is often contingent, and that the choice of this solution may be influenced or shaped by specific values or interests. Often, too, there are concerns that top-down approaches contribute to increased differences or conflicts where local views or interests appear to be ignored. The emphasis on oceans policy as a means to manage conflicts indicated greater weight being given to a process that encourages a wider search for alternatives to resolve differences. Recognising the constraints in the traditional approach to decision-making provides an opportunity to develop an approach that emphasises the process as much as it does the outcome, and gives increased opportunities for policy learning.

The lack of a mechanism to facilitate coordination between different activities, uses and interests was identified as a problem:

> It is intended that New Zealand's Oceans Policy will fill that gap. It will link the several things that New Zealanders want and need to do with the marine environment and allow an understanding, in advance, of how, why and by whom choices will be made. It will act as the ridgepole over the house – the tahuhu over the whare – to provide a framework for several supports, each of which in itself is essential to a complete and functional structure. The house itself must accommodate the range of interests, values and activities that New Zealanders have in relation to their marine environment. (MACOP 2001, p. 10)

The use of a metaphor associated with Maori dwellings, together with the MAC's charter and actions, to engage and consult with the Maori was significant. As in Australia where the Oceans Policy process was seen by indigenous groups as an important opportunity to express their views over 'sea country' and assert interests and rights to be part of the management, the Maori used the consultation process to maintain these interests in the coast and seas. The Treaty of Waitangi commitments, providing major differences in policy development in New Zealand as opposed to Australia, were nonetheless severely challenged in the lead-up to, the debates surrounding, and the response following the enactment of the Foreshore and Seabed Act 2004.

The MAC was charged with designing and implementing a consultation process as a central element of stage one of the policy development. This was guided by the terms of reference provided to the members of the MAC that emphasised an open and inclusive process (MACOP 2001, pp. 53–5). While the terms of reference provided strong statements in relation to public involvement, they may well have encouraged heightened expectations amongst participants over the scope and outcomes of the process. This also reinforces a key point identified by the MAC: the values and interests held by protagonists are important factors in managing a consultation process. The New Zealand process paid considerable attention to ensuring that all interests were recognised and 'all views were accorded respect' (ibid., p. 54). Different values and beliefs will mean that stakeholders shape and prioritise problems differently and frame them in different ways. Recognising these characteristics of problems may alert policy analysts to the possible unanticipated consequences that may follow from policies based on the right solution to the wrong problem, or even vice versa (Dunn 1994, p. 142).

These issues were noted by the MAC in its comments that New Zealanders 'want to have confidence in decision making' (MACOP 2001, p. 6) and seek a policy framework that minimises conflict and costs, enabling engagement with the process without necessarily resorting to 'adversarial processes that do little to contribute to enduring solutions' (ibid.). The MAC recognised that 'finding a balance between local input and central governance will be a challenge' (ibid.). It outlined, for example, the strong and 'rigidly stated' positions and tensions between different fishing interests (MACOP 2001, p. 31). The MAC also stated that despite public statements such as the reluctance from recreational fishing organisations to compromise on rights to fish, 'compromise will be required of everyone' (ibid,). The MAC noted that in the case of recreational fishing, the fishers themselves must take responsibility for participating in processes to find solutions, to avoid solutions being imposed on them, thus 'ensuring their activities are free of the regulation and bureaucrats they so clearly dislike' (ibid.). The conflict over fishing and the interests of recreational fishers is not unique to New Zealand, with similar positions and issues being raised in Australia. The management of conflicting uses and activities was clearly an important issue and reiterated the need for a policy framework that could accommodate and manage these differing interests. The MAC encapsulated the community's desire for an effective policy framework in the following:

> A simple, principled and flexible framework is required that focuses on the effects of activities in an integrated way, is not unduly prescriptive and is efficient, durable and adaptable. (MACOP 2001, p. 6)

The New Zealand Oceans Policy process was characterised by a focus on public consultation. Forty-seven meetings and 24 hui (Maori gatherings) were held across New Zealand, including meetings on Stewart Island and on Chatham Island from 25 June to 13 August 2001. Over 2000 people attended these meetings, with 1160 written submissions being received by the MAC and 300 000 downloads from the MAC consultation website (MACOP 2001). Eight hundred submissions (69 per cent of the total) were individual submissions and there were 360 submissions (31 per cent of the total) from groups – ranging in size from two to 31 000 members. The MAC was required to report to the oceans policy Ministerial Group on the results of the consultation by 30 September 2001. The consultation process was extensive and significant, with the MAC's report providing useful 'insights' from the consultation. Importantly, these insights included discussion of 'consultation overload', and a degree of cynicism in the effect of consultation. It also identified the problems of 'consultation fatigue' among the Maori, and concern at the lack of coordination among government consultation processes (MACOP 2001, p. 44).

The MAC emphasised New Zealanders' links to the coastal and marine environment, with the nation's physical setting as a group of islands in 'a corner of the world's largest ocean' (MACOP 2001, p.15) giving its people a close connection to the sea. The MAC noted the spiritual and physical connection the Maori placed on their relationship to the oceans, and the need for oceans policy to recognise and incorporate *tangata whenua* – the Maori worldview. The MAC noted the importance placed on 'a healthy sea' as the basis for the Oceans Policy by many contributors to the consultation. The MAC also noted that in addition to providing an essential resource, the 'oceans support a complex infrastructure that a modern society and economy need to function'. This focused the MAC to establish the link between oceans policy and 'a healthy society'. The development of the vision underpinning New Zealand's oceans policy was adopted by Cabinet as: 'healthy oceans, wisely managed for the greatest benefit to New Zealand, now and in the future' (Benson-Pope 2005). Following the conclusion of the first phase of the process, attention was directed at policy development and implementation.

DEVELOPING THE OCEANS POLICY

In the early months of 2002, the challenge for the New Zealand government was to keep stakeholders involved in oceans policy development. In February the Minister for Fisheries, Pete Hodgson, addressed the Ngai Tahu Waipounamu Treaty Festival and outlined the key issues for stage two policy development. These included:

First is the identifications of models for integrated management. We need to look at systems for consistent decision-making across a wide range of issues. Second is the need for holistic management systems. New Zealanders have a very wide range of values in relation to the sea: cultural, economic, aesthetic, spiritual and more. We need to identify management systems that can take account of them all, as well as the very diverse physical qualities of the marine environment. We need to determine how we are going to bring about compliance with these management systems – and enforce them if necessary. Policies that encourage voluntary compliance will be a high priority. (Hodgson 2002)

Other key issues included: decision-making models; the co-existence of the Oceans Policy and Treaty of Waitangi; the development of an information management framework; and policy monitoring (Hodgson 2002). The Oceans Policy Secretariat commissioned Enfocus Ltd, URS New Zealand and Hill Young Cooper to prepare a 'stocktake' of the oceans in November 2002. The purpose of this research was provide an overview of the strengths and weaknesses of the oceans management approaches in New Zealand. Secondly, it examined key themes across legislation. Unlike Australia and Canada's state and provincial issues integrating approaches across jurisdictions, New Zealand's focus was on the extent of legislative cohesion on ocean issues. The *Ocean Policy Stocktake Part 1 – Legislation and Policy Review* (Enfocus Ltd et al. 2002) outlined New Zealand's oceans management strengths as being:

- single, uncontested jurisdiction;
- comprehensive legal framework;
- some ability to create consistent regulatory regimes;
- integrated coastal zone management;
- the Treaty of Waitangi; and
- relatively efficient allocation mechanisms for fisheries.

Weaknesses included:

- absence of an overriding goal;
- inconsistent decision-making structures and opportunities for participation;
- inconsistent management of 'like' activities (and potential effects), particularly beyond the territorial sea;
- The Treaty of Waitangi Act and aboriginal rights;
- ecologically arbitrary spatial management units and a general lack of integrated management; and
- lack of information.

Whilst cross-jurisdictional issues were not an issue for New Zealand, the disadvantages were reminiscent of oceans management problems being experienced in Australia, Canada and the United States. The report also concluded that the legal instruments and government strategies have 'no unifying thread or theme' and that 'each has been developed for a different purpose and therefore has a different utility' (Enfocus Ltd et al. 2002, p. 43).

On 14 March 2003 the Oceans Policy Secretariat released a series of 11 working papers as part of the second stage of the Oceans Policy process. Meetings were held in Auckland and Wellington in late March 2003 with a hui also held in Wellington. The Oceans Policy Secretariat provided a document summarising feedback from the meeting and from written comment in April 2003 (Oceans Policy Secretariat 2003). In addition to the feedback and a summary report the 11 working papers covered the following topics:

- Paper One: Information Issues;
- Paper Two: Ocean Use Rights;
- Paper Three: Maori and Oceans Policy;
- Paper Four: Environmental Issues;
- Paper Five: The Land–Sea Interface;
- Paper Six: Marine Biosecurity;
- Paper Seven: Marine Cultural Heritage;
- Paper Eight: Participation in Oceans Management;
- Paper Nine: Adapting to Future Changes;
- Paper Ten: Encouraging New Opportunities in the Ocean; and
- Paper Eleven: International Oceans Issues (Oceans Policy Secretariat 2003).

This included consideration of new institutional structures to facilitate implementation and operation of the policy. The following institutional arrangements were suggested in 2003:

- Ad Hoc Ministerial Group;
- Oceans Policy External Reference Group;
- Officials Steering Group;
- Oceans Policy Secretariat;
- working groups;
- Oceans Policy Group Chair; and a
- Departmental Reference Group (see Vince 2008).

The opportunity to learn from the Australian experience is clearly shown in the proposed institutions and their interrelationships. While the titles of each institution differ from Australian oceans policy arrangements (at least from 1999 to 2005) their structure and functions were very similar. For example, the Ad Hoc Ministerial Group was to be made up of relevant ministers, as was Australia's Oceans Ministerial Board. The Oceans Secretariat has a structure and function that mirrored the initial model of the Australian National Oceans Office (to which it returned following the 2005 restructuring – see Chapter 4). These similarities in language, shared elements and organizational forms highlight the significance of policy transfer in the development of New Zealand's Oceans Policy, reinforcing the relevance of McAdam and Rucht's argument that one of the key conditions for transfer or diffusion is through the sharing of specifiable common elements (McAdam and Rucht 1993, p. 66).

New Zealand was able to closely follow Australia's Oceans Policy development process through its participation in relevant Ministerial Councils and the associated standing committees of officials. New Zealand had active involvement in the Australian and New Zealand Environment and Conservation Council (ANZECC) and the Natural Resource Management Ministerial Council during the development and implementation of Australia's Oceans Policy (Environment Australia 2003). Being part of the main process oceans of policy implementation has meant that New Zealand had 'inside' access to policy decisions and institutional development.

OBSERVATIONS ACROSS THE TASMAN

New Zealand officials readily engaged with and utilised opportunities to learn from their Australia counterparts. This included visits to and working with the National Oceans Office (NOO) as well as the more formal linkages through the ANZECC. New Zealand officials were thus able to experience the challenges of developing an integrated policy model. A number of lessons were learned, including those related to the institutional structure established to implement the Oceans Policy. New Zealand officials were not surprised that the location of the NOO in Hobart, Tasmania, and its executive agency status provided challenges (Vince 2008). The decision to move the NOO from executive agency status to the Department of Environment and Heritage in 2005 did not surprise New Zealand officials, as they had anticipated that this would eventuate (ibid.).

The Australian government's decision not to develop an Oceans Act, but instead rely on establishing a policy framework, was an important lesson. New Zealand officials believed that this weakened the implementation of regional marine plans; as one official commented: 'a legislative framework is necessary to make the plans happen' (ibid.). New Zealand also drew on the Canadian experience with regard to oceans legislation, and recognised that a synthesis of both approaches would utilise specific strengths. New Zealand's environmental non-governmental organisations (NGOs) also noted developments in Australia and elsewhere. Australia provided an excellent kick-start to New Zealand's policy process, and that the ability to watch and learn from Australia had great benefits (Vince 2008; see also Cozens 2000).

Australia began the implementation of its oceans policy by mapping the continental shelf. Similarly, New Zealand began mapping its continental shelf boundary through Oceans Survey 20/20, an oceans information-gathering project coordinated by Land Information New Zealand (LINZ). Oceans Survey 20/20 is a programme that is to be completed by 2020 and supports nine key themes: sovereignty; coastal stewardship and management; natural hazards and risk management; maritime safety and security; fisheries; biodiversity and ecosystems; hydrocarbons; minerals and other physical resources; and climate (LINZ 2006). LINZ had close linkages with Geoscience Australia and benefited from work done by this agency in defining the Australian continental shelf. Australia and New Zealand agreed to combine their interests in ocean surveying and both countries contributed to the New Zealand and Australia Norfolk Ridge–Lord Howe Rise Biodiversity Voyage (NORFANZ) voyage which explored deep-sea habitats in the Tasman Sea in 2003. The delineation of New Zealand's continental shelf was completed in April 2006.

In May 2003, the research report *Oceans Management at the Local Level* produced for the Oceans Policy Secretariat by Enfocus Ltd summarized the findings of surveys completed by local authorities and Department of Conservation conservancies. This report was indicative of the 'bottom-up' approach to implementation being pursued by the Secretariat. Following this, on 30 June 2003, the Centre for Advanced Engineering released a report prepared for the Secretariat titled *Economic Opportunities in New Zealand's Oceans: Informing the Development of Oceans Policy* (CAENZ 2003). The myriad of reports released by the Oceans Secretariat to mid 2003 demonstrated its thoroughness and aim to 'leave no stone unturned' in oceans policy development. This followed Australia's approach in releasing numerous background documents prior to the release of the oceans policy in 1998. A comprehensive overview of oceans management during policy development was recognized as one strength of Australia's oceans policy process by New Zealand and Canadian officials (Vince 2008). The work undertaken from 2000 to 2003 in New Zealand provided an important base to policy development and implementation. 'This includes designing a policy that gives effect to the vision put forward after the Ministerial Advisory Committee on Oceans Policy – chaired by Dame Catherine Tizard – talked to thousands of New Zealanders' (Benson-Pope 2005).

OCEANS POLICY: SHOALS, SQUALLS AND THE QUESTION OF FORESHORE AND SEABED TITLE

The policy development process was abruptly terminated in mid-2003. Following the New Zealand Court of appeals decision in *Ngati Apa, Ngati Koata & Ors* v *Ki Te Tua Ihu Trust & Ors* (the *Ngati Apa* case) in June 2003 the New Zealand government took the view that issues regarding the ownership of the foreshore and seabed between the Maori and the Crown needed to be resolved before any further oceans policy development continued. The *Ngati Apa* case saw a long-standing legal precedent relating to status of Maori title over coastal and seabed areas challenged by the Court of Appeal. The decision in the *Ninety Mile Beach* case ([1963] NZLR 261), handed down in 1963, 'shut down Maori claims to customary title in the foreshore by ruling that any customary interests in the foreshore and seabed were extinguished by implication, if the adjoining dry lands were investigated by the Native Land Court, the Maori Land Court's predecessor' (Charters and Erueti 2005, p. 261). *Ngati Apa* also centred on the jurisdiction of the Maori Land Court. The Maori Land Court was first established in 1865 to investigate ownership of tribal lands and to grant freehold title to those owners. Almost all of customary title to dry land had been converted into freehold by 1900 (Charters and Erueti 2005).

While the *Ngati Apa* case focused on an application 'to seek declaratory orders that certain land below mean high water mark in the Marlborough Sound is Maori customary land' (NZCA [2003] 117 para 3), the principal legal question was whether the Maori Land Court had the authority to exercise jurisdiction in relation to the foreshore and seabed (Charters and Erueti 2005). The Court of Appeal found that the Maori Land Court had jurisdiction, with the court also overturning the decision in the *Ninety Mile Beach* case. This latter aspect of the case was seen as opening up claims to freehold title to coastal and seabed areas by the Maori, and caused significant public and political controversy. New Zealand's unitary political system has enabled land-based coastal issues that affect the state of the oceans to be an important aspect of debates over coastal and oceans policy (Mansell 2004, p. 5).

Soon after the Court of Appeal decision the New Zealand government 'announced that it would introduce legislation to overrule the decision' (Charters and Erueti 2005, p. 262). In August 2003 the government announced that it was proposing legislation that would 'declare the entire foreshore and seabed public domain, guarantee a general right of access along the foreshore', and alter the Maori Land Court's jurisdiction (Charters and Erueti 2005, p. 262). The Foreshore and Seabed Bill was introduced into the New Zealand parliament in early 2004. Prior to this the matter had been taken up by the Waitangi Tribunal that made strong criticism of both the policy underpinning the proposed legislation and the process undertaken by the government. In July 2004 Maori organisations submitted a request to the United Nations Committee on the Elimination of Racial Discrimination to review the bill.

The bill was referred to a select committee that invited public submission. Charters and Erueti comment that: 'the Select Committee revived just fewer than 4000 submissions of which over 94 percent [were] opposed [to] the FS Bill' (Charters and Erueti 2005, p. 263). The select committee could not agree on amendments to the Bill, being 'sharply divided along party lines' (Charters and Erueti 2005, p. 264), although 'substantial amendments' were presented when the bill returned to parliament for a second reading on 16 November 2004 (Charters and Erueti 2005, p. 264). The Foreshore and Seabed Act, a landmark piece of legislation in New Zealand's history of conflict over land ownership, was finally enacted on 24 November 2004. The United Nations Committee on the Elimination of Racial Discrimination, although its decisions are not enforceable against New Zealand (Charters and Erueti 2005), brought down its decision in March 2005, determining that the Foreshore and Seabed Act discriminates against the Maori. This determination was rejected and opposed by the New Zealand government. The lack of resolution over Maori concerns is likely to shape oceans governance debates into the future. The Minister, perhaps responding to the acrimonious political and public debate over the Foreshore and Seabed Act, stated that his intension 'for the development of oceans policy to continue to be an inclusive process' (Benson-Pope 2005).

The two and half years interregnum in oceans policy development that arose from the consequences of the *Ngati Apa* case, including the fallout from the *Foreshore and Seabed* Act, did provide further opportunities for policy learning and information-gathering processes. At the same time New Zealand's legislative and administrative system has provided opportunities for its initiatives to provide learning opportunities for others. The Environmental Defence Society (EDS) noted that: 'oceans policy is a hot policy development topic and there is great interest in the New Zealand model (we don't have the complexities of federal government or an enormous population). The thinking is that if we can get it right the crowd will follow' (EDS 2005).

The close links between New Zealand and Australian government officials enabled the transfer of oceans policy ideas and terminology, institutional structures, and policy development approaches and implementation tools. The formal and informal communications between officials were the catalyst for policy learning. Formal and informal contact between Australian and New Zealand officials exists, and this contact continues to facilitate oceans policy development.

NEW ZEALAND'S OCEAN POLICY: IMPLEMENTING A FRAMEWORK

On 11 February, 19 March and 4 June 2004, the Ministry of Environment held informal workshops to 'test ideas' on oceans policy priority. Participants included representatives from government agencies, consultants and NGOs. The outcomes of these workshops were summarised in two papers: *Getting Our Priorities Right: The Role of Information in Setting Priorities for Management of New Zealand's Ocean* (Ministry for the Environment 2005a) and *Offshore Options: Managing Environmental Effects in New Zealand's Exclusive Economic Zone* (Ministry for the Environment. 2005b) – both released in June 2005 by the Ministry for the Environment. The *Priorities* paper began by referring to the Draft Oceans Policy, which at the time was yet to be passed by Cabinet. It stated that the policy was: 'a first step towards identifying a preferred, adaptive approach for setting future ocean priorities, together with specific actions needed to build information, tools and concepts that might underpin this approach' (Ministry for the Environment 2005a, p. vi). It recommended, among other things, that there needed to be stronger links between the Oceans Policy process and the Ocean Survey 20/20 project to 'ensure there is no duplication in effort and ... address the range of barriers to accessing and using existing information' (Ministry for the Environment 2005a, p. 37).

The *Offshore Options* paper focused on: current environmental legislation in the EEZ and management gaps; international environmental management of activities in the EEZ; and options for improving the environmental management in the EEZ (Ministry for the Environment 2005b). Of the latter, it identified four options for improving environmental management:

- *Option 1 – the voluntary approach:* government would work with industries operating in the EEZ to develop appropriate environmental management procedures. Compliance with these procedures would be voluntary (at least initially).
- *Option 2 – filling the gaps in current legislation:* this would involve putting in place new legislation to cover activities not already covered,

and improving the environmental management provisions of existing legislation as necessary.

- *Option 3 – one Act to manage all resources in the EEZ:* all of the current legislation applying in the EEZ would be replaced by one Act controlling resource management (including the allocation of resources and/or management of their effects) in the EEZ.
- *Option 4 – an 'umbrella' Act:* a new statute would be developed requiring environmental assessments to be carried out for all activities with potentially significant environmental effects (similar to the approach taken under Australia's Environmental Protection and Biodiversity Conservation Act 1999). Detailed regulation of specific activities through existing legislation would continue. (Ministry for the Environment 2005b, p. v)

The Ministry for the Environment recommended in the paper that a voluntary approach be taken along with the development of an 'umbrella Act'. Interestingly, the voluntary approach reiterated the aims highlighted by Minister Hodgson in 2002. The *Offshore Options* paper instigated the new approach of the third stage of oceans policy implementation (see below).

On 21 November 2005 the Seachange 05: Managing our Coastal Waters and Ocean*s* Conference was held in Auckland. This conference was organised by the EDS with the aim to 'evaluate recent national policy developments affecting the management for New Zealand's coastal and marine areas' (EDS 2005). The EDS had undertaken its own analysis of oceans policy initiatives in Australia, Canada and the USA to help inform and focus on issues facing new Zealand's development of 'an effective oceans policy' (EDS 2005; see also Peart 2005). A key speech from the New Zealand Minister for the Environment, the Hon. David Benson-Pope, announced that the Oceans Policy development process had resumed:

> To develop oceans policy a cross-government project team of officials has been assembled. The team is led by the Ministry for the Environment and includes the Department of Conservation, the Ministry of Fisheries, the Ministry of Economic Development, Te Puni Kokiri, the Treasury and the Department of Prime Minister and Cabinet. Other Departments are also involved as required to offer relevant expertise such as the Ministry of Foreign Affairs and Trade, Ministry of Justice and Maritime New Zealand. (Benson-Pope 2005)

The recommencement of the Oceans Policy resulted in a change to the original plans for the third implementation stage. The *Offshore Options* paper steered the Oceans Policy in a direction away from a broad plan to one that was more focused and targeted the management of New Zealand's EEZ.

The New Zealand government had 'agreed that oceans policy development will focus on fixing the most pressing marine problems in the short term while taking a more coordinated and integrated approach to

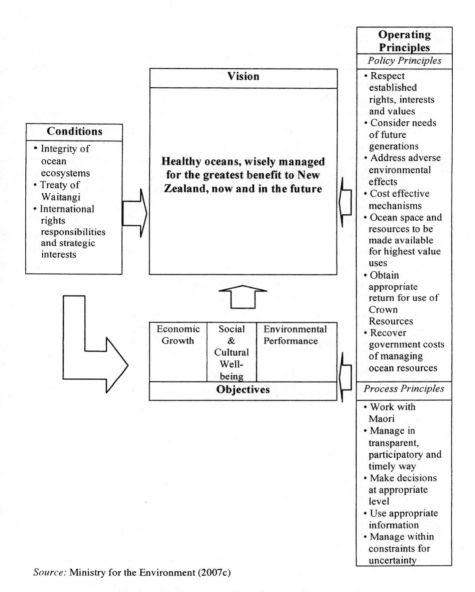

Source: Ministry for the Environment (2007c)

Figure 6.2 Draft Oceans Policy Framework – New Zealand

marine management over time' (Ministry for the Environment, 2007a). The decisions dealing with marine issues are to be made within the scope of the Draft Oceans Policy Framework (see Figure 6.2), a one page overview of the 'vision', 'conditions', 'operating principles' and 'process principles' that will guide the sustainable development of New Zealand's oceans (Ministry for the Environment 2007a).

As recommended by the Ministry for the Environment in the *Offshore Options* paper, voluntary approaches to managing the environmental impacts of marine activities in the EEZ were developed. In March 2006, the *Environmental Best Practice Guidelines for the Offshore Petroleum Industry* paper was released and it stated that 'until there is an oceans policy, industry and government agree to voluntary principles to manage environmental impacts beyond New Zealand's territorial sea' (Ministry for the Environment 2006, p. 2).

In August 2007, the first step towards a legislative component to the oceans policy was explored through the release of the discussion paper *Improving Regulation of Environmental Effects in New Zealand's Exclusive Economic Zone* (Ministry for the Environment 2007b). The paper was open for public comment until 30 September 2007, with a summary of submissions released later in the year. This discussion paper identified two different options for legislative change to the *Offshore Options* paper. Instead of an 'umbrella Act', the discussion paper recommended:

- Option 1: the establishment of legislative mechanisms focused on filling key gaps in EEZ environmental regulation and promoting a consistent approach across statues, including the assessment of cumulative effects; or
- Option 2: Develop an entirely new regime for managing all activities in the EEZ (Ministry of the Environment 2007, p. 10).

Whilst these options were open for public comment, the discussion paper emphasised that the 'preferred option' would be option 1, to fill in the key gaps in existing legislation. The paper outlined some key questions to be considered if this option were to be implemented, including: 'who should make the final decisions on 1) rules, 2) applications? The minister, the administering department or an independent agency?' In addition, there was a call for discussion to whether an existing agency or a new agency be developed to administer the legislation. Ironically, this is a similar debate to that held during the development of the Oceans Policy by the Oceans Policy Secretariat.

CONCLUSION: NEW ZEALAND'S OCEANS POLICY: SAFE HARBOUR OR A LEE SHORE?

When the Oceans Policy process began in New Zealand in 2000, New Zealand officials and international observers felt optimistic about a new approach to oceans management that would combine the best features of oceans policies that had been implemented elsewhere. Learning from Canada, Australia and the United States was integral in the development of New Zealand's Oceans Policy. The stalling of the development of the policy in 2003 provided a pause to refocus the direction of the policy. However, this pause also ceased the initial momentum and enthusiasm that the development of the policy generated. Beggs and Hooper (2005) rightly claim that 'development of New Zealand's oceans policy has been ambitious and visionary', yet 'progress has been comprised by several "too hard" issues'.

At one level one can mount an argument that the New Zealand experience reinforces the fact that much policy work is reactive, responding to political agendas set by government through election promises or programme commitments, or responding to issues forced onto the political agenda by the pace of events. This argument is supported by the rapid pace of development following the October 1999 election, and more starkly the government's decision to abandon this process following the *Ngati Apa* case, and its actions that led to the Foreshore and Seabed Act 2004.

At another level, though, the role of the policy analyst in the prioritisation of problems and developing options and policy is clearly important and thus the analysis is clearly proactive. In this case the analyst produces material, data and scenarios and helps guide government decisions. Obviously, too, in current public sector arrangements much policy development is delegated to the public sector to develop and implement with only broad involvement from ministers or Cabinet. The New Zealand experience also supports this viewpoint. The decision to restart the oceans policy process in late 2005 built on the preceding work and expertise within the public sector, helped, too, by the opportunities to observe activities in both Australia and Canada.

7. United States

As the United States of America (USA) emerged as the major ocean power in the twentieth century, its maritime interests shaped its attitudes towards oceans policy and governance. The development of USA sea power in the first half of the twentieth century and its significant role in the Second World War was matched by the role of the USA Navy in the Cold War, and in the post-Cold War era. USA domestic interests have also been influential. Concern over management of the USA's maritime domain has led to periods of intense government activity, first in the mid-to-late 1960s – with concomitant policy and legislative innovation and administrative reform in the early 1970s – and more recently in the decade from the late 1990s. The USA's oceans jurisdiction is significant – an extensive coastline, borders on three oceans, and important Pacific Ocean interests (see Figure 7.1) – and its maritime interests are equally extensive.

Oceans governance in the United States of America has, as in Australia and Canada, centred on questions over jurisdiction between the federal government and the states, leading to what were termed the 'tidelands dispute' and 'seashore federalism'. These questions have given rise to ongoing political conflict between the federal government and the states. As in the cases of Australia and Canada, the struggle over 'seashore federalism' in the United States has involved judicial review, extensive intergovernmental disputation and political 'settlement' of the struggle. The US federal government has launched initiatives in relation to coastal zone management and marine sanctuaries but has yet to conclude a comprehensive oceans governance regime.

INTERNATIONAL ISSUES: THE LAW OF THE SEA

The USA has also lagged behind other states in relation to its ratification of the Law of the Sea Convention (LOSC), despite its active involvement in the third United Nations Conference on the Law of the Sea (UNCLOS III in 1972–82 – see Chapter 2). The USA's participation occurred despite ambivalence towards the attempts to establish UNCLOS III, and concluded with hostility to specific seabed mining provisions within the LOSC.

The concern over seabed mining and perceived constraints on the operation of the US Navy and its maritime interests contributed to the failure to ratify by the Reagan and Bush (Snr) administrations, although the USA did, under President Reagan, proclaim a 200 mile exclusive economic zone (EEZ) in March 1983. Despite more positive views by the Clinton administration – reinforced by the passage of the 1994 implementing agreement (the 'Boat Paper') discussed in Chapter 2, and more recently by active support from President George W. Bush – the USA has yet to ratify the LOSC.

Figure 7.1 United States of America – maritime jurisdiction

The USA's interests in maintaining freedom of navigation and passage for its merchant and more specifically its naval fleet has meant that despite its reluctance to ratify the LOSC the USA acts assertively to challenge coastal states' actions in relation to claims made under the LOSC. The USA also expressed concern and suspicion over the aims of debates at the United Nations in the late 1960s (Wenk 1972). As noted in Chapter 2, Ambassador Pardo's advocacy that the world's sea and oceans be designated as the common heritage of mankind, delivered in the wake of increasingly visible problems of ocean pollution after the *Torrey Canyon* disaster, was of direct concern to senior US officials.

Opposition to the LOSC from within the United States Senate was significant and held up attempts for ratification under the Clinton and George W. Bush administrations, despite support for this action from the respective administrations. Attempts from within the Senate, including the powerful Foreign Relations Committee, to gain a 'floor vote' on the matter in the 108th Congress failed in October 2003. A further attempt within the Senate was made in September 2007, buttressed by strong statements in support of such actions by President Bush in May 2007, where President Bush 'urged the Senate to act favorably on US accession to the United Nations Convention on the Law of the Sea during this session of Congress' (Bush, 2007). This statement noted that 'joining will serve the national security interests of the United States' (ibid.), directly countering the main focus on opposition within the Senate. The case for ratification was strongly supported by the work of the Joint Ocean Commission Initiative (see below).

Despite its reluctance to ratify the LOSC, the US can be seen to have been particularly influential in actions to codify the law of the sea in the second half of the twentieth century. President Truman's Presidential Proclamation No. 2667 of 28 September, 1945 *Policy of the United States with Respect to the Natural Resources of the Subsoil and Sea Bed of the Continental Shelf*, the 'Truman Proclamation', *inter alia*, noted:

Having concern for the urgency of conserving and prudently utilizing its natural resources, the Government of the United States regards the natural resources of the subsoil and sea bed of the continental shelf beneath the high seas but contiguous to the coasts of the United States as appertaining to the United States, subject to its jurisdiction and control. In cases where the continental shelf extends to the shores of another State, or is shared with an adjacent State, the boundary shall be determined by the United States and the State concerned in accordance with equitable principles. The character as high seas of the waters above the continental shelf and the right to their free and unimpeded navigation are in no way thus affected. (Presidential Proclamation No. 2667 of 28 September 1945).

This proclamation, and similar actions in subsequent years by other states, including Australia, led to the establishment of the first United Nations Conference on the Law of the Sea (UNCLOS I), as discussed in Chapter 2. The US action in asserting jurisdiction over its continental shelf may have indicated a broadening of interest in understanding this new frontier. Edward Wenk, who was later to play a major role in shaping US oceans law and policy, noted however that 'through the 1950s exploration of the sea was a feeble, delicate, loosely knit enterprise' (Wenk 1972, p. 38). Increased interest and growth in scientific disciplines such as oceanography and the establishment of institutions such as the Scripps Institution of Oceanography at the University of California, San Diego, the Woods Hole Oceanographic Institute at Cape Cod and Columbia University's Lamont Geological Observatory, were to play important roles in US ocean science in the coming decades.

One argument for an increased impetus in US attention toward the ocean was driven by concern over the rise of the Soviet Union's technological capabilities, as epitomised by 'the issues of Sputnik and the science–math gap' (Knecht et al. 1998, p. 1). The decision by the Soviet Union (USSR) to participate in the International Geophysical Year (IGY), beginning in 1957 (Walton 1987, p. 32) posed a challenge for the USA. The IGY developed from an initiative of the International Council of Scientific Unions (ICSU) that established the Comité Spéciale de l'Année Géophysique Internationale (CSAGI) to coordinate programming and participation. The Antarctic, by virtue of the paucity of existing scientific information, was singled out for special treatment, as was outer space. In 1955 the Soviet Union registered its intention to participate in the Antarctic programmes of the IGY and then, in 1957, launched its first *Sputnik* spacecraft (Quigg 1983, p. 47). The launching of *Sputnik* saw a rapid energising of US science towards outer space, and the establishment of the National Aeronautical and Space Administration (NASA), and while US advocates pushed for a similar focus on marine science it was not until the following decade that a new era in oceans affairs was ushered in, as Wenk describes, 'impelled more by logic than crisis' (Wenk 1972, p. 5).

DOMESTIC INTERESTS AND THE CONFLICT OVER JURISDICTION: 'THE EBB AND FLOW OF SEASHORE FEDERALISM'

As indicated, US oceans governance has been influenced by both conflict and collaboration between the federal and state governments. The term 'ebb and flow of seashore federalism' is taken from Weller's evocative, and accurate, description of similar struggles over jurisdiction in Australia (Weller 1989, p. 293). We have noted (in Chapter 4) that these struggles in Australia were markedly similar to those undertaken in the United States, allowing for obvious differences surrounding the use of the presidential veto in the US political system. The conflict over offshore oil and gas development centred first on issues of jurisdiction, similar issues that were also to be faces in Australia and Canada. The 'tidelands' and 'outer continental shelf' disputes related to proposals to develop offshore oil and gas resources in the Gulf of Mexico and later similar proposals off the coast of California. Initially conflict centred on the question of sharing oil and gas revenues, but later, after the Santa Barbara oil spill, conflict occurred over the question of environmental protection and control.

The 'tidelands' dispute first surfaced in the late 1930s when the federal government questioned state ownership of what was termed 'submerged lands'. After tortuous congressional wrangling, including vetoes by President Truman on bills attempting to return ownership to the states in 1946 and 1952 (see Barker 1962, p. 350), these disputes went to the United States Supreme Court in 1947 (*United States* v *California*) and 1960 (*United States* v *Louisiana, Alabama, Mississippi, Texas and Florida*).

President Eisenhower, elected in 1952, had campaigned in support of the states and in 1953 signed the Submerged Lands Act into law (Barker 1962, pp. 350–51). This Act provided for state jurisdiction within 'their historic boundaries ... that were defined as extending three miles [offshore], except the Act recognized that in certain circumstances states bordering the Gulf of Mexico may lay claim to more than three miles but not exceeding ten and one-half miles' (Barker 1962, p. 351). The legal picture was clarified when, as Barker noted:

> Concurrent with the Submerged Lands Act and as a corollary to it, Congress enacted the Outer Continental Shelf Lands Act. This law provided for federal jurisdiction and control of lands and resources seaward of state boundaries and extending to the edge of the continental shelf. (Barker 1962, p. 351)

Warren Christopher, writing in 1953, called the Outer Continental Shelf Lands Act an 'epochal statute', commenting that the 'mineral resources and food potential of this area have been said to make the acquisition more important than the Louisiana Purchase' (Christopher 1953, p. 23). Christopher, later to become Secretary of State in the Carter Administration during the deliberations at UNCLOS III, believed that the act provided a unique combination of US law and addressed an emerging issue in international law (Christopher 1953, p. 23). The question of offshore development, particularly off the California coast, has continued to be a major issue, with proposals for offshore oil and gas projects restricted on environmental grounds, and recent court cases that limited the use of sonar by the US Navy on the grounds of its effects on cetaceans.

While the early phases of US oceans governance were punctuated by ongoing conflict between the states and Washington, it is also important to recognise the significant initiatives that occurred in the late 1960s and 1970s. While the federal government continued to assert its interests offshore and, increasingly, in the coastal zone, this period saw improved collaboration between the federal and state governments. Collaboration developed through innovative programmes that provided federal funding for states to develop and implement plans for their coastal zones under the provisions of the Coastal Zone Management Act (CZMA) of 1972.

DEVELOPMENTS IN US OCEANS GOVERNANCE

This legislation and the administrative processes that it supported provided significant opportunities to address problems in the coastal zone and near shore areas. The CZMA was one of a number of actions that developed from a milestone federal government enquiry into oceans and coastal management in the US that began in 1966, and was to have far-reaching consequences for oceans governance in that country.

The enactment of the Marine Resources and Engineering Development Act in 1966 by the US Congress led to the establishment of the Commission on Marine Science, Engineering, and Resources. This commission, 'chaired by Julius Stratton and commonly termed the Stratton Commission, issued its influential report *Our Nation and the Sea* in January 1969' (Juda 2003, p. 165), has been described as a 'turning point' (Wenk 1972, p. 4) in US oceans governance.

While its outcomes were to be pivotal, the factors leading to what became wide-reaching concern with marine affairs contrasted markedly with those of a decade earlier with the USA's entry into the 'space race'. The security of the US was not 'menaced significantly by the maritime power of another, no underwater Sputnik triggered a frantic response ... and while the promise of sudden wealth was espoused by some enthusiasts it did not serve as a spur' (Wenk 1972, p. 5).

While the preceding decade had been marked, as noted above, by conflict between the President and Congress, and between the federal and state governments over the question(s) surrounding offshore jurisdiction, the Marine Resources and Engineering Development Act of 1966 overcame existing inertia by establishing 'a cabinet-level policy-planning council chaired by the Vice-President of the United States and a Presidentially appointed public advisory commission' (Wenk 1972, p. 5). Gaining President Johnson's support for this legislation, in the face of limited enthusiasm within government, 'with no supporters within the administration, and Navy, in particular, was very much opposed' (Knauss 1998, p. 10), and was regarded by many as a major achievement in its own right. The legislation was a compromise from within Congress, merging proposals developed in the Senate and House of Representatives. Senator Magnuson, a key proponent of the legislation, had a close friendship and working relationship with President Johnson. Magnuson and Johnson had worked together while the latter was in the Senate and Johnson was best man at Magnuson's wedding. This friendship was seen as particularly influential in ensuring passage of the Bill (see Wenk 1972; Knauss 1998, p. 10).

While its supporters, particularly Senator Magnuson, provided strong support within Congress, leadership from Vice-President Hubert Humphrey's emerging role as the 'nation's chief oceanographer' (Wenk 1972, p. 119) was significant. The support provided by the Cabinet committee (the National Council of Marine Resources and Engineering Development) again was important though the council itself was to be temporary (Hinkel 1998, p. 4). The Commission on Marine Sciences, Engineering and Resources (COMSER) was 'to guarantee continued high-level review of the ocean program' (Hinkel 1998, p. 4). While Vice-President Humphrey's personal commitment ensured that the issues of marine affairs achieved prominence, the appointment of Julius Stratton, former President of the Massachusetts Institute of Technology (MIT) and serving as Chairman of the Ford Foundation when appointed as chair of the COMSER by President Johnson (Hinkel 1998), provided strong leadership and a touch of 'genius' (Knauss 1998, p. 10).

This period also saw the development of the innovative Sea Grant Program, modelled on an earlier successful terrestrial programme (Land Grant) that provided funding for agricultural research and development, and supported funding for related educational programmes (Wenk 1972, pp. 92–3). The Sea Grant concept was introduced by Senator Claiborne Pell in a bill that 'would authorize establishment and operation of the Sea Grant colleges and programs, initiating and supporting programs of education, training, and research in the marine sciences and a program of advisory services relating to activities in the marine sciences' (Wenk 1972, pp. 92–3). This proposed legislation immediately attracted interest from a number of members of Congress (from both major parties), with that result, in Wenk's words that: 'for the first time more than a handful saw that their constituency had a stake in the Sea Grant outcome' (Wenk 1972, p. 93). After significant debate, including over the 'administrative home' for the Sea Grant Program, that saw a high level of bureaucratic manoeuvring and internal politics almost derail the concept, the Sea Grant Program was included as an amendment to the new Marine Resources and Engineering Development Act.

The inclusion of the Sea Grant Program in this legislation occurred as a result of opportunities provided by President Johnson's speech in July 1996, which in addition to 'emphasizing freedom of the seas' gave notice of his wish that that National Council of Marine Resources and Engineering Development should begin its work immediately (Wenk 1972, p. 94). The council then provided a vehicle for oversight of the Sea Grant Program, with funding managed through the National Science Foundation. The Sea Grant Program eventually passed through Congress, despite some differences between the House of Representatives and the Senate. The programme provides significant resources in a range of oceans-related research endeavours, including those in the social sciences. This research effort continued to provide the well-spring for ongoing discussion over oceans management and governance into the twenty-first century, 40 years after its initiation.

THE STRATTON COMMISSION

The Stratton Commission completed a report that 'was the product of a much broader examination of ocean activities than that suggested in the mandate establishing the Commission' (Juda 2003, p. 165) and, as a result, provided the foundation for significant legislative and policy initiatives by the USA into the 1970s. The Stratton Commission found that ocean and coastal management was fragmented both within federal and state governments, with overlapping departmental responsibilities leading to conflict, in short: 'there was believed to be neither rhyme nor reason in the manner is which responsibilities for ocean affairs had evolved' (Juda 2003 p. 165).

The 15-member Commission, appointed by President Johnson under the Marine Resources and Engineering Development Act, included nominees from federal and state governments, industry and universities (Hinkel 1998, p. 5). The initial number of support staff provided under the budget allocation was insufficient to cope with 'the scope and pace of the work'. Additional staff resources were gained by 'borrowing individuals from government agencies' (Hinkel 1998, p. 5). The Commission eventually had 35 staff, 'triple the initial allocation of the budget bureau' (Hinkel 1998, p. 5). The majority of the work of the Commission was undertaken by working panels, with the exception of 'the question of government reorganization which the Commission chose to approach as a committee of the whole'

(Hinkel 1998, p. 5). Seven panels of between two and four members were established, with Panels on:

- Basic Science;
- Environmental Monitoring and on Management and Development of the Coastal Zone;
- Manpower, Education and Training;
- Industry and Private Investment;
- Marine Engineering and Technology;
- Marine Resources; and the
- International Panel.

The Stratton Commission identified the traditional, sectoral-based approach to developing and managing ocean and coastal use as leading to the situation where issues 'were addressed in isolation, without reference to the ocean environment and its uses taken as a whole ... [with] such an approach obviat[ing] the possibility of long-term rational management' (Juda 2003, p. 165). While the Stratton Commission focused on management of uses, within what is now understandably seen as a traditional approach to governance, it did recognise the importance of what would later be seen as an integrated ecosystem approach (Juda 2003; see also Scheiber 1998). The Stratton Commission focused on the opportunities for administrative reform, and for new legislative and regulatory approaches to overcome what it perceived as limitations in current US ocean management.

The Stratton Commission Report, *Our Nation and the Sea* (COMSER 1969), made 120 recommendations that helped shape US oceans policy for the next three decades. While some recommendations – such as that regarding the establishment of a new federal agency for the oceans – were modified (see below), and other funding recommendations were ignored, Wenk comments: 'it is hard to measure [the] performance of the Stratton Commission because there has been no evaluation of responses to its ... recommendations' (Wenk 1998, p. 22).

The Stratton Commission recommended the establishment of a new federal independent agency, the National Oceans and Atmospheric Agency to 'provide a central and integrated focus for civilian, ocean-related programs' (Juda 2003, p. 166). Following release of the Stratton Commission Report *Our Nation and the Sea,* President Nixon established the National Oceans and Atmospheric Administration (NOAA) in 1970. NOAA was not established as an independent agency but placed within the Department of Commerce:

Although the creation of NOAA represented a significant step toward ocean policy centralization, it did not eliminate the reality that a number of civilian federal government departments and agencies still maintained important jurisdictional and programmatic responsibilities relating to ocean/coastal matters. (Juda 2003, p. 166)

DEVELOPMENTS IN THE 1970S – PROVIDING A PLATFORM FOR OCEANS GOVERNANCE

The early 1970s saw significant legislative and administrative development, spurred by the recommendations of the Stratton Commission, with its report *Our Nation and the Sea*, released as the newly elected President Nixon took office. The Nixon administration enacted a raft of important and keystone environmental instruments that provided new approaches to terrestrial and marine environmental management. This legislation included the National Environmental Policy Act taking effect 1 January 1970; the very significant and influential Coastal Zone Management Act in 1972; the Marine Mammal Protection Act in 1972; the Endangered Species Act in 1973; the Ocean Dumping Act in 1973; and the Fisheries Conservation and Management Act in 1977, taking effect 1 March 1977. The Endangered Species Act and the Ocean Dumping Act reinforced and supported international action in these respective areas, providing the vehicle for US ratification of, respectively, the Convention on the International Trade in Endangered Species of Wild Fauna and Flora (CITES), and the London Dumping Convention. The Fisheries Conservation and Management Act (FCMA) established a 200 nautical mile fishery conservation zone off the USA, with this zone later replaced by a 200 nautical mile exclusive economic zone.

Legislative developments in the early to mid-1970s provided innovative administrative and programmatic solutions to emerging issues and problems. The Coastal Zone Management Act (CZMA) provided a framework for 'the management of the nation's coastal resources, including the great lakes and balances economic development with environmental conservation' (OOCRM – NOAA 2007). There is detailed literature on the CZMA (see, for example, Cicin-Sain and Knecht 1998) and the national Coastal Zone Management Program that it established. The provision of funding to develop, implement and evaluate coastal management programmes has seen 34 such programmes established by state governments (OOCRM – NOAA 2007).

The CZMA's 'federal consistency' provision was an innovative and central element in encouraging: first, the take-up of the coastal zone programme by state governments; and second, although admittedly more arguably, the development of a collaborative intergovernmental regime. In short this mechanism ensured that federal government activities were to be 'consistent to the maximum extent possible with the enforceable policies of approved state management programs' (Beatley et al. 1994, p. 68). Much of the struggle over resources management in the 1980s centred on the use of the consistency provision by state governments to limit federal government actions in the coastal and offshore area. While Beatley et al. recorded that '[i]mplementation of the [consistency] doctrine has been generally successful', they also noted disputes over oil and gas exploration and development, dredge-spoil disposal and incineration activities (Beatley et al. 1994, p. 69).

The CZMA's objectives 'remain balanced to preserve, protect, develop and where possible, to restore or enhance the resources of the national coastal zone' (OOCRM – NOAA 2007). While its provisions and operations were challenged by the Reagan administration (see below) the CZMA has provided an innovative and strongly supported approach to management of the coastal zone. The CZMA has provided an important framework for development of programmes and practices to manage the coastal zone through a 'spatial and not a sectoral approach to management of the coastal zone, one in which uses are not to be considered in isolation but in relation to other uses and with consideration of their impacts on the broader environment' (Juda 2003, p. 166). As such it has provided a model that has been widely analysed and discussed, particularly as the emphasis of coastal management shifted toward improving integration between uses and users.

The call for integrated approaches to management of the coast, including addressing the problem of cumulative impacts, gained impetus in the 1980s and 1990s though the work of the World Commission on Environment and Development (WCED), also known as the Brundtland Commission, and its report *Our Common Future* (WCED 1990). This report encouraged development of more integrated approaches to coastal management. The development of the CZMA regime in the USA indicates, however, that translation of these objectives into feasible programmes is not a simple matter, as even if effective programmes are devised, implementation becomes a significant problem in itself (Davis and Haward, 1994).

The FCMA also provided a mechanism to link federal and state action through the establishment of Regional Fishery Management Councils. The regional councils are responsible for establishing plans for the management of fisheries and other species, as approved by the Secretary of Commerce (FWS 2007).

THE 1980s AND 1990s: SWINGS OF THE PENDULUM

The election of President Reagan saw the pendulum swing back on oceans policy, with a commitment to a reduced role for the federal government in programmes and expenditure, within what was termed 'New Federalism'. This led to a winding back of federal funding in a range of policy areas and concomitantly a retreat from federal funding of oceans initiatives. The CZMA regime was directly challenged by the Reagan administration, through its controversial attempt to open up offshore oil and gas leases that had been subject to a moratorium. This challenge was defeated through action in the Supreme Court and within the Congress, with this strong congressional support leading to the reauthorisation of the CZMA. These domestic offshore oil and gas controversies were paralleled at the international level with the Reagan Administration's concerns over the LOSC's provisions on deep-seabed mining, to the extent that the US did not sign the convention at its conclusion in December 1982. As noted above, issues associated with the ratification of the Law of the Sea Convention continued to dominate discussion of US oceans policy for the next two-and-a-half decades. The proclamation of a 12 mile territorial sea in 1988 again raised issues of jurisdiction between federal and state governments (Koester 1990, p. 196). Koester commented that the

> only way to forestall this new round in the continuing Seaweed Rebellion is to create a management system that provides sufficient incentives to virtually compel cooperation between the states and federal government. (Koester 1990, p. 207)

This issue, that had focused much of the work of the Stratton Commission in the mid-1960s, was to remain central in discussion on US oceans policy in the first decade of the new century.

Knecht et al. characterised the Reagan era as one where 'the ocean policy window closes'. Drawing on the work of United States academic John Kingdon, they use his insight that policy is determined by interaction between three different 'streams' – the problem, the politics and the policy stream to analyse challenges to the development of a US national ocean policy in the 1980s, and possible opportunities in the next decade (Knecht et al.1988, pp. 113–14). The presence of key policy actors to take advantage of opportunities in the policy process to advance proposals (individuals designated by Kingdon as 'policy entrepreneurs') was important, as was the emergence of opportunities – 'policy windows' – that occurs when the three streams coalesce (see Kingdon 1984). Kingdon identified the importance of both regular events such as elections and budget cycles, and the more random external events or 'accidents' which create 'windows of opportunity' for skilled policy entrepreneurs to shape and develop the policy agenda (Kingdon 1984).

Knecht, et al. identify the importance of strong national government leadership in USA oceans policy efforts in the preceding 20 years, and the allocation of programme funding by the Nixon, Ford and Carter administrations to ensure that problems that had been identified by the Stratton Commission were addressed (Knecht et al. 1988, p. 121). The role of policy entrepreneurs in taking advantage of a number of policy windows can be seen in the development and outcomes from the Stratton Commission. The Reagan administration's cutting back of government expenditure was part of a broad 'drastic shrinking of governmental programs, activities and regulations the implementation of tax cuts and rigorous budgetary control exercised by the Office of Management and Budget (OMB)'. Knecht et al. note that 'ocean and coastal programs were targeted for heavy hits by the [Office of Management and Budget] OMB' (Knecht et al. 1988, p. 121).

Despite congressional attempts to establish a new oceans commission in the late 1980s, and arguments for action from within the academic community (see Belsky 1989), the next policy window took some time to open fully, with both internal and external events in the late 1990s building on a groundswell of support for action, leading to serious discussion on US national oceans policy. Knecht et al. noted and recognised the need for well-developed policy proposals to take advantage of the next 'window of opportunity' (Knecht et al. 1988, p. 137) including the 'need for explicit national oceans goals and priorities' (ibid., p. 136).

In the early 1990s interest in reviving discussion on US oceans policy saw the formation of the Ocean Governance Study Group (OGSG). The OGSG 'was created in 1991 to re-examine the status of ocean governance in the United States and to develop management options for achieving responsible stewardship of our oceans and coasts' (Knecht et al. 1998, p. 81). The OGSG comprised 31 'ocean policy experts' from US universities, led by an eight-person steering committee with two members each from the University of Delaware, the University of California at Berkeley, the University of Hawaii and the University of Massachusetts. The OGSG included international advisers from the United Kingdom, Sweden, Australia, Italy and Peru. 'The work of the Ocean Governance Study Group has been primarily supported by the Sea Grant Programs of California, Delaware, Florida, Hawaii, Louisiana, Maine, Massachusetts, Mississippi-Alabama, North Carolina, Oregon, Rhode Island, Texas, and Washington' (University of Delaware 2007).

The OGSG continued to promote debate on US oceans governance through a range of publications and conferences (Lowry 1994; Scheiber 1999), taking part in a series of activities during the 1998 International Year of the Ocean. This involved the study group partnering other research institutions and government agencies in a number of influential forums, including an important workshop on lessons that could be learned from the work and outcomes of the Stratton Commission (see below). An early publication outlined the OGSG's 'basic premise ... that national ocean management requires a new vision; a vision that focuses on the oceans as a whole and not merely as discrete sectors' (Lowry 1994, p. 2). Lowry states further that:

> The emphasis of the Study Group is on governance – the collective array of strategies, policies and practices of national, state and local governments, non-governmental organizations, and the private sector to guide the use of the ocean and coastal resources and space under national jurisdiction, to the edge of the 200-mile Exclusive Economic Zone. (Lowry 1994, p. 2)

The International Year of the Ocean encouraged the National Oceans and Atmospheric Administration (NOAA) to initiate a 'National Dialogue' on US oceans policy. This dialogue was supported by NOAA releasing Year of the Ocean discussion papers. In February 1998 the Federal Ocean Agencies Report provided a review of current practice. The H. John Heinz Center for Science, Economics and the Environment released its report *Our Ocean Future* in May 1998 (Heinz Center 1998). The Heinz Center, established in December 1995, is 'dedicated to improving the scientific and economic foundation for environmental policy' (Heinz Center 2008), and has developed an action agenda for coasts and oceans.

One of the most interesting elements of the national dialogue on oceans policy in 1998 was the convening of what was titled the 'Stratton Roundtable'. The Stratton Roundtable was a seminar with a sub-title Looking Back, Looking Forward: Lessons from the 1969 Commission on Marine Science Engineering and Resources, sponsored by the Centre for the Study of Marine Policy at the University of Delaware, NOAA, and the Ocean Governance Study Group, held in Washington on 1 May 1998. This seminar focused, *inter alia*, on lessons that could be drawn from the Stratton Commission, and included presentations by key personnel involved in the establishment and/or operation of the Stratton Commission: Ed Wenk, John Knauss and Samuel Lawrence.

The appraisal of the achievements of the Stratton Commission provided useful 'lessons' for attempts to re-energise debate on US oceans policy. The combination of timing, leadership and luck were highlighted as critical elements by key Stratton Commission alumni. Concern with the need to boost science in the wake of the USSR's achievements meant that the Commission 'rode a wave of enthusiasm for support for science generated by Sputnik and a true awakening of interest in ocean matters by a group of dedicated members of both the House and Senate' (Knauss 1998).

The involvement and engagement of the Executive Branch was seen as crucial by Wenk, Knauss and Lawrence who all commented on President Johnson's and Vice-President Humphrey's active involvement in oceans issues through, for example, the State of the Union Address. Vice-President Humphrey's personal commitment to ocean issues was unprecedented. This commitment from the Executive Branch was matched, as noted above, by leadership from members of the Congress in supporting the Stratton Commission. Stratton's leadership style, too, was seen by Knauss and Wenk as the singular contribution to the success of the work of the Commission. A further lesson was provided by Lawrence who focused on the important role of the chair and commission members and staffers in energising government. As Samuel Lawrence recorded, 'documents do not decide things, people do' (Lawrence 1998, p. 27).

These lessons from the Stratton Commission resonate with the analysis of oceans policy provided a decade earlier by Knecht et al. The International Year of the Ocean provided an opportunity to reconsider US oceans policy, with Executive Branch support, congressional action and increasing public concern over the oceans providing strong support for action. The work in the mid-to-late 1990s highlighted similar problems to those that confronted the Stratton Commission in the 1960s. Oceans management in the 1990s was affected by similar problems of overlapping and conflicting agency responsibilities, a growing bureaucracy and increasing regulatory environment. As one observer pointed noted: 'the Stratton Commission spawned many children which are now in need of spiritual guidance' (Froelich 2002).

President Clinton and Vice-President Gore attended the National Oceans Conference held in June 1998. President Clinton noted that:

> through innovation and prudence we've proved that we can clean the water, the air, protect marine sanctuaries and wildlife refuges, phase out deadly pesticides and ozone eating chemicals, and do it while still producing he world's strongest, most competitive economy ... With partnerships and persistence ... we must extend this record of success to our oceans. If we want our children to inherit the gift of living oceans we must make the 21st century a great century of stewardship of our seas. (NOAA 1998, p. 1)

Key states within the USA were also active in developing coastal and oceans policies. Hersham identified Alaska, California, Florida, Hawaii, Maine, Massachusetts, Mississippi, North Carolina, Oregon and Washington as 'activist states' (Hershman 1996, p. 31). These states had developed innovated programmes, had improved capacity for ocean management and had defined a greater role for themselves in national decision-making concerning ocean resources (Hershman 1996, pp. 28–9). The Western Governors Association was an important mechanism by which West Coast states continued to work together on coastal matters (see Juda 2003).

The late 1990s saw increased US public concern over the oceans and coasts, with this concern matched by congressional action, with legislation introduced into the 105th Congress that sought 'to undertake a process similar to the comprehensive review of ocean and coastal policy conducted by the Stratton Commission in the late 1960s' (Buck 1998, p. 1.) This legislation included S.1213 sponsored by Senator Hollings, which called for 'the development and implementation of a coherent, comprehensive and long-range national policy to explore, protect and use ocean and coastal resources' (US Senate Committee on Commerce, Science and Transportation 1997). S.1213 also provided for the establishment of an Oceans Commission. Related legislation was introduced into the House of Representatives (H.R.3445). S.1213 was subject to an amendment that addresses concerns over the appointment of members of the Oceans Commission. An amendment proposed by Senator McCain increased 'the size of the Commission to 16 members and provided for Presidential appointment of Commission members directly and from lists provided by the Congressional leadership' (US Senate Committee on Commerce, Science and Transportation 1997). This amendment was 'adopted by voice vote and the bill, as amended, was unanimously adopted by voice vote'. S.1213 was passed in the Senate on 13 November 1997, and the bill was sent to the House of Representatives on 27 January 1998. The House undertook committee review of the bill, but the proposed legislation lapsed at the ajournment of the 105th Congress in January 1999.

Senator Hollings reintroduced legislation in the 106th Congress, with S.2327 ('A bill to establish a Commission on Ocean Policy and for other purposes'). This bill, with minor amendment, passed the Senate with 'unanimous consent' on 26 June 2000, and was sent to the House of Representatives on the same day. The House Committee on Resources completed its review and on 25 July 2000 the bill was agreed to by voice vote in the House, and 'cleared for the White House' on the same day. President Clinton signed this bill into law as P.L. 106-256 on 7 August 2000.

THE NEW CENTURY – THE OCEAN COMMISSIONS

In response the first years of the new century saw concerted investigations into the current state of US oceans policy, management arrangements and problems. Two Commissions of Inquiry were established, the first mandated through the Oceans Act of 2000 that took effect from 20 January 2001. This Act had been championed and sponsored by Senator Fritz Hollings (South Carolina) whose interests in oceans policy went back to the implementation of the Stratton Commission's work in 1969–70. The Oceans Act established a Commission on Ocean Policy 'to make recommendations to the U.S. government for a coordinated and comprehensive ocean policy' (*American Journal of International Law* 2004, p. 590). The second commission was established by the Pew Charitable Trust while the Ocean Act was making its way through Congress (Froelich 2002).

The Commission on Ocean Policy

The Commission on Ocean Policy had 16 members drawn from government, the military, academic and private sectors 'appointed by President in coordination with the majority and minority leaders of Congress' (*American Journal of International Law* 2004, p. 590). Retired US Navy Admiral James Watkins chaired the Commission (*American Journal of International Law* 2004; Juda 2003).

> Within 120 days of receipt of the final Commission report, the President is required to provide Congress with proposals to implement or respond to what is termed 'the Commission's recommendations for a coordinated, comprehensive, and long-range national policy for the responsible use and stewardship of ocean and coastal resources for the benefit of the United States'. (Juda 2003, p. 169)

The Commission on Ocean Policy released its preliminary report in April 2004 (see *American Journal of International Law* 2004, pp. 590–91). This report noted 'the need for solutions that transcend local and state political boundaries and emphasize the need to move towards an ecosystem-based management approach' (Watkins 2004). The preliminary report 'addressed 200 recommendations covering governance, science, education, fisheries, marine commerce and emerging offshore uses' (Watkins 2004). A key element identified by the Chair of the Commission was the 'imperative' for the United States to ratify the Law of the Sea Convention, and noted that this action had already gained support of the Bush administration.

The Commission on Ocean Policy's final report, *An Ocean Blueprint for the 21st Century*, was submitted to President Bush on 20 September 2004.

The Commission prefaced its work by the comment that: 'America is a nation intrinsically connected to and immensely reliant on the ocean' (Commission on Ocean Policy 2004, p. 1). The Commission noted the values of the ocean and coast to the American peoples and recognised that there was 'trouble in paradise'. To overcome these 'troubles' the Commission on Ocean Policy 'recommended moving to an ecosystem-based management approach by focusing on three cross-cutting themes'. These themes were:

1. a new, coordinated national oceans policy framework to improve decision-making;
2. cutting-edge ocean science and data translated into high quality information for managers; and
3. life-long oceans-related education to create well-informed citizens with a strong stewardship ethic (Commission on Ocean Policy 2004, p. 5).

These themes were supported by a set of 'overarching principles' to guide national ocean policy. These principles were:

- sustainability;
- stewardship;
- ocean–land–atmosphere connections;
- ecosystem-based management;
- multiple use management;
- preservation of marine biodiversity;
- best available sciences and information;
- adaptive management;
- understandable laws and clear decisions;
- participatory governance;
- timeliness;
- accountability; and
- international responsibility (Commission on Oceans Policy 2004, p. 6).

In an echo of the Stratton Commission, the Commission on Ocean Policy identified the fragmented and uncoordinated nature of current policy and decision-making. It recommended the creation of a 'National Ocean Council within the Executive Office of the President – chaired by an assistant to the President – and composed of cabinet secretaries of departments and administrators of independent agencies with relevant ocean- and coastal-related responsibilities' (Commission on Oceans Policy 2004, p. 7).

On 17 December 2004, as required under its enabling legislation, President Bush provided his response to the Commission on Ocean Policy's work. President Bush launched the Ocean Action Plan as a vehicle to redirect efforts toward the oceans. The President signed an Executive Order establishing a Committee on Ocean Policy and released the US Ocean Action Plan. In addition to the creation of the Committee on Ocean Policy, the President

> directs the Executive Branch agencies to facilitate, as appropriate, coordination and consultation regarding ocean-related matters among Federal, State, Tribal, Local Governments, the private sector, foreign governments and international organizations. (Ocean Action Plan 2004, p. 4)

The Committee on Ocean Policy (COP) was given responsibility:

> to coordinate the activities of executive branch departments and agencies regarding ocean-related matters in an integrated and effective manner to advance the environmental and economic interests of present and future generations of Americans. The Chairman of the Council on Environmental Quality (CEQ), James L. Connaughton, also serves as Chairman of this Committee. (Council on Environmental Quality 2007a)

The COP was a high-level body, with its membership drawn from key departments and agencies. It included the Secretaries of State, Defense, the Interior, Agriculture, Health and Human Services, Commerce, Labor, Transportation, Energy, Homeland Security and the Attorney General:

> Other members of the Committee include the Administrator of the Environmental Protection Agency, the Director of the Office of Management and Budget, the Administrator of the National Aeronautics and Space Administration, the Director of National Intelligence, the Director of the Office of Science and Technology Policy, the Director of the National Science Foundation, and the Chairman, Joint Chiefs of Staff; and the Assistants to the President for National Security Affairs, Homeland Security, Domestic Policy, Economic Policy, and an employee of the Office of the Vice President. (Council on Environmental Quality 2007b).

The COP membership provided opportunities for input across relevant agencies but its size and complexity raise questions over the ability of such bodies to effectively provide effective advice in terms of coordinating policy across government. The US Ocean Action Plan provided 88 actions and a set of principles to guide those actions, centred on the following areas:

- enhancing ocean leadership and coordination;
- advancing our understanding of oceans, coasts and the Great Lakes;

- enhancing the use and conservation of ocean, coastal and Great Lakes resources;
- managing coasts and their watersheds;
- supporting maritime transportation; and
- advancing international oceans science and policy (Committee on Oceans Policy 2007, p. 1)

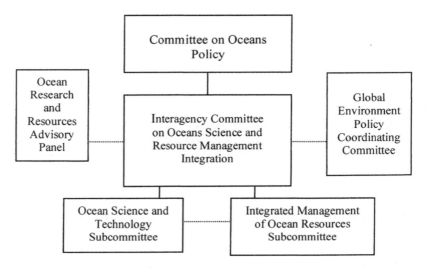

Source: Council on Environmental Quality (2007b).

Figure 7.2 Coordinating oceans governance structure – United States of America

In a similar approach to that adopted in Australia with the release of the *Australia's Ocean Policy: Specific Sectoral Measures* document (see Chapter 4), many of the recommendations contained within the Ocean Action Plan 'are summaries of existing programs or past initiatives ... however the *Plan* does support the codification of NOAA' (Gove 2005, pp. 35–6).

The Ocean Action Plan 'highlights' were:

- establish a new Cabinet-level Committee on Oceans Policy;
- promote greater use of market-based systems in fisheries management;

- build a Global Earth Observation Network, including an Integrated Oceans Observation system;
- develop an Oceans Research Priorities Plan and Implementation Strategy;
- support accession to the United Nations Convention on the Law of the Sea;
- implement Coral Reef Local Action Strategies;
- support a regional partnership in the Gulf of Mexico;
- seek passage of the NOAA Organic Act establishing NOAA within the Department of Commerce: and
- implement the Administration's National Freight Action Agenda (Ocean Action Plan 2004).

The Ocean Action Plan was assessed by the Commission on Ocean Policy as a 'promising first step towards implementation of a comprehensive ocean policy' (Commission on Ocean Policy 2004). The US Commission on Ocean Policy 'expired' on 19 December 2004 as provided within the provisions of the Oceans Act 2000. President Bush was to note two-and-a-half years later that following 'the release of my Ocean Action Plan in 2004, my Administration has made great strides in ocean conservation by working with State, tribal, and local governments, the private sector, and our international partners in the spirit of cooperative conservation' (Bush 2007).

The Pew Oceans Commission

The Pew Oceans Commission had a 'focus on improving oceans stewardship through recommendations that sustain marine life' (Froelich 2002). Leon Panetta, a former White House Chief of Staff to President Clinton, chaired the 18-member Pew Oceans Commission, with Commission members drawn from the fishing industry, science, business and philanthropic organisations. Panetta had previously served eight terms in the US Congress, representing a California district, and had long-standing interests in coastal and marine issues. The Pew Oceans Commission's mission was 'to identify policies and practices necessary to restore and protect living marine resources in US waters and the ocean and coastal habitats on which they depend' (Pew Oceans Commission 2003, p. ix).

The Pew Oceans Commission was organised into four committees investigating core issues of:

- governance;
- fishing;
- pollution; and

- coastal development.

In addition the Commission investigated marine aquaculture, invasive species, ocean zoning, climate change, science and education (Pew Oceans Commission 2003, p. ix). This work was facilitated by input from scientists in determining 'priority issues' and 'summarizing the best available scientific information available on those subjects' (Pew Oceans Commission 2003, p. ix). The Pew Oceans Commission also undertook a 'national dialogue on oceans issues', including 15 regional meetings around the US coast, including Hawaii and Alaska, and 12 focus groups with fishermen including a meeting in Alaska.

The Pew Oceans Commission report, *America's Living Oceans: Charting A Course for Sea Change*, was released in May 2003. The report's Executive Summary began with the words: 'America's oceans are in crisis and the stakes could not be higher' (Pew Oceans Commission 2003, p. v). Despite identifying 'expressions of hope and signs of success' in the 'midst of crisis' the report argued for a new course in oceans management to ensure that these 'proven workable solutions' become more than 'exceptions' (Pew Oceans Commission 2003, p. v). The Pew Oceans Commission's 'fundamental conclusion' was:

> that this nation needs to ensure healthy, productive and resilient marine ecosystems for present and future generations. In the long term, economic sustainability depends on ecological sustainability. (Pew Oceans Commission 2003, p. x)

The Commission identified five priority objectives:

1. declare a principled, unified national ocean policy based on protecting ecosystem health and requiring sustainable use of ocean resources;
2. encourage comprehensive and coordinated governance of ocean resources and uses at scales appropriate to the problem to be solved;
3. restructure fisheries management institutions and reorient fisheries policy to protect and sustain the ecosystems on which our fisheries depend:
4. protect important habitats and manage coastal development to minimise habitat damage and water quality impairment; and
5. control sources and pollution, particularly nutrients, that are harming marine ecosystems (Pew Oceans Commission 2003, x).

The report elaborated a series of actions to address these objectives, centred on the following areas:

- 'Governance for Sustainable Seas';
- 'Restoring America's Fisheries';
- 'Preserving Our Coasts';
- 'Cleaning Coastal Waters';
- 'Guiding Sustainable Marine Aquaculture'; and
- 'Science, Education, and Funding'.

The brief survey of the content and recommendations of the two commission reports in the preceding discussion reinforces the comment that they had 'identified remarkably similar core priorities and made complementary recommendations in a number of key areas' (Joint Ocean Commission Initiative 2005).

The Aftermath – the Joint Ocean Commission Initiative

From late 2004 into early 2005 members of both commissions worked to develop a 'collaborative effort to catalyze ocean policy reform' (Joint Ocean Commission Initiative 2005), leading to what was termed the *Joint Ocean Commission Initiative*. The Joint Commission is made up of ten members – five from the Commission on Ocean Policy and five from the Pew Oceans Commission. Admiral Watkins and Leon Panetta provide co-chairs for the initiative. The Joint Ocean Commission Initiative's 'primary goal is to accelerate the pace of change that results in meaningful ocean policy reform' (Joint Ocean Commission Initiative 2005).

To this end the Joint Ocean Commission Initiative has developed and released its *US Ocean Policy Report Cards* for 2004–05 and 2006 (Joint Ocean Commission Initiative 2006a, 2007). The report cards were reinforced by a request on 16 March 2006 from the US Senate to provide a report that answered three key questions to help guide the Senate's ongoing work on oceans policy (Joint Ocean Commission Initiative 2006b). These questions were:

1. 'What are the top 10 actions Congress should take to implement the recommendation made by the US Commission on Ocean Policy and the Pew Oceans Commission?'
2. 'What are the highest priorities for funding needed to support the development and implementation of ocean policies that are consistent with the recommendations of the US Commission on Ocean Policy and the Pew Oceans Commission?'
3. 'What are the priority changes to law and the federal budgeting process needed to establish a more effective and integrated ocean and coastal governance approach?'

The Joint Ocean Commission Initiative reported to the Senate in June 2006. This report, *From Sea to Shining Sea* (Joint Ocean Commission Initiative 2006b) is a detailed and frank assessment of the challenges facing the US in developing and implementing oceans policy recommendation. The Joint Ocean Commission Initiative addressed the Senate's question on the 'top ten actions' for Congress by recommending the following:

1. Adopt a statement of national oceans policy.
2. Establish the National Oceanic and Atmospheric Administration (NOAA) in law and work with the administration to identify and act upon opportunities to improve federal agency coordination on oceans and coastal issues.
3. Foster ecosystem-based regional governance.
4. Reauthorise an improved Magnuson–Stevens Fishery Conservation and Management Act.
5. Enact legislation to support innovation and competition in oceans-related research and education consistent with key initiatives in the Bush administration's Oceans Research Priorities Plan and Implementation Strategy.
6. Enact legislation to authorise and fund the Integrated Ocean Observing System (IOOS).
7. Accede to the United Nations Convention on the Law of the Sea.
8. Establish an Oceans Trust Fund in the US Treasury as a dedicated source of funds for improved management and understanding of oceans and coastal resources by federal and state governments.
9. Increase base funding for core ocean and coastal programmes and direct development of an integrated oceans budget.
10. Enact ocean and coastal legislation that has already progressed significantly in the 109th Congress (Joint Ocean Commission Initiative 2006b, pp. 8–10).

In relation to the Senate's second question – 'What are the highest priorities for funding needed to support the development and implementation of oceans policies that are consistent with the recommendations of the US Commission on Oceans Policy and the Pew Ocean Commission?' – the Joint Ocean Commission Initiative noted that several of the ten priorities identified would not need additional funding. In relation to ecosystem-based regional governance the Joint Commission identified an additional $41 million needed to implement this action, and $429 million to support the reauthorisation of an improved Magnuson–Stevens Fishery Conservation and Management Act. The Joint Commission endorsed the recommendation of the US Commission on Ocean Policy for $138 million to fund the Integrated Ocean Observing System (IOOS). Accession to the Law of the Sea Convention would require $3 million for US contributions to specialist institutions established by the convention. The Joint Commission recommended an addition $536 million in new funding for additional activities to support implementation of a new national Oceans Policy, meaning a total funding commitment of $747 million over 2006 levels to address the need for increased base funding for core ocean and coastal programmes and direct development of an integrated oceans budget (Joint Ocean Commission Initiative 2006b, pp. 10–12).

In response to the Senate's third question – 'What are the priority changes to law and the federal budgeting process needed to establish a more effective and integrated oceans and coastal governance approach?' – the Joint Ocean Commission Initiative report noted 'the lack of coordination, coherence and focus' in the nation's oceans governance system (Joint Ocean Commission Initiative 2006b, p. 12). It encouraged Congress and the Administration to address issues related to national oceans governance reform, regional and state oceans governance reform, fisheries management reform, and to increase focus on research, science and education, emphasise the US role in international leadership on oceans, and address the need for new funding for oceans policy and programmes (Joint Ocean Commission Initiative 2006b, p. 12).

Ongoing evaluation of progress towards implementation of the Ocean Action Plan is enhanced by the publication of the *US Ocean Action Plan Implementation Update* by the Committee on Ocean Policy (Committee on Oceans Policy 2007). The Committee reported progress on the identified actions within the Action Plan and identified new actions and priorities and activities.

The Chair of the Committee on Oceans Policy, James L. Connaughton, noted that commitments for 73 of the 88 actions had been met, and that the four larger multi-action items had 'nearly met' their commitments. Of the remaining 11 items, 'the schedule for one has been adjusted while the remaining 10 items are proceeding on schedule' (Committee on Ocean Policy 2007, p.1).

PRESIDENTIAL ACTIONS: OCEAN POLICY INITIATIVES

The three years following the conclusion of the Commission on Ocean Policy lifted oceans governance higher on the political agenda, with initiatives and actions from the Executive Branch, and action within Congress matching efforts in the halcyon period of the late 1960s and early

1970s following the Stratton Commission's work. It is of course to soon to evaluate the impact of these latter initiatives, or to make definite judgement on the effectiveness of this work, but President George W. Bush has placed oceans issues high on the domestic agenda, and built on the foundation established in the latter period of the Clinton administration.

A number of important actions took place in mid-2006. President Bush declared 4–10 June 2006 to be National Oceans Week. The President 'called on the people of the United States to learn more about the vital role the oceans play in the life of our country and how they can conserve their many natural treasures' (Council on Environmental Quality 2007b). In the same month, on 15 June 2006, President George Bush signed a Proclamation establishing the Northwestern Hawaiian Islands Marine National Monument:

> to celebrate the area's natural, cultural, and historical importance. The tropical waters of the Papahânaumokuâkea Marine National Monument are a sanctuary for 7000 marine species. This important Monument is our Nation's largest single conservation area and the largest protected marine area in the world. (Bush 2007)

President Bush also took action on fisheries, noting that he was 'proud to sign into law' the Magnuson–Stevens Fishery Conservation and Management Reauthorization Act 2006. This Act was the latest reauthorisation of a key part of the oceans governance framework from the 1970s. The Magnuson–Stevens Fishery Conservation and Management legislation had governed USA fisheries policy and influenced oceans resource management for three decades. The 2006 reauthorisation was fine-tuned to address contemporary problems identified in both the Commission on Oceans Policy and Pew Oceans Commission reports, and at the same time introduce new tools to the task: 'to end over-fishing and rebuild our Nation's fish stocks through more effective, market-based management' (Bush 2007).

President Bush also proclaimed June 2007 as National Oceans Month of the United States of America. In his proclamation on 30 May 2007 the President noted specific achievements:

> Internationally, we continue to lead in protecting the maritime environment while preserving the navigational freedoms essential to the security and prosperity of every nation. By working to build a well-managed system of offshore aquaculture, we can provide a healthy source of food and reduce pressure on our ocean ecosystems. (Bush 2007)

President Bush commented that:

> During National Oceans Month and throughout the year, we recognize all who are dedicated to making our oceans, coasts, and Great Lakes cleaner, healthier, and

more productive, including the many Federal agencies that make up the Committee on Ocean Policy. One of these agencies, the National Oceanic and Atmospheric Administration, celebrates two centuries of dedicated research and conservation of coastal and marine environments. By continuing to work together, we can conserve and enjoy the splendor of these magnificent waters now and for generations to come. (Bush 2007)

CONCLUSION

The United States has provided important innovations that have help shaped both the international and domestic oceans governance agenda. These innovations – the use of commissions of enquiry, administrative change and reform directed towards improved oceans policy-making, innovative legal mechanisms and financial assistance and engagement of stakeholders – provide examples of the range of instruments and tools available for governance of the oceans and coastal zone. The United States experience also emphasises the importance of political commitment and the work of 'policy champions' including the President and/or Vice-President, members of Congress and policy advocates within and outside the bureaucracy (Knauss 1998; Wenk 1998).

Members of Congress such as Senator Fritz Hollings, for example, provided long-standing support for oceans policy initiatives. Hollings's first input was in the late 1960s in relation to the implementation of recommendations from the Stratton Commission (Knauss 1998). He also sponsored the Oceans Act in 2000 (Froelich 2002). In noting the importance of Executive Branch engagement, Edward Wenk (a major figure in the development of United States' oceans policy in the 1960s and 1970s) records: 'if there is any single individual who helped elevate the strength and visibility of marine affairs it is Vice President Humphrey' (Wenk 1998, p. 18).

The long march to a US Oceans Policy indicates the complexities of policy development in federal systems, and the influential nexus between international and domestic policy. This latter point is emphasised through the difficulties in gaining support for ratification of the Law of the Sea Convention from within the US Senate, despite widespread support from the Executive Branch and within Congress. At the same time the US has, through the work of the oceans commissions, provided the basis for the development of a comprehensive national Oceans Policy. It remains to be seen whether these initiatives continue to develop and prove to be a worthy successor to the innovative Stratton Commission, and provide the foundation for US oceans governance in the twenty-first century.

Conclusion

This book has outlined the major developments in oceans governance in the three decades from the 1980s. We have noted that the period from 1992 to the present has seen increasing attention to institutional arrangements and policy outcomes affecting the governance of the world's seas and oceans. In examining these developments at international, regional and national scales, we have seen governance as focusing on four elements:

- setting priorities;
- coherence, consistency and coordination in policy development;
- application of policy instruments and an implementation strategy; and
- ensuring effective accountability for and evaluation of policy.

At the same time we have identified the important relationship between international and regional initiatives and national policy, recognising that this relationship is often two-way, and the influence of policy learning and transfer as means by which the 'oceans agenda' has been broadened. We have also identified the link between policy development and institutional capacity. This draws attention to tools, instruments and approaches underpinning effective and efficient institutional arrangements necessary to ensure implementation. Many of these instruments incorporate principles such as sustainable development, reflecting the pervasive influence of the post-United Nations Conference on Environment and Development (UNCED) agenda as well as reflecting a broader government reform agenda that saw government moving more to incorporate market and/or collaborative-oriented forms of governance to supplement, extend or replace traditional state-directed regulatory arrangements.

We have noted, too, the agenda set by UNCED Agenda 21 Chapter 17. This agenda encouraged new approaches to marine and coastal area management that are 'integrated in content and are precautionary and anticipatory in ambit' (Agenda 21 Chapter 17.1). We have also noted the challenges facing governments attempting to implement this agenda.

The empirical cases discussed in preceding chapters provide detailed discussion of institutional arrangements and the policy processes centred on national and regional efforts towards oceans governance. While each case is unique, reflecting specific historical, political, geographical and social factors, there are some more general similarities. Traditionally oceans and coastal policy in each case has been developed in a fragmented, generally uncoordinated manner by sectoral agencies with clearly defined responsibilities. This pattern of management has led to strong regulatory arrangements for each sector but it has been less successful in addressing new issues, or those issues that cut across these pre-existing administrative mandates:

> While each of the sectoral regimes has specific and immediate tasks and challenges it is also important to focus on one major outstanding issue, the need to provide integrated management of the oceans. Such management arrangements are not easy to establish or maintain. Integration involves a vertical dimension linking international instruments and regimes to national legislation and practices. Within national jurisdictions integration also involves an important horizontal dimension ensuring that national and sub-national government agencies are working together to ensure appropriate governance of coastal and ocean areas. (Haward 2000, p. 128)

Prior to assessing the extent to which our case examples have moved 'beyond the buzzwords' (Chircop and Hildebrand 2006) towards a more integrated model of oceans governance, we need to revisit and expand on our key analytic criteria.

SETTING PRIORITIES

Government determine priorities in response to complex dynamics – driven either by internal or external factors, by election mandates or by the political salience of an issue. Issues can emerge onto the policy agenda in different ways. An issue or problem may be 'discovered' and become the focus of intense attention. For example the 'discovery' of the ozone hole and the damage to the Earth's ozone layer by chlorofluorocarbons in the mid 1980s led to concerted action by governments and corporations. Alternatively the 'problem' may have existed for a considerable time and become incorporated into government programmes, for example the problem of poverty. These dynamics were identified by Downs as being part of what he termed 'the issue-attention cycle' (Downs 1972). Cobb and Elder, in one of the classic studies on agenda setting, distinguished between all issues meriting public attention and within the jurisdiction of government as forming a broad systemic agenda as opposed to those issues explicitly set up for active and serious consideration and authoritative decision-making – the institutional agenda (Cobb and Elder 1983).

Oceans policy development conforms to this general model. While problems of oceans management have been well known and specific issues identified and addressed, the formation of an institutional agenda, with the problems of ocean management seen as a priority occurred in the mid-1990s, with an early initiative being Canada's Ocean Act of 1997. This action was given impetus by the considerable attention given to marine resource management in Canada. The policy agenda was also influenced by the declaration of the International Year of the Ocean in 1998. The preceding chapters illustrate how this initiative provided impetus for setting priorities in all our exemplar countries, with some, particularly Australia, progressing further during this year in policy development than others.

Policy actors will perceive issues differently, a point that has been identified in several studies from the 1970s to the present. Part of this may relate to differences over the nature of the problem, the fact that in the development of policies 'antagonists can rarely agree on what the issues are' (Schattschneider 1960, p. 84). Schattschneider also identified the importance of what he termed the 'mobilisation of bias'; 'some issues are organised into politics while others are organised out of politics' (1960, p. 71). As Schattschneider also observed, the more visible an issue the more intense the interaction over it (Schattschneider 1957). Schattschneider also commented that the treatment of issues relates to their direction and scope, the extent to which the issue reinforces, or cuts across, existing political cleavages and debate. Thus issues that are more tractable, and able to be dealt with without increasing cleavages or conflict, will more likely be dealt with by governments than intractable issues.

The management of oceans policy reinforces Schattscheider's insights. Part of the problem with attempting to develop integrated policy in Australia and Canada reflects the difficulties of establishing new policy settings that cut across existing management arrangements and legislative and administrative mandates and responsibilities. Issues or options that open up existing cleavages during the oceans policy process have led to conflict, and derailing of the process. This was most clear in relation to declaration of marine protected areas under the regional planning process in south-east Australia. Resource access and allocation issues were also problematic. Indigenous peoples in Australia were unsuccessful in using the oceans policy process to provide greater access to marine areas or resources (Clark 2006; Dillon 2006). Maori claims to foreshore and coastal seabed areas effectively stalled the New Zealand policy development process.

Schattschneider's argument is exemplified by the failure of the Australian states to work within the oceans policy framework. This is the single most limiting factor in an attempt to provide an integrated approach to oceans management in Australian process, yet is explicable as it reflects and reinforces decades of intergovernmental conflict. Similar issues can be expected in the implementation of oceans policy in the USA, and with ongoing development and implementation of the EU's Maritime Policy.

The structuring of the problem is important in helping to set priorities. Dunn makes the pertinent observation that: 'the reason that problem structuring is so important is that policy analysts seem to fail more often because they solve the wrong problem than because they get the wrong solution to the right problem' (Dunn 1994, p. 138). This occurs because 'problems' are complex and priorities often difficult to isolate. In the Australian case the political imperative of the Commonwealth government structured the problem of Australia's Oceans Policy as its responsibility, rather than placing its within an intergovernmental framework. Dunn alerts us to the consequences that may follow from policies based on the right solution to the wrong problem (Dunn 1994, p. 142).

POLICY DEVELOPMENT, INSTRUMENTS AND IMPLEMENTATION

We have noted the importance of coordination in policy development, through the pattern and influence of interaction between the components of the political system. These components can either be the differing agencies within a government, or in multi-jurisdictional arrangements the constituent governments of the political system. Implementation is challenging, and as noted below 'failures' are a major force for arguments for greater coordination. There are, however, opportunities posed by these arrangements. Involving multiple jurisdictions in policy-making reduces the possibility of policy failure (the concept of redundancy) and provides a range of possible models or programmes to tackle specific problems. Innovations introduced in one place can be applied or modified to fit a number of other situations:

> organisations can be viewed for some purposes as collections of choices looking for problems, issues and feelings looking for a decision situation in which they might be aired, solutions looking for issues to which they might be an answer and decision makers looking for work. (Cohen et al. 1972, p. 1)

Policy instruments are important 'tools of government':

> Selecting the right tool for the job often turns out to be a matter of faith and politics rather than of certainty. Indeed it not uncommon to find that the choice of 'instruments' attracts much hotter political debates than the ends being sought. (Hood and Margetts 2007, p. 13)

The introduction of market-type forms of activity is a visible feature of contemporary governance. This is most notable in shifts to 'user pays' and other economic instruments in the place of former regulatory-based approaches to governance. Economic instruments can be effective in governance arrangements, provide efficient means of dealing with public policy issues, without the high costs of establishing and enforcing rules. Fees, taxes and charges are obvious examples of economic instruments, and have long-standing use in the implementation of policy, particularly in fisheries management. The use of tradeable rights and the creation of quasi-market approaches by such 'trades' in fisheries management, for example, has clearly provided an alternative paradigm for both fishers and fisheries managers. In the 1990s the New Zealand and Australian governments increased the use of economic instruments, chiefly through the introduction of individual transferable quotas, fishing rights and resource rent recovery. These instruments were integral to the oceans policy initiatives in both countries. In the USA the Ocean Action Plan endorsed by President Bush emphasises the use of economic instruments in marine resource management.

Of course the use of economic instruments does not mean that regulation is not needed; indeed most economic instrument are implemented by laws or regulations passed by formal institutions of government. As shown in the preceding chapters market-based and co-management tools provide more than just an opportunity to increase resource rents to government (and the community) or placate resource user through symbolic participation in decision-making. Neither regulation nor use of economic instruments is necessarily mutually exclusive; nor do they preclude the development of a third set of instruments, those commonly associated with user self-management or co-management arrangements.

Although implementation of a policy is often seen as an end point – where problems have been addressed and priorities determined – non-governmental stakeholders or interests may continue to urge changes or to highlight perceived weaknesses or limitations in the policy. The stakeholders may be important agents for identifying areas where policy change may be needed, or where policy failure has occurred. This role may well contribute to the emergence of new issues as part of the continuation of the policy cycle.

ACCOUNTABILITY AND EVALUATION

Accountability is one of the most interesting and confusing concepts in public policy and public administration. As with many key concepts in the social sciences there is no single, recognised definition of accountability. One of the outcomes of the introduction of the new public management or managerialism has been a debate focused on the issues of accountability. The role and functions of the public servant have changed as new forms of governance have been introduced. Improving accountability is one aim of the management model through the development of programme focus in planning and budgeting – transparency in government activities, hence delegation of authority and responsibility, gives greater responsibility to junior and middle managers who under the traditional model were anonymous (see Hughes 2003).

The examples of oceans policy development described in the preceding chapters have been developed within their respective public sector frameworks. Parliamentary scrutiny (in Australia, New Zealand and Canada) is an important form of accountability, as is congressional oversight in the USA. Failure to maintain reporting to parliament was highlighted in the Canadian Auditor-General's report on *Canada's Oceans Management Strategy* (Auditor General of Canada 2005b) New Zealand's parliament was embroiled in a debate over Maori claims to foreshore and coastal seabed areas, cutting across a process that had emphasised engagement with the Maori.

A second, and related, issue is the need to be able to evaluate achievements or developments in the public sector, and establish frameworks that facilitate understanding of impacts, and provide information on performance and achievement of goals, objectives and targets. This has been a critical part of the development of the managerial paradigm with a focus on measurable indicators, and an overarching concern with efficiency and effectiveness, and integral to programme-focused budget models. One common criticism is that the development of quantitative indicators (numbers) has taken precedence over qualitative indicators that are by definition more value-focused and thus harder to 'measure'. Efficiency and effectiveness can be assessed through quantitative indicators, measuring outcomes in relation to inputs with monitoring to ensure maximum outcomes for a given level of inputs, or through qualitative indicators criteria such as accuracy, comprehensiveness, timeliness, responsiveness, clarity and practicality. Quantitative and qualitative elements are integral to programme evaluation within public sector planning.

While many of the examples of oceans policy discussed in this book are in the developmental phase, the two 'most mature cases', Australia and

Canada, have undertaken evaluation of their oceans policy processes. These evaluations have focused on performance of key agencies as well as outcomes and have been used to help steer the respective processes, and have resulted in new structures and directions in Australia, and a recommitment to the oceans management strategy and additional funding by the Canadian federal government.

MANAGING THE BLUE PLANET: OCEANS GOVERNANCE IN THE TWENTY-FIRST CENTURY

We have noted in Chapter 1 that the traditional institutional framework governing ocean management has considerable strength and resilience. In all cases oceans governance arrangements are very effective at the sectoral level, with these arrangements providing stability and consistency. There is less evidence of success in relation to the attempt to implement integrated arrangements across sectors and across jurisdictions, simply because issues of horizontal and vertical governance have not been satisfactorily resolved. Challenges remain, as we have noted, in addressing the demands of integrated management (Haward 2003, p. 49). One immediate challenge is providing frameworks and processes that can accommodate, and resolve, conflicts between the vast range of oceans-related interests and values. These frameworks may also be tested by emergent issues such as indigenous peoples' concerns over access to resources and sea claims; issues that have been central in oceans policy debates in Canada, Australia and particularly in New Zealand.

One important effect of the development of the oceans policy framework has been the examination of new tools and approaches to governance – regional management, increasing analysis of market-based approaches (Greiner et al. 1997), and a focus on co-management in its various forms – and the increasing policy learning and transfer. This is most clearly evident in relation to oceans policy development in Australia, Canada and New Zealand (Vince 2008), although the impact of these experiences is likely to be broader result of the work of forums such as the Ocean Policy Summit, discussed in Chapter 2.

We identified two cross-cutting themes – first, institutional design and policy capacity; and second, policy frameworks for integrated oceans management – as key parameters in the development of effective ocean governance. In earlier chapters we have noted positively the considerable efforts, and the range of initiatives or actions developed to manage the world's seas and oceans. While progress has been slow, and in some cases justifiably criticised, the pace of implementation refects the challenges on introducing new approaches to oceans management. Not surprisingly the case studies of national policy development are notable more for the problems in implementation than their successes.

We have noted previously that in the case of Australia 'the oceans policy and the regional marine planning process have clearly identified goals and objectives ... [and that] these objectives will provide a yardstick for ongoing assessment of performance' (Haward 2003, p. 49). The review of Australia's Oceans Policy (prior to completion of the South-eastern Regional Marine Plan) noted significant achievements in relation to 'key initiatives'. We would concur with this assessment, but note that many of the 390 sectorally-oriented commitments identified in the Oceans Policy documents in 1998 have been achieved without necessary reference to the regional (now bioregional) marine planning focus. There is less evidence of success in relation to the attempt to implement integrated arrangements across sectors and across jurisdictions, simply because the question of jurisdiction has not been satisfactorily resolved.

In the case of Canada similar constraints were identified. The review by the Canadian Auditor General found that implementation of the Oceans Act and its related oceans management strategies had not been a priority for government and that there were difficulties in 'implementing a workable approach to integrated oceans management'. In addition the review raised significant questions over the ability of the Canadian parliament to monitor progress or be able to hold the Department of Fisheries and Oceans accountable for its Oceans Act responsibilities. The Auditor General noted that commitment to report periodically on the state of the oceans had not been met. Further efforts were needed to improve horizontal governance, and improve coordination of efforts. The Department of Fisheries and Oceans' competing mandates for 'fisheries' and 'oceans' was identified as an ongoing challenge in governance.

The discussion of these attempts at reform of national oceans governance invites an assessment of achievements, and consideration of the effectiveness of these initiatives. We have noted the difficult and at times tortuous path of policy development, and recognise, too, that the process is partial (in the case of Australia) or incomplete (New Zealand) or still in development (in the USA and Europe). Even in Canada, a 'mature case' of national ocean policy development, progress towards integrated oceans management has required additional funding. The concept of effectiveness is complex, and at its most basic relates to the extent to which an instrument successfully performs its function or solves the problems that led to its establishment (Underdal 2002, p. 5).

As Young and Levy note, effectiveness 'can mean a number of things, and some of the meanings require difficult normative, scientific and historical judgements' (Young and Levy 1999, p. 3). Young and Levy identify a number of approaches to the study of effectiveness: problem solving, legal, economic, normative and political (Young and Levy 1999, pp. 4–6). From these approaches, Young and Levy emphasise 'political effectiveness' as an important yardstick. 'Effective regimes cause changes in the behaviour of actors, in the interests of actors, or in the policies and performance of institutions in ways that contribute to positive management of the targeted problems' (Young and Levy 1999, p. 5). While most studies of effectiveness have focused on the analysis of international environmental regimes, their insights are particularly apposite for examining 'collective problems calling for joint solutions' (Underdal 2002, p. 3), the essence of the governance arrangements (and dilemmas) integral to oceans policy implementation.

Underdal defines 'effectiveness of a ... regime as a function of the stringency and inclusiveness of its provisions, the level of compliance on the part of its members and the side effects it generates' (Underdal 2002, p. 6). In simple terms the more stringent and inclusive the policy, leading to high levels of compliance and generating positive side effects, the more effective it will be. The 'stringency and inclusiveness' of management provisions, 'level of compliance' and the impact of side-effects produced by the instrument centres attention on the processes of decision-making, the outputs and outcomes deriving from these decisions, and the impacts of these outcomes from the oceans policy process.

These issues return to Young and Levy's insight that effectiveness is related to 'changes in the behaviour of actors, in the interests of actors, or in the policies and performance of institutions in ways that contribute to positive management of the targeted problems' (Young and Levy 1999, p. 5). The period from 1992 has seen major changes in the behaviour of actors and institutions towards the maritime domain, leading to increased governmental attention at national, regional and international scales to these 'problems'.

While implementing integrated oceans management remains a policy ideal, there are ongoing developments in each country and within regional or supra-national organisations that have the potential to provide sound vessels and charts for further policy 'voyages'. It is likely that these vessels will face new and emergent challenges in addition to meeting commitments to integrated management. One emergent challenge will arise from the impacts of climate variability and change. Changes in ocean temperature may lead to changes in marine ecosystems, with direct effects on activities such as fishing and aquaculture operations, as well as increasing the frequency and intensity of extreme weather events affecting coastal and marine environments. Warming of the oceans impacts on global ocean currents, the mechanism by which the Earth's climate is moderated. At the same time rises in ocean temperature contribute to extreme weather events, such as cyclones or severe storms, that in coastal and estuarine areas can lead to inundation of coastal land.

We do not underestimate the scale and scope of future challenges. This book has emphasised the complexities in oceans policy development and implementation. While each political system is different, shaped by constitutional and jurisdictional frameworks, as well as by political and judicial decisions, each case emphasises that developments in oceans governance centres attention on the processes of decision-making, the outputs and outcomes deriving from these decisions, and the impacts of these outcomes on 'the blue planet'.

References

ABARE (Australian Bureau of Agricultural and Resource Economics). 2007. *Australian Fisheries Statistics 2006*, Canberra, ABARE.

ACIUCN (Australian Committee for IUCN). 1998. *Conserving Australia's Oceans: Development of an Oceans Policy for Australia: Outcomes of a National Workshop, 15–17 May 1997*, ACIUCN Occasional Paper Number 7, March.

ACF (Australian Conservation Foundation). 2004. '*South-East Regional Marine Plan*'. www.acfonline.org.au/articles/news.asp?news_id=377. Accessed 27 July 2007.

ACF (Australian Conservation Foundation). 2006. *Out of the Blue: A Discussion Paper for an Australian Oceans Act*, Melbourne, ACF.

AFMA (Australian Fisheries Management Authority). 2008. Management Advisory Committees, www.afma.gov.au/management/partnerships/macs.htm. Accessed 13 May 2008.

Allison, G. 1992. 'Public and Private Management: Are They Fundamentally Alike in All Unimportant Respects', in R.J. Stillman Jr. (ed.), *Public Administration: Concepts and Cases*, 5th edn, Boston, Houghton Mifflin: 292–8.

American Journal of International Law. 2004. 'Report of US Commission on Oceans Policy', *American Journal of International Law*, 98, 3: 590–91.

APEC (Asia-Pacific Economic Cooperation). 2005. *Bali Plan of Action: Towards Healthy Oceans and Coasts for Sustainable Growth and Prosperity of the Asia–Pacific Community*, Joint Ministerial Statement, Bali, 2nd APEC Oceans Related Ministerial Meeting, 16–17 September.

Arctic Council. 2008. *About Arctic Council*, http://www.arctic-council.org, Accessed 21 January 2008.

ASOC (Antarctic and Southern Ocean Coalition). 2002. *Report of the Antarctic and Southern Ocean Coalition (ASOC) to the Twenty–First Meeting of the Commission for the Conservation of Antarctic Marine Living Resources*, www.asoc.org/Portals/0/pdfs/CCAMLR2002/ ASOC. Report. CCAMLR02.doc.

Auditor General of Canada. 2005a. *Report of the Commissioner of the Environment and Sustainable Development to the House of Commons:*

The Commissioner's Perspective – 2005, Ottawa, Office of the Auditor General of Canada.

Auditor General of Canada. 2005b. *Report of the Commissioner of the Environment and Sustainable Development to the House of Commons: Chapter 1 Fisheries and Oceans Canada – Canada's Oceans Management Strategy*, Ottawa, Office of the Auditor General of Canada.

Australian Democrats. 1994. 'The Coast's Major Inquiry's Recommendation "Beached"', Media Release, 28 November.

Bache, S., L. Munz, S. Rajkumar and M. Tsamenyi. 2003. *Current Developments in Integrated Oceans Management and Governance in APEC Member Economies*, Final Report to the Marine Resources Conservation Working Group, Asia-Pacific Economic Cooperation.

Bain, R. 1984. 'Prospects, Policies and Problems for the Australian Fishing Industry: a Commonwealth View', paper presented at The Australian Fishing Industry – Today and Tomorrow Conference, Launceston, Australian Maritime College, July.

Bakvis, H. 1997. 'Pressure Groups and the New Public Management: From "Pressure Pluralism" to "Managing the Contract"', in M. Charih and A. Daniels (eds), *Canadian Public Administration and New Public Management*, Toronto, Institute of Public Administration of Canada: 293–315.

Barker, L.J. 1962. 'The Supreme Court as Policy Maker: The Tidelands Oil Controversy', *Journal of Politics*, 24, 2: 350–66.

Barry, L. 1986. 'Offshore Petroleum Agreements: An Analysis of the Nova Scotian and Newfoundland Experience', in J.O. Saunders (ed.), *Managing Natural Resources in a Federal State: Essays From the Second Banff Conference on Natural Resources Law*, Toronto, Carswell.

Bateman, S. 1997. 'Marine Industry Development and Oceans Policy in Australia', paper presented at COSU Conference, Singapore, 12–14 May.

Beatley, T., D.J. Brower and A.K. Schwab. 1994. *An Introduction To Coastal Zone Management*, Washington, DC, Island Press.

Beggs, M. and G. Hooper. 2005. 'Development of New Zealand's Oceans Policy', ICPC Conference, March.

Belsky, M.H. 1989. 'The Ecosystem Model: Mandate for a Comprehensive US Ocean Policy', *San Diego Law Review*, 26, 3: 417–96.

Bennett, C. and M. Howlett, 1992. 'The Lessons of Learning: Reconciling Theories of Policy Learning and Policy Change', *Policy Sciences*, 25: 275–94.

Benson-Pope, D. 2005. 'SeaChange 05 – Oceans Policy Recommended', speech to SeaChange 05 Conference, Auckland, New Zealand, 21 November.

Bergin, A. and M. Haward. 1996. *Japan's Tuna Fishing Industry: A Setting Sun or New Dawn?* New York, Nova Science Publishers.

Bergin, A. and M. Haward. 1999. 'Australia's New Oceans Policy', *International Journal of Marine and Coastal Law*, 14, 3: 387–98.

Bergin, A. and M. Haward. 2000. *Australia and International Fisheries Management Issues – Future Directions*, Canberra, Fisheries Resources Research Fund, Bergin and Associates, University of Tasmania.

Bergin, A., M. Haward, D. Russell and R. Weir. 1996. 'Marine Living Resources', in L. Kriwoken, M. Haward, D. VanderZwaag and B. Davis (eds), *Oceans Law and Policy in the Post-UNCED Era: Australian and Canadian Perspectives*, London, Kluwer Law International: 173–214.

Berkes, F., D. Feeney, B. McKay and J.M. Acheson. 1989. 'The Benefits of the Commons,' *Nature*, 340, 13: 91–3.

Birnie, P.W. and A. Boyle. 1995. *Basic Documents on International Environmental Law*, Oxford, Clarendon Press.

Borg, J. 2006. 'Current Difficulties and Long Term Perspectives for the Fisheries Sector', speech at meeting with representatives of Europêche, Europêche, Brussels, 19 May, http://ec.europa.eu/fisheries/press_corner/speeches/speech06_04a_en.htm . Accessed 19 May 2008.

Brown, D. 2005. *Salmon Wars: The Battle for the West Coast Salmon Fishery*, Madeira Park, British Columbia, Harbour Publishing.

Bryson, L. and M. Mowbray. 1981. 'Community: The Spray–on Solution', *Australian Journal of Social Issues*, 16, 4: 255–67.

Buck, E.H. 1998. 'Oceans Act in the 105th Congress: Bills Relating to a US Ocean Policy', *CRS Report for Congress*, reprinted by National Council for Science and the Environment, Washington, NCSE.

Burmester, H. 1995. 'Australia and the Law of the Sea', in J. Crawford and D.R. Rothwell (eds), *The Law of the Sea in the Asian Pacific Region*, Dordrecht, Martinus Nijhoff Publishers: 51–64.

Bush, G.W. 2007. 'President's Statement on Advancing US Interests in the World's Oceans', 15 May, Washington, The White House.

Byrne, J. 1985. 'The Decision Making Structure for Fisheries Management: the Role of Government and State and Commonwealth Authorities', paper presented at Australian Fisheries Conference, January, Canberra.

CAENZ 2003 (Centre for Advanced Engineering New Zealand) 2003. *Economic Opportunities in New Zealand's Oceans: Informing the Development of Oceans Policy*, www.caenz.com/ocean/ocean.html. Accessed 25 May 2008.

Campbell, E. 1960. 'Regulation of Australian Coastal Fisheries', *University of Tasmania Law Review*, 1, 3: 405–78.

Carson, R. 1951. *The Sea Around Us*, New York, Oxford University Press.

CCAMLR (Commission for the Conservation of Antarctic Marine Living Resources). 2002. *Report of the Twenty-First Meeting of the Commission*, Hobart, CCAMLR.

Chapman, R.J.K. 1990. 'Public Policy, Federalism, Intergovernmental Relations: The Federal Factor', *Publius*, 20, 4: 69–84.

Charles, A. 1997. 'Fisheries Management in Atlantic Canada', *Ocean and Coastal Management*, 35, 2–3: 101–19.

Charters, C. and E. Erueti. 2005. 'Report from the Inside: The CERD Committee's Review of the Foreshore and Seabed Act 2004', *Victoria University of Wellington Law Review*, 36: 257–90.

Chircop, A. 1996. 'Canada and the Law of the Sea: Perspectives and Issues for Canadian Accession', in L. Kriwoken, M. Haward, D. VanderZwaag and B. Davis (eds), *Oceans Law and Policy in the Post-UNCED Era: Australian and Canadian Perspectives*, London, Kluwer Law International: 75–96.

Chircop, A. and L. Hildebrand. 2006. 'Beyond the Buzzwords: A Perspective on Integrated Coastal and Oceans management in Canada', in D.R. Rothwell and D. VanderZwaag (eds), *Towards Principled Oceans Governance: Australian and Canadian Approaches and Challenges*, Abingdon, Routledge.

Chircop, A., H. Kindred, P. Saunders and D. VanderZwaag. 1996. 'Legislating for Integrated Marine Management: Canada's Proposed Oceans Act of 1996', *Canadian Yearbook of International Law*, 33: 305–31.

Christopher, W.M. 1953. 'The Outer Continental Shelf Lands Act: Key to a New Frontier', *Stanford Law Review*, 6, 1: 23–68.

Chronicle-Herald. Halifax NS Canada.

Cicin-Sain, B. and R.W. Knecht. 1998. *Integrated Coastal and Oceans Management: Concepts and Cases*, Washington, Island Press.

Clark, G. 2006. 'Indigenous Rights in the Sea: The Law and Practice of Native Title in Australia', in D.R. Rothwell and D. VanderZwaag (eds), *Towards Principled Oceans Governance: Australian and Canadian Approaches and Challenges*, Abingdon, Routledge: 315–32.

CMS (Convention on Migratory Species of Wild Animals). 2008. 'Convention on Migratory Species', http://www.cms.int/. Accessed 25 May 2008.

Cobb, R.W. and C.D. Elder. 1983. *Participation in American Politics: The Dynamics of Agenda Building*, 2nd edn, Baltimore, Johns Hopkins University Press.

Cohen, M.J., J. March and J. Olsen. 1972. 'A Garbage Can Model of Organisational Choice', *Administrative Science Quarterly*, 17: 1–25.

Coleridge, S.T. 1797–99. *The Rime of the Ancient Mariner.* www.online-literature.com/coleridge/646/. Accessed 25 May 2008.

Collis, B. 1997. 'Ocean Awaits Policy Wake Up Call', *Canberra Times,* 18 January.

Commission on Ocean Policy (United States Commission on Ocean Policy). 2004. *An Ocean Blueprint for the 21st Century,* Washington, Commission on Ocean Policy.

Committee on Ocean Policy. 2007. *US Ocean Action Plan Implementation Update,* Washington, Committee on Ocean Policy.

Commonwealth of Australia. 1967. *Agreement Relating to the Exploration for and Exploitation of, the Petroleum Resources, and Certain Other Resources, of the Continental Shelf of Australia and of Certain Other Territories of the Commonwealth and Certain other Submerged Land,* Canberra, Commonwealth of Australia.

Commonwealth of Australia. 1995. *Living on the Coast: The Commonwealth Coastal Policy,* Canberra, Department of Environment, Sport and Territories.

Commonwealth of Australia. 1997a. *Australia's Oceans Policy: Oceans Facts and Figures, A Primer on Australia's Oceans and Exclusive Economic Zone,* Background Paper 1, Canberra, Environment Australia.

Commonwealth of Australia. 1997b. *Australia's Oceans, New Horizons, Oceans Policy Consultation Paper,* Canberra, AGPS.

Commonwealth of Australia. 1998a. *Australia's Oceans Policy – An Issues Paper,* Canberra, AGPS.

Commonwealth of Australia. 1998b. *Australia's Oceans Policy: Caring, Understanding and Using Wisely,* Canberra, AGPS.

Commonwealth of Australia. 1998c. *Australia's Oceans Policy: Specific Sectoral Measures,* Canberra, AGPS.

Commonwealth of Australia, 1999. *Australia's Marine Science and Technology Plan,* Canberra, AGPS.

COMSER (Commission on Marine Sciences, Engineering and Resources [Stratton Commission]). 1969. *Our Nation and the Sea,* www.lib.noaa.gov/noaainfo/heritage/stratton/contents.html. Accessed May 27 2008

Connor, R.D. 2004. 'Individual Transferable Quota in Fisheries Management', unpublished PhD thesis, Canberra, Australian National University.

Conservation Sector. 2004. 'Conservation Sector Submission on the Draft South-east Regional Marine Plan'.

Cordonnery, L. 2005. 'Implementing the Pacific Islands Regional Ocean Policy: How Difficult is it Going to be?' *Victoria University of Wellington Law Review,* 36: 723–31.

Costanza, R., F. Andrade, P. Antunes, M. van den Belt, D. Boersma, D.F. Boesch, F. Catarino, S. Hanna, K. Limburg, B. Low, M. Moliror, J.G. Pereira, S. Rayner, R. Santos, J. Wilson and M. Young. 1998. 'Principles for Sustainable Governance of the Oceans', *Science*, 281: 198–9.

Council on Environmental Quality. 2007a. 'About the Committee on Ocean Policy', http://ocean.ceq.gov/about/welcome.html. Accessed 22 October 2007.

Council on Environmental Quality. 2007b. 'Committee on Ocean Policy', http://ocean.ceq.gov/. Accessed 22 October 2007.

Cozens, P. 2000. 'An Australasian Oceans Policy?' *Maritime Studies*, 115: 15–20.

CPAWS (Canadian Parks and Wilderness Society). 2004. 'Ocean Action Plan in Speech from the Throne', Media Release, 4 February.

Crowley, R.W. and R.C. Bourgeois. 1989. 'The Rationale and Future Direction of Canada's Oceans Policy: Domestic Aspects', in D. McRae and G. Munro (eds), *Canadian Oceans Policy: National Strategies and the New Law of the Sea*, Vancouver, University of British Columbia Press: 253–68.

Cullen, R. 1990. *Federalism in Action: The Australian and Canadian Offshore Disputes*, Sydney, Federation Press.

Cullen, R. 1996. 'Rights to Offshore Resources after Mabo 1992 and the Native Title Act 1993 (Commonwealth)', *Sydney Law Review*, 18, 2: 125–51.

DAFF (Department of Agriculture, Fisheries and Forestry). 2007. 'Fisheries' http://www.daff.gov.au/fisheries. Accessed 10 October 2007.

Davis, B.W. 1996. 'National Response to UNCED Outcomes: Australia', in L. Kriwoken, M. Haward, D. VanderZwaag and B. Davis (eds), *Oceans Law and Policy in the Post-UNCED Era: Australian and Canadian Perspectives*, London, Kluwer Law International: 25–40.

Davis, B.W. and M. Haward 1994. 'Oceans Policy and Overlapping Regimes', in P.G. Wells and P.J. Ricketts (eds), *Coastal Zone Canada 94: 'Cooperation in the Coastal Zone' Conference Proceedings*, Coastal Zone Canada Association, Bedford Institute of Oceanography, Dartmouth Nova Scotia, Vol. 1: 155–64.

Daw, T. and T. Gray. 2005. 'Fisheries Science and Sustainability in International Policy: A Study of Failure in the European Union's Common Fisheries Policy', *Marine Policy*, 29: 189–97.

DFO (Department of Fisheries and Oceans Canada). 1987. *Oceans Policy for Canada: A Strategy to Meet the Challenges and Opportunities on the Oceans Frontier*, Ottawa, DFO.

DFO (Department of Fisheries and Oceans Canada). 2000. 'Dhaliwal Announces Advisory Council on Oceans', News Release 8 June NR-HQ-

00-29E, www.dfo-mpo.gc.ca/media/newsrel/2000/hq-ac29_e.htm. Accessed 24 May 2008.

DFO (Department of Fisheries and Oceans Canada). 2002. *Canada's Oceans Strategy*, Ottawa, DFO.

DFO (Department of Fisheries and Oceans Canada). 2005a. *Canada's Oceans Action Plan: For Present and Future Generations*, Ottawa, Communications Branch DFO.

DFO (Department of Fisheries and Oceans Canada). 2005b. *Strategic Plan 2005–2010*, Ottawa, Communications Branch DFO.

DFO (Department of Fisheries and Oceans Canada). 2007. 'Canada's New Government Announces New Activities to Protect the Health of the Oceans', Media Release, 9 October, Vancouver, DFO.

Dillon, R. 2006. 'Aboriginal Peoples and Oceans Policy in Australia: The Indigenous Perspective', in D.R. Rothwell and D. VanderZwaag (eds), *Towards Principled Oceans Governance: Australian and Canadian Approaches and Challenges*, Abingdon, Routledge: 333–46.

Dimas, S. and J. Borg. 2007. 'World Oceans Day: Healthy Oceans are Key to Europe's Future, say Commissioners Dimas and Borg', Brussels 8 June. http://ec.europa.eu/maritimeaffairs/press/press_rel080607_en.html. Accessed 25 May 2008.

DOALOS (Division of Oceans and the Law of the Sea – United Nations). 2007. *United Nations Open–Ended Informal Process on Oceans and the Law of the Sea*, www.un.org/Depts/los/consultative_process/consultative_process.htm. Accessed 8 August 2007.

Dodds, K. 1997. *Geopolitics in Antarctica: A View From the Southern Ocean Rim*, New York, Wiley.

Dolowitz, D. and D. Marsh. 2000. 'Learning From Abroad; the Role of Policy Transfer in Contemporary Policy-Making', *Governance*, 13, 1: 5–24.

Doucet, G.J. 1984. 'Canada–Nova Scotia Offshore Agreement: One Year Later', *Alberta Law Review*, 22, 1: 132–9.

Downs. A. 1972. 'Up and Down with Ecology: The Issue–Attention Cycle', *Public Interest*, 28: 38–50.

Dunn, W.N. 1994. *Public Policy Analysis: An Introduction*, 2nd edn, Englewood Cliffs, N.J. Prentice Hall.

EDS (Environmental Defence Society). 2005. Seachange 05 – Managing our Coastal Waters and Oceans Conference, 21–22 November.

Enfocus Ltd, Hill Young Cooper Ltd and URS NZ Ltd. 2002. *Oceans Policy Stocktake: Part 1 Legislation and Policy Review*, Wellington, Oceans Policy Secretariat.

Environment Australia. 1997. *Australia's Oceans Policy. Analysis of the Submissions to the Oceans Policy Consultation Paper*, Background Paper 3, Canberra, Environment Australia.

ESDSC (Ecologically Sustainable Development Steering Committee) 1992. *National Ecologically Sustainable Development Strategy*, Canberra, AGPS.

Europa. 2007. http://ec.europa.eu/maritimeaffairs/policy_en.html. Accessed 27 October 2007.

Europa. 2008. 'Common Fisheries Policy', http://ec.europa.eu/fisheries/cfp_en.htm. Accessed 19 May 2008/

European Commission. 2002. *Communication from the Commission on the Reform of the Common Fisheries Policy – Roadmap.* Luxembourg, European Commission.

European Commission. 2006. *Communication: Improvement of the Economic Situation in the Fishing Industry*, COM(2006) 103 Final, Brussels, European Commission.

European Commission. 2007. *An Integrated Maritime Policy for the European Union*, COM(2007) 575 Final 2007, Brussels, European Commission.

Evans, M. 2004. *Policy Transfer in a Global Perspective*, Aldershot, Ashgate Publishing.

Evans, M. and J. Davies. 1999. 'Understanding Policy Transfer: A Multi-Level, Multi-Disciplinary Perspective', *Public Administration*, 77, 2: 361–85.

Evans, N. 1998. 'Jurisdictional Disputes and the Development of Offshore Petroleum Legislation in Australia', unpublished PhD thesis, Hobart, University of Tasmania.

Fanning, L., R. Mahon, P. McConney, J. Angulo, F. Burrows, B. Chakalall, D. Gil, M. Haughton, S. Heileman, S. Martinez. L. Ostine, A. Oviedo, S. Parsons, T. Phillips, C.S. Arroya, B. Simmons and C. Toro. 2007a. 'A Large Marine Ecosystem Governance Framework', *Marine Policy*, 31: 434–43.

Fanning, L., R. Mahon, P. McConney and C. Toro. 2007b. 'The Caribbean Large Marine Ecosystem (CLME) Project: Governance Framework, Project Structure and Challenges', paper presented at International Conference on Ocean Security in the Wider Caribbean, Corpus Christi, Texas 10–12 February.

FAO (Food and Agriculture Organization). 1999. 'Rome Declaration on the Implementation of the Code of Conduct for Responsible Fisheries', Adopted by the FAO Ministerial Meeting on Fisheries, Rome 10–11 March 1999.

FAO (Food and Agriculture Organization). 2000. *Stopping Illegal, Unreported and Unregulated (IUU) Fishing*, Rome, FAO.

FAO (Food and Agriculture Organization). 2002. *Implementation of the International Plan of Action to Prevent, Deter and Eliminate Illegal, Unreported and Unregulated Fishing*, FAO Technical Guidelines for Responsible Fisheries, No. 9, Rome, FAO.

FAO (Food and Agriculture Organization). 2007. *The State of World Fisheries and Aquaculture 2006*, Rome, FAO.

Ferguson. J.R. 1997. 'The Expanses of Sustainability and the Limits of Privatarianism', *Canadian Journal of Political Science*, 30, 2: 285–306.

Fløistad, B. 1990. 'Communication Between Science and Decision Makers: The Advisory Function of the International Council for the Exploration of the Sea', *International Challenges*, 10, 4: 22–8.

Foster A.M. 2002. 'New Zealand's Oceans Policy', LLB (Hons) Research Paper, Wellington, Victoria University of Wellington Law School.

Foster A.M. 2003. 'New Zealand's Oceans Policy', *Victoria University of Wellington Law Review*, 34: 469–96.

Foster, E. and M. Haward. 2003. 'Integrated Management Councils: A Conceptual Model for Ocean Policy Conflict Management in Australia', *Ocean and Coastal Management*, 46: 547–63.

Foster, E., M. Haward and S. Coffen-Smout. 2005. 'Implementing Integrated Oceans Management: Australia's South East Regional Marine Plan (SERMP) and Canada's Eastern Scotian Shelf Integrated Management Initiative (ESSIM)', *Marine Policy*, 29: 391–405.

Francis, J. and E. Torell. 2004. 'Human Dimensions of Coastal Management in the Western Indian Ocean Region', *Ocean and Coastal Management*, 47: 299–307.

Froelich, A. 2002. 'A Sea Change for US Ocean Policy?' *American Institute of Biological Sciences Washington Watch*. www.aibs.org/washington-watch/washington_watch_2002_03.html. Accessed 8 August 2007.

FWS (Fish and Wildlife Service). 2007. *Digest of Federal Resource Laws of Interest to the US Fish and Wildlife Service*. http://www.fws.gov/lawsdigest.htm. Accessed 26 September 2007.

Gale, F. and M. Haward. 2004. 'Public Accountability in Private Regulation: Contrasting Models of the Forest Stewardship Council (FSC) and Marine Stewardship Council (MSC)', Proceedings of the Australasian Political Studies Association Conference, Adelaide, South Australia, http://www.adelaide.edu.au/apsa/papers/#Pubpol.

GEF (Global Environment Facility). 2007. 'International Waters', http://www.gefweb.org/. Accessed 10 October 2007.

George, A. 1979. 'Case Studies and Theory Development: The Method of Structured, Focused Comparison', in P.G. Lauren (ed.), *Diplomacy*, New York, Free Press: 43–68.

Gibbs, N. and K. Woods. 2003. 'Facilitating Tradeoffs Between Commercial Fishing and Aquaculture Development in New Zealand', Rights and Duties in the Coastal Zone Conference, Stockholm, 12–14 June.

Global Forum (Global Forum on Oceans, Coasts and Islands). 2005. *Agenda for 2005–2010*, Newark, Delaware International Coastal and Ocean Organization, http://www.globaloceans.org. Accessed 8 August 2007.

Global Forum (Global Forum on Oceans, Coasts and Islands). 2007. *Report on Activities 2005–2007 and Future Directions*, Newark, Delaware International Coastal and Ocean Organization, http://www.globaloceans.org. Accessed 8 August 2007.

Globe and Mail. Toronto, Canada.

Gove, M. 2005. 'A Comprehensive National Ocean Policy: America's Next Step?' Unpublished Masters of Environmental Management thesis, Duke University, Durham, NC, USA.

Gray, T. and J. Hatchard. 2003. 'The 2002 Reform of the Common Fisheries Policy's System of Governance – Rhetoric or Reality?' *Marine Policy*, 27: 545–54.

Green Paper. 2006. *Towards a Future Maritime Policy for the Union: A European Vision for the Oceans and Seas*. Commission of the European Communities, Brussels, 7.6.2006 COM(2006) 275 Final.

Greiner, R., M. Young, A. McDonald and M. Brooks. 1997. *Australia's Oceans Policy: Oceans Planning and Management, Management Instruments for Marine Allocation and Use*, Issues Paper 2, Canberra, Environment Australia.

Haas, P. 1989. 'Do Regimes Matter? Epistemic Communities and Mediterranean Pollution Control', *International Organization*, 43: 377–403.

Hall, H.R. and M. Haward. 2001. 'Enhancing Compliance with International Legislation and Agreements Mitigating Seabird Mortality on Longlines', *Marine Ornithology*, 28: 183–90.

Hanf, K. and A. Underdal. 1998. 'Domesticating International Commitments: Linking National and International Decision Making', in A. Underdal (ed.), *The Politics of International Environmental Management*, Dordrecht, Kluwer Academic Publishers: 149–70.

Hardin, G. 1968. 'The Tragedy of the Commons', *Science*, 162: 1243–8.

Harris, M. 1998. *Lament for an Ocean: The Collapse of the Atlantic Cod Fishery – A True Crime Story*, Toronto, McClelland & Stewart.

Harrison, A.J. 1982. 'Marine Resource Policy in Tasmania', in R.A. Herr, R. Hall and B.W. Davis (eds), *Issues in Australia's Marine and Antarctic*

Policies, Public Policy Monograph, Department of Political Science, Hobart, University of Tasmania.

Harrison A.J. 1991. *The Commonwealth in the Administration of Australian Fisheries: 'A Sort of Mongrel Socialism'*, National Monograph Series 6, Royal Australian Institute of Public Administration, Canberra, RAIPA.

Harrison, P. and F. Kwamena. 1979. *Canada's Offshore Resources: Introduction and Bibliography*, Research Note 25, Department of Geography, Ottawa, University of Ottawa.

Haward, M. 1989. 'The Australian Offshore Constitutional Settlement', *Marine Policy*, 13, 4: 334– 8.

Haward, M. 1990. 'Intergovernmental Relations and Coastal Zone Management', submission to House of Representatives Inquiry into the Protection of the Coastal Environment, verbal presentation, Hobart, September.

Haward, M. 1991a. 'Intergovernmental Relations and Offshore Resources Policy in Australia and Canada,' *Australian–Canadian Studies*, 9, 1–2: 35–51.

Haward, M. 1991b. 'The Offshore', in B. Galligan, O. Hughes and C. Walsh (eds), *Inter-Governmental Relations and Public Policy*, Sydney, Allen & Unwin: 109–28.

Haward, M. 1992. 'Federalism and the Australian Offshore Constitutional Settlement', unpublished PhD thesis, Hobart, University of Tasmania.

Haward, M. 1995. 'Institutional Design and Policy Making "Down Under": Developments in Australian and New Zealand Coastal Management', *Ocean and Coastal Management*, 26, 2: 87–117.

Haward, M. 1996. 'Institutional Framework for Australian Ocean and Coastal Management', Special Issue, *Ocean and Coastal Management*, 19–39.

Haward, M. 1998. 'Political Constraints on Fisheries Management', paper prepared for National Fisheries Officers Course, Beauty Point, Australian Maritime College.

Haward, M. 2000. 'Outstanding Issues with Regimes for Oceans Governance', in D. Wilson and R. Sherwood (eds), *Oceans Governance and Maritime Strategy*, Sydney, Allen & Unwin: 121–8.

Haward, M. 2001. 'Developing Australia's Ocean Policy', *Ocean Yearbook*, 15: 523–39.

Haward, M. 2003. 'The Ocean and Marine Realm', in S. Dovers and S. Wild River (eds), *Managing Australia's Environment*, Sydney, Federation Press: 35–52.

Haward, M. 2004. 'IUU Fishing: Contemporary Practice', in A.G. Oude Elferink and D.R. Rothwell (eds), *Oceans Management in the 21st Century*, The Hague, Martinus Nijhoff Publishers: 87–105.

Haward, M. (forthcoming). 'Marine and Coastal Environmental Security in the Indian Ocean Context', in T. Doyle and M. Risely (eds), *Crucible for Survival: Environmental Security in the Indian Ocean Region*, New Brunswick, NJ, Rutgers University Press.

Haward, M. and B.W. Davis. 1994. 'Recent Developments in Australian Coastal Zone Management', in P.G. Wells and P.J. Ricketts (eds), *Coastal Zone Canada 94: 'Cooperation in the Coastal Zone' Conference Proceedings*, Coastal Zone Canada Association, Bedford Institute of Oceanography, Dartmouth Nova Scotia, Vol. 1: 19–29.

Haward, M. and R.A. Herr. 2000. 'Australia's Oceans Policy: Policy and Process', ACORN Phase 2 Workshop, Vancouver, 10–11 December.

Haward, M. and L.P. Hildebrand. 1996. 'Integrated Coastal Zone Management', in L. Kriwoken, M. Haward, D. VanderZwaag and B. Davis (eds), *Oceans Law and Policy in the Post-UNCED Era: Australian and Canadian Perspectives*, London, Kluwer Law International: 141–72.

Haward, M. and J. Jabour. 2007. 'Science and Politics in the Polar Regions', paper presented at International Studies Association Conference, Chicago, 28 February–3 March.

Haward, M. and D. VanderZwaag. 1995. 'Implementation of UNCED Agenda 21 Chapter 17 in Australia and Canada: A Comparative Analysis', *Ocean and Coastal Management*, 29, 1–3: 279–95.

Haward, M. and M. Wilson. 2000. 'Co-Management and Rights-Based Fisheries', in R. Shotton (ed.), *Use of Property Rights in Fisheries Management, Proceedings of the FishRights99 Conference*, Fremantle, WA 11–19 November 1999, FAO Fisheries Technical Paper No 404/2 Rome, FAO: 155–9.

Haward, M., A. Bergin and H.R. Hall. 1998. 'International Legal and Political Bases to the Management of the Incidental Catch of Seabirds', in G. Robertson and R. Gales (eds), *Albatross: Biology and Conservation*, Chipping Norton, NSW, Surrey Beatty & Sons Ltd: 255–66.

Haward, M., R. Dobell, A. Charles, E. Foster and T. Potts. 2003. 'Fisheries and Oceans Governance in Australia and Canada: From Sectoral Management to Integration', *Dalhousie Law Journal*, 26, 1: 6–45.

Healey, M.C. and T. Hennessy. 1998. 'The Paradox of Fairness: The Impact of Escalating Complexity on Fishery Management', *Marine Policy*, 22, 2: 109–18.

Heinz Center (H. John Heinz Center for Science, Economics and the Environment). 1998. *Our Ocean Future*, Washington, DC, H. John Heinz Center for Science, Economics and the Environment.

Heinz Center (H. John Heinz Center for Science, Economics and the Environment). 2008. *Project Description – The Nations Coasts: a Vision and Action Agenda for the Future*, http://www.heinzctr.org. Accessed 14 January 2008.

Herman, A. 2004. *To Rule the Waves: How the British Navy Shaped the Modern World*, New York, Harper Perennial.

Herr, R.A. 1990. *The Forum Fisheries Agency: Achievements, Challenges and Prospects*, Suva, Institute of Pacific Studies, University of the South Pacific.

Herr, R.A. and B.W. Davis. 1982. 'Of Federations and Fishermen: Australia, Canada and UNCLOS III', in P. Crabb (ed.), *Theory and Practice in Comparative Studies: Canada, Australia: Papers from the first Conference of the Australian and New Zealand Association of Canadian Studies*, Sydney, Australian and New Zealand Association of Canadian Studies and Macquarie University.

Herr, R.A. and B.W. Davis. 1986. 'The Impact of UNCLOS III on Australian Federalism', *International Journal*, 41, 3: 674–93.

Herriman, M., M. Tsamenyi, J. Ramli and S. Bateman. 1997. *Australia's Oceans Policy: International Agreements*, Background Paper 2, Canberra, Environment Australia.

Hershman, M. 1996. 'Ocean Management Policy Development in Subnational Units of Government: Examples from the United States', *Ocean and Coastal Management*, 31, 1; 25–40.

Hilborn, R. and D. Gunderson. 1996. 'Rejoinder – Chaos and Paradigms for Fisheries Management', *Marine Policy*, 20, 1: 87–9.

Hinkel, R. 1998. 'Background on the Stratton Commission', in R.W. Knecht, B. Cicin-Sain and N. Foster (eds), *The Stratton Roundtable, 1998*, Newark, DE, Centre for the Study of Marine Policy, National Oceans Service, NOAA and Oceans Governance Study Group, 3–8.

Hodgson, P. 2002. 'An Oceans Policy for New Zealand – The Next Steps', address to the 2002 Ngai Tahu Waipounamu Treaty Festival, Otakou Marae, Otakou, Otago Peninsula.

Holt, S.J. 2001. 'Sharing the Catches of Whales in the Southern Hemisphere', in R. Shotton (ed.), *Case Studies on the Allocation of Transferable Quota Rights in Fisheries*, FAO Fisheries Technical Paper 411, Rome, FAO: 322–73.

Homeshaw, J. 1995. 'Policy Community, Policy Networks and Science Policy in Australia', *Australian Journal of Public Administration*, 54, 4: 520–32.

Hood, C.C. and H.Z. Margetts. 2007. *The Tools of Government in the Digital Age*, Basingstoke, Palgrave Macmillan.

Hope, R.M. 1975. *The National Estate: Report of the Committee of Inquiry*, Canberra, Government Printer of Australia.

HORSCERA (House of Representatives Standing Committee on Environment, Recreation and the Arts). 1991. *The Injured Coastline: Protection of the Coastal Environment*, Canberra, AGPS.

Hundloe, T. 1998. 'The Environment: How to Solve Problems that Don't Respect Borders', *Australian Journal of Public Administration*, 57, 3: 87–91.

Hughes, O.E. 2003. *Public Management and Administration: An Introduction*, 3rd edn, Basingstoke, Palgrave Macmillan.

Hunt, C. 1989. *The Offshore Petroleum Regimes of Canada and Australia*, Calgary, Canadian Institute of Resources Law.

ICES (International Council for Exploration of the Sea). 2007. *About ICES*, http://www.ices.dk/indexfla.asp. Accessed 26 March 2007.

IISD (International Institute for Sustainable Development). 2005. *The Oceans Policy Summit 2005 Bulletin*, http://www.iisd.ca/SD/TOPS2005/. Accessed 26 March 2007.

IMO (International Maritime Organization). 2007. 'Safe, Secure and Efficient Shipping on Clean Oceans – Home Page', http://www.imo.org. Accessed 20 December 2007.

IUCN (International Union for Conservation of Nature – World Conservation Union). 2007. 'What is the World Conservation Union?' http://cms.iucn.org/about/index.cfm. Accessed 26 March 2007.

IWC (International Whaling Commission). 2007. 'Revised Management Scheme', http://www.iwcoffice.org/conservation/rms.htm. Accessed 26 March 2007.

Jabour, J., M. Iliff and E.J. Molenaar. 2007. 'The Great Whale Debate: Australia's Agenda on Whaling', in L.K. Kriwoken, J. Jabour and A. Hemmings (eds), *Looking South: Australia's Antarctic Agenda*, Sydney, Federation Press: 135–48.

Jacobs, K. and P. Barnett. 2000. 'Policy Transfer and Policy Learning: A Study of the 1991 New Zealand Health Services Task Force', *Governance*, 13, 2: 185–213.

Johnston, D. 1994. 'UNCLOS III and UNCED: A Collision of Mind Sets', paper presented at ACORN Workshop, Halifax, Nova Scotia, 24–25 September.

Johnston, D. 2002. 'The Challenge of International Oceans Governance: Institutional, Ethical and Conceptual Dilemmas', paper presented at ACORN II Conference, Canberra 31 May–2 June.

Johnston, D. n.d. 'Concept Paper: Cooperative Oceans Governance in the APEC Region'.

Johnston, D. and D. VanderZwaag. 2000. 'The Ocean and International Environmental Law: Swimming, Sinking, and Treading Water at the Millennium', *Ocean and Coastal Management*, 43: 141–61.

Joint Ocean Commission Initiative. 2005. 'Background to the Joint Oceans Commission Initiative', www.jointoceancommission.org//webpages/background.html. Accessed 16 August 2007

Joint Ocean Commission Initiative. 2006a. *U.S. Ocean Policy Report Card*, www.jointoceancommission.org/rc-reports.html. Accessed 22 May 2008.

Joint Ocean Commission Initiative. 2006b. *From Sea to Shining Sea: Priorities for Ocean Policy Reform: Report to the United States Senate*, June.

Joint Ocean Commission Initiative. 2007. *U.S. Ocean Policy Report Card 2006*, www.jointoceancommission.org/rc-reports.html. Accessed 22 May 2008.

Jose, J. 2007. 'Reframing the "Governance" Story', *Australian Journal of Political Science*, 42, 3: 455–70.

Joyner, C. 2000. 'The International Ocean Regime at the New Millennium: A Survey of the Contemporary Legal Order', *Ocean and Coastal Management*, 43:163–203.

Juda, L. 2003. 'Changing National Approaches to Ocean Governance: The United States, Canada and Australia', *Ocean Development and International Law*, 34: 161–87.

Juda, L. 2007. 'The European Union and Ocean Use Management: The Marine Strategy and Maritime Policy', *Ocean Development and International Law*, 38: 259–82.

Kay, R. and C. Lester. 1997. 'Benchmarking Future Directions for Coastal Management in Australia', *Coastal Management*, 35, 1: 1–29.

Keating, P.J. 1995. 'Oceans Policy: Statement', Press Release, the Prime Minister, the Hon P.J. Keating, No. 144/95, 8 December.

Kelemen, R.D. 2002. 'Regulatory Federalism: EU Environmental Regulation in Comparative Perspective', *Journal of Public Policy*, 20, 2: 133–67.

Kellow, A. and A. Zito. 2002. 'Steering Through Complexity: EU Environmental Regulation in the International Context', *Political Studies*, 50, 1: 43–60.

Kemp, D. 2002. 'Government to Spend Record $1.8 billion on Environment', Media Release, Federal Minister for the Environment and Heritage, Canberra, 14 May.

Kimball, L.A. 2001. *International Oceans Governance: Using International Law and Organisations to Manage Marine Resources Sustainably*, Gland Switzerland and Cambridge UK, IUCN – World Conservation Union.

Kingdon. J. 1984. *Agendas, Alternatives and Public Policies*, New York, Longman.

Kjær, A.M. 2004. *Governance*, Cambridge, Polity Press.

Knauss, J. 1998. 'The Origins of the Stratton Commission', in R.W. Knecht, B. Cicin-Sain and N. Foster (eds), *The Stratton Roundtable, 1998*, Newark, DE, Centre for the Study of Marine Policy, National Oceans Service, NOAA and Oceans Governance Study Group.

Knecht, R.W., B. Cicin-Sain and J.H. Archer. 1988. 'National Oceans Policy: A Window of Opportunity', *Ocean Development and International Law*, 19, 2: 113–42.

Knecht, R.W., B. Cicin-Sain and N. Foster (eds). 1998. *The Stratton Roundtable, 1998. Looking Back, Looking Forward: Lessons from the 1969 Commission on Marine Science, Engineering and Resources: Proceedings*, Newark, DE, Centre for the Study of Marine Policy, National Oceans Service, NOAA and Oceans Governance Study Group.

Koester, G.T. 1990. 'State–Federal Jurisdictional Conflicts in the US 12-Mile Territorial Sea: An Opportunity to End the Seaweed Rebellion', *Coastal Management*, 18: 195–211.

Koh, T.B. 1983. 'Statement at Final Session of Third UN Conference on the Law of the Sea, Montego Bay December 1982', reprinted in United Nations, *The Law of the Sea: Official Text of the United Nations Convention on the Law of the Sea*, UN, New York.

Kriwoken, L.K., M. Haward, D. VanderZwaag and B. Davis (eds). 1996. *Oceans Law and Policy in the Post-UNCED Era: Australian and Canadian Perspectives*, London, Kluwer Law International.

Lang, A.G. and M. Crommelin. 1979. *Australian Mining and Petroleum Laws: An Introduction*, Sydney, Butterworths.

Larmour, P. 1997. 'Models of Governance and Public Administration', *International Review of Administrative Sciences*, 63: 383–94.

Laughlin, T.L. 2003. 'History of Ecosystems-Based Management Discussions in APEC', paper presented at Ecosystems-Based Management (EBM) Workshop, Beyond Biodiversity – Sustainable Management and Conservation of the Oceans Using EBM, Cairns, Australia, June.

Lawrence, S.A. 1998. 'Timing and Work of the Stratton Commission', in R.W. Knecht, B. Cicin-Sain and N. Foster (eds), *The Stratton Roundtable, 1998*, Newark, DE, Centre for the Study of Marine Policy, National Oceans Service, NOAA and Oceans Governance Study Group. 25–9.

Lee, E.G and D.G. Fraser. 1989. 'The Rationale and Future Direction of Canada's Ocean Policy: International Dimensions', in D. McRae and G. Munro (eds), *Canadian Oceans Policy: National Strategies and the New Law of the Sea*, Vancouver, University of British Columbia Press: 238–52.

Levi-Faur, D. and E. Vigoda-Gadot. 2006. 'New Public Policy, New Policy Transfers; Some Characteristics of a New Order in the Making', *International Journal of Public Administration*, 29, 4–6: 247–62.

LINZ (Land Information New Zealand). 2006. *Ocean Survey 20/20* http://www.linz.govt.nz/home/news/items/20062007-ocean-survey-2020/index.html. Accessed October 2007.

Lowry, K. 1994. 'Introduction to Special Issue on Issues in Ocean Governance', *Ocean and Coastal Management*, 23: 1–6.

McAdam, D. and D. Rucht. 1993. 'The Cross-National Diffusion of Movement Ideas', *Annals of the American Academy of Political and Social Science*, 528: 56–74.

McLean, L. 1995. '$53 Million Coastal Package Flags Labor's Green Comeback', *Australian*, 29 May: 3.

MACOP (Ministerial Advisory Committee on Oceans Policy). 2001. *Healthy Sea: Healthy Society – Towards an Oceans Policy for New Zealand. Report on Consultation Undertaken by the Ministerial Advisory Committee on Oceans Policy*, Wellington.

McRae, D. and G. Munro (eds), 1989. *Canadian Oceans Policy: National Strategies and the New Law of the Sea*, Vancouver, University of British Columbia Press.

Mansell, J. 2004. 'The Voyage Towards National Oceans Policy in New Zealand: Encountering Rocks and Shoals', *Maritime Studies*, 137: 1–12.

Metcalfe, L. 1994. 'International Policy Coordination and Public Management Reform', *International Review of Administrative Sciences*, 60: 271–90.

Michaelis, F. 1998. *International Year of the Oceans – 1998: Australian Policies, Programs and Legislation*, Parliamentary Library Research Paper 6, Canberra, Parliament of Australia.

Miles, E.L. 1999. 'The Concept of Ocean Governances: Evolution Toward the 21st Century and the Principle of Sustainable Ocean Use', *Coastal Management*, 27: 1–30.

Miles. E.L. and W.T. Burke. 1989. 'Pressures on the United Nations Convention on the Law of the Sea of 1982 Arising from New Fishery Conflicts: The Problems of Straddling Stocks', *Ocean Development and International Law*, 20: 343–57.

Minchin, N. 1999. 'Australia's New Vision for Marine Science', Media Release, 25 June.

Ministry for the Environment. 2005a. *Getting Our Priorities Right: The Role of Information in Setting Priorities for Management of New Zealand's Ocean*, Wellington, Ministry for the Environment.

Ministry for the Environment. 2005b. *Offshore Options: Managing Environmental Effects in New Zealand's Exclusive Economic Zone.* Wellington, Ministry for the Environment.

Ministry for the Environment. 2006. *Environmental Best Practice Guidelines for the Offshore Petroleum Industry,* Wellington, Ministry for the Environment.

Ministry for the Environment. 2007a. 'Oceans', http://www.mfe.govt.nz/issues/oceans/.

Ministry for the Environment. 2007b. *Improving Regulation of Environmental Effects in New Zealand's Exclusive Economic Zone: Discussion Paper,* Ministry for the Environment, Wellington.

Ministry for the Environment. 2007c. 'Draft Oceans Policy Framework', http://www.mfe.govt.nz/issues/oceans/current-work/policy-framework.

Ministry of Fisheries. 2001. Press Release, 6 July, Wellington.

NABST (National Advisory Board on Science and Technology). 1994. *Opportunities From Our Oceans: Report of the Committee on Oceans and Coasts*, Ottawa, NABST.

National Oceans Office. 2004. *South–east Regional Marine Plan: Implementing Australia's Ocean Policy in the South–east Marine Region*, Hobart, National Oceans Office.

New Zealand Aquaculture Council. 2006. *The New Zealand Aquaculture Strategy,* Creative Design Advertising Limited, Nelson.

NOAA (National Oceanic and Atmospheric Administration) 1998. 'Clinton, Gore Speak at National Oceans Conference' *NOAA Legislative Informer,* 27: 1-2.

Norse, E. (ed.) 1993. *Marine Biological Diversity: A Strategy for Building Conservation into Decision Making,* Washington DC and Covelo CA, Island Press.

Ocean Action Plan. 2004. *US Oceans Action Plan: The Bush Administration's Response to the US Ocean Commission on Policy,* White House, Executive Office of the President of the United States.

Oceans Commission, 2004. *An Oceans Blueprint for the 21st Century,* Washington.

Oceans Policy Secretariat. 2003. *Feedback Report,* Oceans Policy Secretariat, Wellington.

OECD (Organisation for Economic Co-operation and Development). 2006. *Using Market Mechanisms to Manage Fisheries: Smoothing the Path.* Paris, OECD Publishing.

OECD (Organisation for Economic Co-operation and Development). 2007. 'Members and Partners', www.oecd.org/pages/www.oecd.org/ pages/ 0,3417,en_36734052_36761800_1_1_1_1_1,00.html. Accessed October 2007.

OOCRM – NOAA (Office of Ocean and Coastal Resources – National Ocean and Atmospheric Administration). 2007. 'Congressional Action to Help Manage Our Nation's Coasts', http://coastalmanagement.noaa.gov/czm/czm_act.html. Accessed 26 September 2007.

OSPAR. 2006. *Twenty Questions on OSPAR and the European Marine Strategy*, London, OSPAR Secretariat.

Ostrom, E. 1987. 'Institutional Arrangements for Resolving Commons Dilemmas: Some Contending Approaches', in B.M. McCay and J.M. Acheson (eds), *The Question of the Commons*, Tucson, AZ, University of Arizona Press.

Ostrom, E. 1990. *Governing the Commons: The Evolution of Institutions for Collective Action*, Cambridge, MAS, MIT Press.

Pacific Islands Forum. 2008. 'Pacific Islands Forum Secretariat: About Us', http://www.forumsec.org/pages.cfm/about-us/. Accessed 19 May 2008.

Parliamentary Commissioner for the Environment. 1999. *Setting Course for a Sustainable Future: The Management of New Zealand's Marine Environment*, Office of the Parliamentary Commissioner for the Environment, Wellington.

Parliamentary Library. 2003. 'The Foreshore and Seabed – Maori Customary Rights and Some Legal Issues', Background Note 2003/12, Parliamentary Library, Wellington.

Parliamentary Library. 2005. 'The New Zealand Constitution', Background Note 2001/1, updated 3 October, Parliamentary Library, Wellington.

Parsons, L.S. and J-J. Maguire. 1996. 'Rejoinder – Comments on Chaos, Complexity and Community Management of Fisheries', *Marine Policy* 20, 2: 175–6.

Peart, R. 2005. *Looking Out to Sea: New Zealand as a Model for Ocean Governance*, EDS, Wellington.

Peters, B.G. 1996. *The Policy Capacity of Governments*, Research Paper No. 18, Canadian Centre for Management Development, Ottawa, CCMD.

Peters, B.G. 1998. 'Managing Horizontal Government: The Politics of Coordination', *Public Administration*, 76: 295–311.

Pew Oceans Commission. 2003. *America's Living Oceans: Charting a Course for Sea Change. A Report to the Nation. Recommendations for a New Ocean Policy.* Pew Oceans Commission.

Pierre, J. (ed.). 2000. *Debating Governance*, Oxford, Oxford University Press.

Pierre, J. and B.G. Peters. 2005. *Governing Complex Societies: Trajectories and Scenarios*, Basingstoke, Palgrave Macmillan.

Pollard. G.B. 1985. *Managing the Interface: Intergovernmental Affairs Agencies in Canada.* Kingston, Ont, Institute of Intergovernmental Relations, Queen's University.

Potts, T. and M. Haward. 2007. 'International Trade, Ecolabelling, and Sustainable Fisheries – Recent Concepts and Practices', *Environment, Development and Sustainability*, 9, 1: 91–106.

Presidential Proclamation 1945. *Policy of the United States with Respect to the Natural Resources of the Subsoil and Sea Bed of the Continental Shelf*, Presidential Proclamation No. 2667, 28 September 1945, http://www.ibiblio.org/pha/policy/1945/450928a.html. Accessed 23 May 2008.

Pross, A.P. 1992. *Group Politics and Public Policy*, 2nd edn, Toronto, Oxford University Press.

Pross, A.P. and S. McQuorquodale. 1987. *Economic Resurgence and the Constitutional Agenda*, Kingston, Ont, Institute of Intergovernmental Relations, Queen's University.

Putnam, D. 1988. 'Diplomacy and Domestic Politics: The Logic of Two-Level Games', *International Organization*, 43, 3: 427–60.

Quigg, P.W. 1983. *A Pole Apart*, New York: McGraw Hill.

Rayfuse, R.G. 2004. *Non-Flag State Enforcement in High Seas Fisheries*, Leiden, Martinus Nijhoff Publishers.

Reichelt, R. and A. McEwan. 1999. 'Australia's Marine Science and Technology Plan: An Action Plan for Australia's Oceans Policy', *Marine and Freshwater Research*, 50, 8: 711–16.

Reid, P.C. 1980. 'Commonwealth–State Relations, Offshore Mining and Petroleum Legislation – Recent Developments: A Historic Milestone or Millstone?' *Australian Mining and Petroleum Law Journal*, 2, 2: 58–76.

Rennie, H.T. 1993. 'The Coastal Environment', in P.A. Memon and H.C. Perkins (eds), *Environmental Planning in New Zealand*, Palmerston North, Dunmore Press, 150–68.

Rhodes, R.A.W. 1985. 'Power–Dependence, Policy Communities and Intergovernmental Networks', *Public Administration Bulletin*, 49: 4–31.

Rhodes, R.A.W. 1995. 'The Institutional Approach', in D. Marsh and G. Stoker, (eds), *Theory and Methods in Political Science*, London, Macmillan.

Rhodes R.A.W. 1996. 'The New Governance: Governing Without Government', *Political Studies*, 44: 652–67.

Rhodes R.A.W. 2000. 'Governance and Public Administration', in J. Pierre (ed.), *Debating Governance*, Oxford, Oxford University Press.

Richardson, J.J. and A.G. Jordan. 1979. *Governing Under Pressure: The Policy Process in a Post-Parliamentary Democracy*, Oxford, Martin Robertson.

Roberts, G.K. 1973. 'Comparative Politics: Strategies and Theories', in P.G. Lewis and D.C. Potter (eds), *The Practice of Comparative Politics*, London, Longman (in association with The Open University Press), 241–59.

Robertson, G. and R. Gales (eds). 1998. *Albatross: Biology and Conservation*, Chipping Norton NSW, Surrey Beatty & Sons.

Rothwell, D.R. and M. Haward. 1996. 'Federal and International Perspectives on Australia's Maritime Claims', *Marine Policy*, 20, 1: 29–46.

Rothwell, D.R. and S.B. Kaye. 2001. 'Australia's Legal Framework for Integrated Oceans and Coastal Management', *Environmental Planning and Law Journal*, 18: 278–92.

Rothwell, D.R. and D. VanderZwaag. 2006. *Towards Principled Oceans Governance: Australian and Canadian Approaches and Challenges*, Abingdon, Routledge.

Sabatier, P.A. 1986. 'Top-Down and Bottom-Up Approaches to Implementation Research: A Critical Analysis and Suggested Synthesis', *Journal of Public Policy*, 6: 21–48.

Sabatier, P.A. and H. Jenkins-Smith. 1993. *Policy Change and Learning: An Advocacy Coalition Approach*, Boulder, Westview Press.

Sainsbury, K., M. Haward, L. Kriwoken, M. Tsamenyi and T. Ward. 1997. *Australia's Oceans Policy: Oceans Planning and Management, Multiple Use Management in the Australian Marine Environment: Principles, Definitions and Elements*, Issues Paper 1, Canberra, Environment Australia.

Sanderson, I. 2002. 'Evaluation, Policy Learning and Evidence-Based Policy Making', *Public Administration*, 80, 1: 1–22.

Sartori, G. 1991. 'Comparing and Miscomparing', *Journal of Theoretical Politics*, 3, 3: 243–57.

Savoie, D. 1995. 'Globalisation, Nation States and the Civil Service', in B.G. Peters and D. Savoie (eds), *Governance in a Changing Environment*, Montreal and Kingston, McGill-Queen's University Press, 82–110.

Sawer, G. 1977. *Federation Under Strain; Australia 1972–1975*, Melbourne, Melbourne University Press.

Schattschneider, E.E. 1957. 'Intensity, Visibility, Direction and Scope', *American Political Science Review*, 51: 933–42.

Schattschneider, E.E. 1960. *The Semi-Sovereign People: A Realist's View of Democracy in the United States*, Hinsdale, IL, Dryden Press.

Scheiber, H.N. 1998. 'The Stratton Commission: A Historical Perspective on Policy Studies in Oceans Governance 1969 and 1998', in R.W. Knecht, B. Cicin-Sain and N. Foster (eds), *The Stratton Roundtable, 1998,*

Newark, DE, Centre for the Study of Marine Policy, National Oceans Service, NOAA and Oceans Governance Study Group.

Scheiber, H.N. (ed.). 1999. *Emerging Issues in National Ocean and Coastal Policy*, Berkeley, CA, University of California for the Ocean Governance Study Group.

SeaViews. 2007. 'Marine Ecosystem Management: Obligations and Opportunities', http://www.converge.org.nz/seaviews/index.html. Accessed 2 October 2007.

SeaWeb. 2007. 'Give Swordfish a Break', http://www.seaweb.org/programs/swordfish. Accessed 4 April 2007.

Sen, S. and J.R. Neilsen. 1996. 'Fisheries Co-Management: A Comparative Analysis', *Marine Policy*, 20, 5: 405–18.

Shotton, R. and M. Haward. 2005. 'Requirements for Managing Deep-Seas Fisheries', in R. Shotton (ed.), *Conference on the Governance and Management of Deep-sea Fisheries Part 1 Conference Reports*, FAO Fisheries Proceedings 3/1 FAO, Rome: 686–710.

Skivington, R. 2006. 'Too Many Boats, Too Few Fish', *Contours*, Department of Agriculture Fisheries and Forestry, Canberra, DAFF: 8–9.

Skjærseth, J.B. 2006. 'Protecting the North-East Atlantic: Enhancing Synergies by Institutional Interplay', *Marine Policy*, 30: 157–66.

Smyth, C., M. Prideaux, K. Davey and M. Grady. 2003. *Oceans Eleven*, Melbourne, ACF.

SPREP (Pacific Regional Environment Programme). 2007. *About the Pacific Regional Environment Programme*, http:www.sprep.org/sprep/about.htm Accessed 20 October 2007.

Starkey, J.C. 1987. 'Australia's Offshore Petroleum Legal and Administrative Regime', *Maritime Studies*, 37: 25–9.

Stokke, O.S. 2000. 'Managing Straddling Stocks: The Interplay of Global and Regional Regimes', *Oceans and Coastal Management*, 43: 205–34.

Stokke, O.S and Ø.B. Thommessen (eds). 2003. *Yearbook of International Co–operation on Environment and Development 2003/2004*, London, Earthscan.

Stommel, H. 1952. 'Review of R. Carson, *The Sea Around Us*', *Geographical Review*, 42, 2: 321–2.

Stone, D. 2000. 'Non-Institutional Policy Transfer: The Strategies of Independent Policy Institutes', *Governance*, 13, 1:45–62.

Sturgess, G. 1997. 'Cooperation Comes Into its Own', *Australian*, 30 January: 11.

Sutinen, J.G., A. Rieser and J.R. Gauvin. 1991. 'Measuring and Explaining Noncompliance in Federally Managed Fisheries', *Ocean Development and International Law*, 21: 335–72.

Tarte, D. 1995. 'Our Sea Our Future ... Major Findings of the State of the Marine Environment Report for Australia', *Waves: Marine and Coastal Community Network Newsletter*, 2, 1: 1–2.

Task Force on Incomes and Adjustment in the Atlantic Fishery. 1993. *Charting a New Course: Towards the Fishery of the Future: Report of the Task Force on Incomes and Adjustment in the Atlantic Fishery*, Ottawa, Communications Directorate Fisheries and Oceans.

Taylor, M. 1982. *Community, Anarchy and Liberty*, Cambridge, Cambridge University Press.

TFG International. 2002. *Review of the Implementation of Oceans Policy*, Hobart, TFG International.

Tønnessen, J.N. and A.O. Johnsen. 1982. *The History of Modern Whaling*, translated from the Norwegian by R.I. Christopherson, London, C. Hurst & Co.

Tonnies, F. 1957. *Community and Society*, translated C. Loomis, East Lancing, MI, Michigan State University Press.

TOPS (The Ocean Policy Summit). 2005. *The Ocean Policy Summit 2005 Bulletin*, http://www.iisd.ca/sd/tops2005/ymbvol117num1e.html. Accessed 26 March 2007.

Treaty of Waitangi. 2007. *Treaty of Waitangi – New Zealand History Online*, http://www.nzhistory.net.nz.category/tid/133. Accessed 20 October 2007.

Underdal, A. 2002. 'One Question, Two Answers', in E.M. Miles, A. Underdal, S. Andresen, J. Wettesad, J.K. Skjaeseth and E.M. Carlin (eds), *Environmental Regime Effectiveness: Confronting Theory With Evidence*, Cambridge, MA, MIT Press: 3–45.

UNDOALOS (United Nations Division for Ocean Affairs and the Law of the Sea). 2007. *Agreement relating to the implementation of Part XI of the United Nations Convention on the Law of the Sea of 10 December 1982: Overview*, www.un.org/Depts/los/convention_agreements/conven tion_agreements/convention_overview_part_xi.htm. Accessed 25 March 2007.

UNEP (United Nations Environment Programme). 2007. *Regional Seas Programme*, http://www.unep.org/DEPI/programmes/regionalseas.html, Accessed 12 December 2007.

United Nations. 1983. *The Law of the Sea: Official Text of the United Nations Convention on the Law of the Sea*, New York, United Nations.

United Nations General Assembly. 1970. *Resolution 2749 (XXV)*, 17 December, New York, United Nations.

United Nations General Assembly. 2005. *Resolution Adopted by the General Assembly*, A/Rs/59/25, New York, United Nations.

United Nations General Assembly. 2007. *Oceans and the Law of the Sea: Report of the* Secretary-General, A/62/66/Add.2, New York, United Nations.

United Nations International Law Commission 2007. *Agenda for the 4th Session*, A/CN.5/52 (4 June–8 August 1952), http://untreaty.un.org/ilc/se ssions/4/4sess.htm. Accessed 26 September 2007.

University of Delaware. 2007. 'Ocean Governance Study Group' http://www.ocean.udel.edu/cmp/pages/us_ocean_policy.html.   Accessed 26 September 2007.

US Senate Committee on Commerce, Science and Transportation. 1997. *Oceans Act 1997: Report of the Committee on Commerce, Science and Transportation on S. 1213*, November 8 1997 105th Congress 1st Session.

VanderZwaag, D. 1983. 'Canadian Fisheries Management: A Legal and Administrative Overview', *Ocean Development and International Law*, 13, 2: 171–211.

VanderZwaag, D. (ed.). 1992. *Canadian Ocean Law and Policy*, Toronto, Butterworths.

Vallega, A. 2001. 'Ocean Governance in Post-Modern Society – A Geographical Perspective', *Marine Policy* 25: 299–414.

Vince, J.Z. 2003. 'Australia's Oceans Policy: Five Years of Integration Across Sectors and Jurisdictions?' *Maritime Studies*, 133: 1–13.

Vince, J.Z. 2004. 'The Development of Australia's Oceans Policy: Change and Stability in a Policy Community', unpublished PhD thesis, Hobart, University of Tasmania.

Vince, J.Z. 2005. 'Policy Transfer in Ocean Governance: Australia, Canada and New Zealand', Proceedings of the Australasian Political Studies Association Conference, Dunedin, New Zealand, Tasmania, September.

Vince J.Z. 2006. 'The South East Regional Marine Plan: Implementing Australia's Oceans Policy', *Marine Policy*, 30: 420–30.

Vince J.Z. 2008. 'Policy Transfer in Oceans Governance: Learning Lessons From Australia's Oceans Policy Process', *Ocean Year Book*, 22: 159–81.

Wallace, C. and B. Weeber. 2005. 'The Devil and the Deep Sea – Economics, Institutions and Incentives: The Theory and the New Zealand Quota Experience in the Deep Sea', in R. Shotton (ed.), *Conference on the Governance and Management of Deep-sea Fisheries Part 1 Conference Reports*, FAO Fisheries Proceedings 3/1, Rome, FAO: 511–43.

Walton, D.W.H. (ed.). 1987. *Antarctic Science*, Cambridge, Cambridge University Press.

Warhurst, J. 1983. 'Intergovernmental Managers and Cooperative Federalism: The Australian Case', *Public Administration*, 61, 3: 308–17.

Watkins, J.D. 2004. 'An Ocean Blueprint for the 21st Century', *Global Issues* April, at http://usinfo.state.gov/journals/itgic/0404/ijge/gj04.htm. Accessed 10 September 2007.

WCED (World Commission on Environment and Development). 1990. *Our Common Future*, Australian edn, Melbourne, Oxford University Press.

Weiss, E. Brown and H.K. Jacobson (eds). 1998. *Engaging Countries: Strengthening Compliance with International Environmental Accords*, Cambridge, MA, MIT Press.

Weller, P. 1989. *Malcolm Fraser PM: A Study in Prime Ministerial Power in Australia*, Ringwood, Penguin.

Wescott, G. 2000. 'The Development and Initial Implementation of Australia's "Integrated and Comprehensive" Oceans Policy', *Ocean and Coastal Management*, 43: 853–78.

Wenk, E. 1972. *The Politics of the Ocean*, Seattle, University of Washington Press.

Wenk, E. 1998. 'Creating the Stratton Commission – a Reprise', in R.W. Knecht, B. Cicin-Sain and N. Foster (eds), *The Stratton Roundtable, 1998*, Newark, DE, Centre for the Study of Marine Policy, National Oceans Service, NOAA and Oceans Governance Study Group.

Wilson, J.A., J.M. Acheson, M. Metcalfe and P. Kleban. 1994. 'Chaos, Complexity and Community Management of Fisheries', *Marine Policy*, 18, 3: 291–305.

Wolman, H. 1992. 'Understanding Cross National Policy Transfers: The Case of Britain and the US', *Governance*, 5, 1: 27–45.

World Bank. 1999. *World Development Report 1999–2000*, Washington, DC, World Bank.

World Bank. 2000. *World Development Report 2000–01 – Overview. Attacking Poverty: Opportunity, Empowerment and Security*, Washington, DC, World Bank.

World Bank. 2007. 'The First PROFISH Forum', http://web.worldbank.org/WBSITE/EXTERNAL/TOPICS/EXTARD/0,,contentMDK:21292984~pagePK:210058~piPK:210062~theSitePK:336682,00.html. Accessed 26 May 2008.

Wright, A., N. Stacey and P. Holland. 2006. 'The Cooperative Framework for Ocean and Coastal Management in the Pacific Islands: Effectiveness, Constraints and Future Direction', *Ocean and Coastal Management*, 49: 739–63.

Young, O.R. and M.A. Levy. 1999. 'The Effectiveness of International Environmental Regimes', in O.R. Young (ed.), *The Effectiveness of International Environmental Regimes*, Cambridge, MA, MIT Press: 1–32.

Zann, L. 1997. *Our Sea Our Future: Major Findings of the State of the Marine Environment Report for Australia*, Ocean Rescue 2000 Programme, Canberra, Department of Environment, Sport and Territories.

Index